Unequal Opportunity

* Learning to Read in the U.S.A.

Jill Sunday Bartoli

Foreword by RICHARD L. ALLINGTON
Afterword by JANE HANSEN

 Teachers College
Columbia University
New York and London

Published by Teachers College Press, 1234 Amsterdam Avenue
New York, New York

Library of Congress Cataloging-in-Publication Data

Bartoli, Jill.
    Unequal opportunity : learning to read in the U.S.A. / Jill Sunday
  Bartoli ; foreword by Richard L. Allington ; afterword by Jane Hansen.
      p.   cm—(Language and literacy series)
  Includes bibliographical references and index.
    ISBN 0-8077-3385-7. — ISBN 0-8077-3384-9 (pbk.)
    1. Educational equalization—United States. 2. Reading—United
States. 3. Educational accountability—United States. I. Title.
II. Series: Language and literacy series (New York, N.Y.)
LC213.2.B37 1994
370.19'34'0973—dc20   94-31500

ISBN 0-8077-3385-7
ISBN 0-8077-3384-9 (Pbk.)

Printed on acid-free paper
Manufactured in the United States of America

99 98 97 96 95   8 7 6 5 4 3 2 1

Contents

Foreword

American schools have never been very successful educating poor children. Today the situation remains largely unchanged. It is poor children who predominantly populate our remedial classes and programs for children identified as handicapped. Although both remedial and special education programs generate additional funds for use in educating eligible children, the evidence on the academic benefits of participation are slim. In other words, the additional funds have not routinely resulted in higher quality, more intensive educational programs for poor children. Actually, the most obvious characteristic of these special programs is that participating children are segregated from their nonparticipating peers for part or all of the school day.

But segregating harder-to-teach children has a long history in American education as well. There have been a myriad of exclusionary practices, from "truant classes," to immigrant schools, and separate schools for "coloreds," to name but a few. Along the way there have been a number of legal victories achieved by advocates for such children, the most recent being the Education of Handicapped Children Act of 1975. Thus, only 20 years ago were all children granted an entitlement to a free public education in the least restrictive educational environment. However, schools have always managed to find ways to continue segregatory educational practices while technically complying with the new laws. This point is well made by Mehan and his colleagues (1986) in their studies of how committees on special education actually operate to decide whether referred students are handicapped and in determining special education placements. Similarly, Denny Taylor (1991) painfully documents the experiences of one family as they battle to have their son educated only to lose the battle in the end. In my own work, my colleagues and I (Allington, 1994; Allington & Walmsley, 1994; Cunningham & Allington, 1994; McGill-Franzen & Allington, 1993) have documented the shattered hopes many held for special programs and the manipulation of rules and regulations to better serve the needs of schools, not children.

In the past 30 years much additional funding has been allocated to better educate children who find learning to read difficult, whether they are served in remedial classes, special education programs, or bilingual education efforts. The most obvious result has been the expansion of a "second system" of special teachers and other educational personnel—additional professional staff to work with "special needs" children. Between 1960 and 1990 the number of adults working in American elementary schools doubled! Class size, however, remained relatively stable. In 1992, the National Center for Educational Statistics reported that for the first time in U.S. history, the number of staff who were not classroom teachers exceeded the number of those who were classroom teachers. We have more specialists than ever before, and this situation has produced a number of unintended effects.

First, there has been a reduced sense of professional responsibility for the education of all children on the part of classroom teachers and regular education administrators. At times I think that many in charge of regular education actually believe that unless the state or federal government makes money available there is no local responsibility to educate all children, especially those who are harder to teach.

Second, the expansion of the "second system" has narrowed educational definitions of normalcy. As we added category after category of specialists and programs, classroom teachers found more and more deviant children. In too many schools, the majority of children are served by one or more special programs created for children who deviated from the norm in some way. Of course, the shortest route into such programs is for a child to experience some sort of difficulty learning to read. Today such children become candidates for segregation from their peers.

Third, our focus on labeling has expanded our reliance on tests to describe children as learners. This, when coupled with the increased accountability testing, has resulted in ever rising enrollments in remedial and special education classes. Skrtic (1991) argues that special programs allow schools to continue to operate as they always have while identifying children as the problem. Schools too rarely alter classroom instructional efforts, even when large numbers of children fail to thrive in their classrooms. Instead we add more specialists and more special programs to repair the "damaged goods" that some parents deliver to the school. Special education provided a release valve for the increased accountability pressure schools felt across the last decade. Virtually every state excuses special education students from statewide testing programs or excludes those students' results from school accountability reports. One effect, which we (McGill-Franzen & Allington, 1993) documented, was an increase in early identification of children as handicapped so as to remove the lowest-achieving students from the accountability reports. Thus, special education was used to "vanish" the lowest-achieving students from accountability rolls, thereby enhancing re-ported average achievement levels in the schools.

American schools have always served poor children less well than they served more advantaged children. Perhaps the situation today is no worse than it was 50 years ago, perhaps even modestly better. But the situation today is still far removed from the democratic principle of equal opportunity for all. In this moving volume Jill Bartoli addresses inequities in American education, the inequities that stare us directly in the face whenever we pause to look past that first glance at our schools. This book is not easy to read because it challenges all of us—teachers, administrators, researchers, teacher educators, legislators, and ordinary citizens—to take a good look at our schools and at the school responses to those children who most need good schools and large amounts of high quality instruction. Equity is not essen-tially achieved until our schools work equally well for all children, regardless of the parents they have. A just school is a school where advantaged kids have no consistent achievement advantage over poor children. A just school is one where ethnicity does not predict achievement. A just school, then, works as well for harder-to-teach children as it does for those children's peers. These are the schools that Bartoli hopes to help build.

REFERENCES

Allington, R. L. (1994). What's special about special programs for children who find learning to read difficult? *Journal of Reading Behavior, 26,* 1–21.

Allington, R. L., & Walmsley, S. A. (1994). *No quick fix: Rethinking literacy programs in American elementary schools.* New York: Teachers College Press.

Cunningham, P. M., & Allington, R. L. (1994). *Classrooms that work: They all can read and write.* New York: HarperCollins.

McGill-Franzen, A., & Allington, R. L. (1993). Flunk'em or get them classified: The contamination of primary grade accountability data. *Educational Researcher, 22,* 19–22.

Mehan, H., Hartweck, A., & Meihls, J. L. (1986). *Handicapping the handicapped.* Stanford, CA: Stanford University Press.

Skrtic, T. M. (1991). The special education paradox: Equity as the way to excel-lence. *Harvard Educational Review, 61,* 148–206.

Taylor, D. (1991). *Learning denied.* Portsmouth, NH: Heinemann.

Richard L. Allington
SUNY at Albany

Acknowledgments

I would like to both acknowledge and express my sincere appreciation to the following people, without whom this book could not have been written:

> to Morton Botel—creator of the Critical Experiences approach to learning, mentor, master teacher, friend, and inspiring model for all of us in education of continuous, hopeful persistence in school reform for 45 years;
>
> to my family—my heroic husband, Jim, and our incredibly wonderful sons and daughter (David, Daniel, Stephen, Patrick, and Catherine), who have made it possible for me to have the time to read, observe, think, and write about learning;
>
> to "James" and his family, who have so patiently and generously helped me to better understand their perception of the world, thereby enlarging my own;
>
> to the many teachers, specialists, and administrators whose creativity, caring, hard work, and persistence continue to inspire me;
>
> and to the administration and faculty in James's school district and in the inner-city school for allowing me the opportunity to observe, interview, be involved, and learn about the ecology of schooling. Without the permission and access granted by the administration, and without the participation of the faculty in sharing their stories, this book would not exist.

In addition, I would like to thank two "long distance" friends and colleagues for their ongoing support and encouragement as this book was in process:

> Gerry Coles, for his excellent research and writing that continue to inspire my thinking, for his thoughtful and thorough critiques of my work, and for being my phone colleague in times of despair over the past 5 years;
>
> and Sarah Biondello, who had faith in my work, who encouraged me to work harder, and whose insightful editing gave shape and coherence to the final product.

Prologue

In the spring of 1988, after Morton Botel and I published our text, *Reading/ Learning Disability: An Ecological Approach,* I gave a new manuscript to our editor at Teachers College Press, Sarah Biondello, when we met with her at the International Reading Association Convention in Toronto. Over the past 5 years, that manuscript has gone through a multitude of revisions, extensions, deletions, and virtual metamorphoses.

It began as an in-depth analysis of the literacy life histories of two students whom I had been observing, interviewing, and gathering ecological data on over a 6-year period. My goal was a full and rich description of the processes of learning to read and learning to fail in traditional suburban schools.

The first major shift in the manuscript, described in the letter that follows, came when I decided to go back into the field—this time as an advocate for change.

August 20, 1988

Dear Sarah:

So much has happened since I last talked with you that I hardly know where to begin. First the bad. I couldn't let those case studies die that I gave you in Toronto. I had this burning need to re-validate, to be sure, to see if what I thought I saw was really still there. So I dug deeper into the "James" case and into the problems of the Black Community in "Smalltown"—not only with the school system but also with their job opportunities, housing problems, financial situation, health and child care needs, social stratification in the community, recreation facilities and needs, drug and alcohol problems, counseling needs (educational, vocational, and emotional), criminal and justice issues—and I was appalled at all that I never knew about Smalltown's lack of response to the crying needs of the Black Community.

I was equally appalled at the continuation of James's 10-year his-

tory of educational deprivation, culminating in the ultimate blame-
the-victim technique: coercing James's mother into psychiatric testing
for a socially/emotionally disturbed placement (Gerry Coles is dead
right that this is not done blind—the psychiatrist was "briefed" before he ever met James). And I was more convinced than ever of the
desperate need to make a change in a school system that has continued to relegate its Black Community to an inferior education and
degrading stereotypes, while simultaneously blaming the victims.

Abandoning my relatively neutral researcher role I began meeting with several Black Community members who share a similar interest in change: a retired (actually he quit in disgust) principal who
saved James from SED placement in fourth grade, a job training counselor who had to fight every step of the way to see that her children
were prepared for college, a crisis counselor who tries to help youth
who have too often been defeated by the system and turned to drugs
or alcohol, and a teacher in the school system whose own children
suffered from low expectations in school. We are presently involved
in trying to prevent James's exclusion from regular education, and last
Wednesday we had our first major defeat.

I talked with teachers, specialists, administrators, and counselors
(and my colleagues did the same), trying to sensitize them to the
larger ecological problems surrounding James's miseducation. We
gave a chapter of Gerry Coles's *The Learning Mystique* to the special
education director, the principal, and the reading supervisor to help
them understand the superficiality of the LD label, we showed them a
chapter from Frank Smith's *Insult to Intelligence* to help them see the
problem with the subskill "education" James has been drowning in,
and I gave the principal (and superintendent) an advocacy-focused
address by Mona Bailey from the spring American Educational Research Association Convention in New Orleans. I sincerely thought
that if they had all the facts and were sensitized to the problem, they
would give James a chance at regular education this year.

The school's position was that James had been a continual disrup-
tion in classes (they did not choose to see that his experiences in the
low track and LD placements, populated with the school's worst behavior problems, had any effect on James's attitude and behavior), that
he was a "leader" in bad conduct such as being tardy to class or being
loud in the halls, and that he got in a fight in school.

The fight was the main problem the principal had with him, so
it seems, because when the principal came up behind James to grab
him (to stop the fight), James threw an elbow and gave the principal a
bloody nose. Bad luck strikes again—just like James's first story called

"Bad Luck." After this incident James was suspended from school, and then allowed in school only until noon for the rest of the year. His year ended in failures in both of his mainstream classes, which will make him ineligible for football, which is his great love.

After I gathered the details of this torrid ninth-grade year, and after I had the support of the retired Black principal, we talked with James and his mother about what we might do to try to keep James in regular education for tenth grade. James admitted that he had been a behavior problem at times, but said that he would try to do better. He said he got into the fight because a kid called him a "nigger," and he even told the kid he didn't want to fight him in school because he didn't want to get kicked out. But the kid hit James anyway, and James said that when his friends were all standing there it was too hard for him not to hit the kid back. The most unfortunate part of it was the principal coming up behind and grabbing James, who thought it was someone else who wanted to fight. This probably led to the principal and counselor bugging James's mother until she relented and let them take her and her son to their psychiatrist. She was never given a written report from this "testing" session, so she assumed that nothing was final.

After talking about the various school options for James, James's mother and my colleagues and I agreed that total removal from his peers and the label of SED (now re-labeled L&A—learning and adjustment), accompanied by a further reduction in education, would be the worst thing for James. So we planned to go as a group to the placement meeting that the school is required to have, to present our alternative. James's mother took the initiative to call the school herself instead of waiting for them to set a meeting time for what we assumed would be the full team meeting to make a decision.

When we arrived last Wednesday, the principal, vice principal, and special education director said they did not know the purpose of the meeting. I discovered later that they not only pushed this family into testing, but they had their required "placement meeting" immediately after the psychiatrist's exam for 15 minutes, telling James's mother that her only option for James was the separate "L&A" placement. I've wondered since about the number of railroad jobs they've done with other cases. Neither James nor his mother was aware (nor were those of us who wanted to help) that, as far as the school was concerned, he was signed, sealed, and delivered with a new label that read, "Oppositional behavior—add Ritalin." The only thing they intended to do at our meeting was to itemize James's transgressions, read James's mother her rights to due process, tell us how much they had done for James throughout the year to "help" him (like throwing him out of school for half days for the last two-and-a-half months of school and confining him to the LD room), and set up a visit to the special school they intended to send James to.

This is the first I have been able to sit down and write about all of this. I'm afraid I've become too involved in this case, and losing James to the school system this past week was like losing one of my own children. I can't tell you how hard this is—and how awful to see.

But now to the good news. I feel more strongly than ever of the direction I need to take: I am convinced that we need a transformation of this highly destructive system of labeling and separation of children from their constitutional right to education, and I would like to rewrite the manuscript I sent you to focus on this transformation. In addition, I think the book should stay with James's study—a 10-year history of inequity and miseducation—so that I could add all of the new data that I have been gathering about the Black Community, wherein we are beginning to work toward transformation as well.

More good news. Morton and I have promises from the state education department for a seed grant to begin working in the inner city with teachers and specialists who want to reintegrate previously labeled and at-risk students back into regular education classrooms. We are excited and encouraged that at least some schools see the vital need to work toward more integration instead of more segregation. It helps to ease the sting of losing in James's school, to an extent. I think I'll tell him that, although we lost this one with his school, at least we may win in the future with others. I just hope to God he does not lose heart in all of this and grow to resent even more the oppressive system that is refusing to adequately educate him.

I once read that if you want to really understand a system, you should try to change it. This is rather a different approach from the more detached observation and documentation with which my work began, but I am no longer content with "pure," quantifiable research that has no benefit to the people being studied. I think the uses to which we put our research are every bit as important as the purity of the methodology—possibly more so. And the use that I want mine put to is to transform the system to one of excellence with equity for all children and families.

The book I am proposing to you is not a book for practice or for better evaluation methods. *Reading/Learning Disability* has that information, and a future revised edition will have even more. Morton is already talking about refinements in the student portfolio and observation methods for evaluation. (Sadly, even informal reading inventories, cloze tests, and miscue analyses can and are used to sort, track, and label students.) This new book is for policy makers, change agents, and transformation leaders who need proof in full ecological detail to both support and direct efforts toward change. We cannot afford more problematic solutions—we are moving toward a permanent underclass of one-third of our population by the twenty-first century.

Sincerely,

Jill

The second major shift in the manuscript came after the first year of the inner-city study from 1989 to 1990, a university–school partnership with the University of Pennsylvania. Having been amazed by the parallels that I found in the schooling processes for African American students in a suburban school and those for Latino students in an inner-city school, I decided on a comparative study that included both.

And the final metamorphosis of this book came after I began teaching at Elizabethtown College and had the opportunity to do collaborative observation with my undergraduate students in a wide variety of classrooms and schools. This broader comparative base, along with the ongoing data from our current college–urban school partnership project, has allowed me to test and extend the themes and issues that emerged from my previous work. I also discovered that my own viewpoint needed to be broadened to understand that what happens in schools and classrooms is only a metaphor for larger societal issues and problems. And I began to understand that part of my own responsibility in working toward change and renewal is to better understand the perspectives of those who are on the front lines of our education system.

So it is to all those from whom I have had the opportunity to learn—those who have been my mentors, collaborators, students, and friends—and to the teachers, students, parents, specialists, and administrators who have shared their views of learning with me, that I dedicate this book, with the hope that our collective understanding of the problems and visions for solutions may help to transform learning to read, learning to learn, and learning to live together in the U.S.A.

Unequal Opportunity

* Learning
to Read
in the U.S.A.

Introduction

This book is an attempt to put learning to read in the U.S.A. into its broader ecological context—the school, the family, and the society. The problematic themes and issues surrounding reading and learning are not isolated from living in this country. Our attempts to disconnect educational questions from their wider ecology have resulted in shortsighted, unsuccessful, and inequitable approaches to schooling and social policy. Consequently, those most in need of help in our schools and society have too often received poorer educations, fewer health and social services, and less adequate housing and employment opportunities.

The central problems and issues in this text pervade all parts of our society in the United States; so we cannot blame those who run the schools for what is, in fact, our collective responsibility as citizens of a pluralistic democracy. As a microcosm of the larger society, the school will reflect these problems; but the solutions will need to come from all parts of the ecology. Individual citizens, parents, teachers, and administrators; corporate and private businesses; public and private agencies and social services; policy makers and political leaders all must be involved. The central issues arise from our national response to the following educational and ethical questions:

How do we define human learning and, in particular, reading?
How do we treat our children and, in particular, those most in need; and what do we want them to be?
What do we value as a nation, and how does the education and treatment of our students in and out of school reflect these values?

As a society nearing the end of the twentieth century, we are beginning to reflect upon and search again for who we are and where we have come from as human beings in our personal and societal quest for meaning, cultural values, and roots. We perceive our universe to be less absolute, morally fixed, and linearly progressive than in the past; racial and economic segregation continues to plague us; and our ideals seem to far outreach our capacities as caring human beings. But, in trying to better understand and solve complex educational and social problems like learning to read—to make meaning or sense—we have the opportunity to reflect upon, reconstruct, and take responsibility for what we truly value, for our treatment of children and families, and for what we want our children and our nation to become.

THE EDUCATIONAL QUESTION: DEFINING LEARNING TO READ

During the twentieth century a convergence of excellent research and theory has emerged about how the human mind works to make sense of life and language, to "read" the world as well as the word. We have both anthropological and biological evidence that the human brain has physically developed through the process of interaction with other human beings. This confirms what good teachers since Socrates's time have known about the power of human dialogue and mediation.

At the same time, across all disciplines an interactive constructivist theory of learning—humans collaboratively building and shaping their own worlds of meaning—is taking prominence over the more passive, receptive, or merely reactive theories. Linked with the thinking of Dewey, Rorty, Cassirer, Langer, and others, Elliot Eisner (1992) describes human knowledge as not *given,* but *made* (hence the use of the term "meaning-making" for reading).

> Knowledge is always constructed relative to a framework, to a form of representation, to a cultural code, and to a personal biography. . . . There is no single, legitimate way to make sense of the world. (p. 14)

What we think we know is a function of the transaction between the world we do not know and our personal experiences and knowledge/schemas/frames of reference. Hence, the use of the phrase "transacting with text" for reading.

Eisner describes humanity's quest for objective certainty in the world—the "right" answer—as a kind of "immaculate perception" that cannot be known. In place of this he suggests the need for multiple voices and people who can understand them, moving us beyond simplified, standardized, controlled interpretations with one right answer.

> Different ways of seeing give us different worlds. Different ways of saying allow us to represent different worlds. . . . Helping people participate in a plurality of worlds made . . . is what education ought to try to achieve. (1992, p. 14)

This is congruent with the literary and philosophical view of human beings as born storytellers in a moral quest for meaning in their lives. And sociolinguistic as well as communication research suggests that this ultimate human quest for meaning involves not only the verbal and even more important nonverbal messages of those around us, but also the mediation or scaffolding that more capable others provide to help us make sense of our lives. Thus, we arrive at a fascinating social theory of human beings learning by interactively constructing their own texts of the world as a larger part of their personal quest for meaning.

Life and learning, then, can be viewed as series of individually created text constructions—created social constructions or dynamic transactions between what we know and what we want to know, who we are and who we want to become. This is quite a different view from the static positivist notion of a more objective, uniform, and measurable reality. This dynamic, meaning-centered, social, constructivist view is not unlike what John Dewey described at the beginning of the twentieth century, and it best describes both the intent and the content of this book. That is, my intent is to construct a text that may help us to make sense in our human quest for meaning-making—and, in particular, our quest to equitably help all children to learn to make meaning in reading.

The lives, or text constructions, of students in both suburban and urban schools, of their teachers and parents, and of myself as a teacher, parent, and researcher are all connected in this book. And the thread that connects us all to each other as we construct the texts of our lives is that of learning to read—making meaning in both life and language. Throughout, readers are invited to transact with the text and construct for themselves a coherent theory from which we can collaboratively build a more successful and democratic way of learning to read for all our children.

The connection among all of the stories and narrators in this book is our common ecology of learning and living in the United States. We will look closely at the classroom, the school, the family, and the community, exploring large and small cities as well as small town communities and suburbs in the Mid-Atlantic states. Reflecting upon this broader cultural context in which all of us are learning, or not learning, to read, we see an ecology of inequity that is badly in need of the kind of attention we have sometimes expended on saving whales and manatees, dying banks and corporations, the earth's streams and lakes, and earthquake, hurricane, or nuclear disaster victims.

Although the stories or text constructions that follow are too often tragic in their depiction of an ecology in need of saving, there are also some encouraging signs of change toward transforming the ecology. These can provide some direction for the future, perhaps serving as a beginning for the kind of interdisciplinary conversation that needs to grow if we are ever to transform the ecology for our most vulnerable children and families.

Following the model of the earliest human form of organizing reality—story, or narrative—this book unfolds the stories of students in the process of trying to learn to read in the United States and of the adults who are trying to help them. These stories are inherently subjective and interpretive, because that is the way we human beings perceive and construct our worlds. Bernstein (1983) suggests that every translation of their stories is "at the same time an interpretation" (p. 141), reminding us of the multiple and complex understandings that are possible as we try to understand each other's stories.

My objective is to present the voices of the students, parents, teachers, specialists, and administrators with whom I have worked over the past decade so that their perspectives are better understood. Scholars and researchers use such terms as ontological hermeneutics, phenomenology, and ethnography for this process of understanding people by "standing behind them and reading over their shoulder the cultural texts from which they themselves are reading" (Cushman, 1990, p. 599; Sass, 1988, p. 250).

Clifford Geertz (1973) uses the term "web of meaning," which is so consistent with the language learning research that describes reading as a highly social, personal, and human process of making meaning. And I have chosen to use the term "ecological" to suggest a more inclusive (of interconnected historical, cultural, economic, and political factors) view of understanding human beings in their interactive contexts. The goal is deeper understanding through careful observation and "thick" description rather than statistical measurement, artificial controls, and a presumed (but ultimately unattainable) objectivity. And taken in combination, I believe that the perceptions and stories of these students, parents, and educators concerning schooling and learning go beyond subjectivity and relativity to a broader pattern that connects (Bateson, 1972; Bernstein, 1983), thereby bringing us closer to the web of meaning that we need to understand as we work toward reform and renewal.

James's case study, for instance, illustrates that a vital issue for student learning is how those in schools perceive, understand, and build relationships with low achieving students and their parents. These stories allow us to look at perceptions and relationships, and to glimpse an interactive ecology that will respond only to intervention efforts that go beyond all of the individual interdependent parts. Going beyond perceptions, curriculum, management, counseling, school structure, student behavior, and academic achievement, we can begin to see how the ecology of schooling all fits together, rather than placing blame on individual parts. For in both family and school systems, and indeed in all of human ecology, the whole is always greater than the sum of its parts.

THE ETHICAL QUESTION

Nationally, a minimum of one-third of our population is not educated sufficiently to participate meaningfully in our democratic process of government. African American, Latino, and Native American children and families are disproportionately represented in this undereducated group, as are poor children and families of all races. Where there is high poverty in the United States, such as in the inner cities, school failure and dropout rates may soar as high as 75–85%. This does not match well with our traditional national value of equal opportunity for all citizens in a democracy.

The problematic and seemingly intractable racial and economic divisions in our schools and communities; the continued racial biases, stereotypes, and deficit assumptions that pervade our classrooms, workplaces, and social groups; and the difficulties we have in understanding fellow citizens who are culturally, ethnically, and racially different from ourselves suggest that we have a distance to travel toward equality and justice for all. The goals of multicultural education cannot be achieved without building respectful, trusting relationships across racial, social, and economic lines. We need to remember our own history, learn from it, and find a multitude of ways to celebrate the cultural diversity that has traditionally been the great strength and resource of our nation.

THE STORY OF MY OWN LEARNING

Since 1981 I have been actively engaged in the process of trying to understand why some children do not learn to read very well in our schools. Before that time my involvement as a college and high school English teacher, and later as a reading specialist, was a less focused watching and wondering. My ethnographic research with students labeled as "disabled" readers (dyslexic, learning disabled, remedial/poor reader) began in earnest during my doctoral study years, and I was taught more by the students I observed closely over time than it is possible to express, even within a Deweyan/Freirean democratic philosophy of learning from and with one's students.

Since that first group of longitudinal case studies from 1981 to 1986, partial data from which were summarized in *Reading/Learning Disability: An*

Ecological Approach (Bartoli & Botel, 1988a) as the "Sunny" and "James" case studies, I have continued to gather more data on those same students (in particular from "James," whose story is in Chapter 3) for a decade-long history of schooling. Also, in collaboration with my students at Elizabethtown College, I have continued to observe and document the learning and nonlearning of over 200 students in other classrooms in suburban, rural, and urban schools.

Over the past 7 years my research has expanded to include documenting the process of teacher learning as it relates to student learning. And since I have been teaching in-service and preservice teachers and specialists in graduate school, college, and school district sites, I have also had the opportunity to collaborate in the research of my graduate and undergraduate students on learning to read.

Between 1987 and 1989 I worked with teachers, specialists, and principals at their suburban, rural, and inner-city schools as they were engaged in on-site graduate seminars. Through their journals, and also through observation in their classrooms, I had the opportunity to be a part of educators' efforts to understand their own teaching as well as the learning of their students. They read, reflected, tried out new classroom practices, and talked together about their successes and failures.

At the inner-city sites I also visited homes to interview parents and children, gathered data from the community, and interviewed school personnel. At the larger city site I collaborated with doctoral students and two other university professors to understand the learning process for Latino students, over half of whom would not graduate from the city school system. Data from this site appear in Chapter 4.

In the process of supervising student teachers and junior practicum students from 1990–1994, I have had the opportunity to personally gather data in over 80 early childhood and elementary classrooms, each with several students who were experiencing difficulty in learning to read. I observed once a week for a semester in half of these classrooms, and four times a semester for the others. Informal observation and interview methods in these contexts allowed me to compare and test my original longitudinal data.

In addition, my undergraduate students in reading and language arts, children's language development, and independent studies gathered data for observational case studies and/or primary language learning records (Barrs, Ellis, Tester, & Thomas, 1989) in 200 different early childhood and elementary classrooms. Their focus was on students who were regarded as off-schedule or low progress learners, often given such labels as poor/slow/remedial reader, learning disability (LD), attention deficit disorder (ADD), or at risk for failure.

I introduced my students to context/field-based observation and to informal child, parent, and teacher interview methods "in the spirit" of ethnography. That is, they read about ethnography (Spradley, 1979, 1980), they read several ethnographic case studies (Bartoli & Botel, 1988a; Taylor & Dorsey-Gaines, 1988), and we discussed several frameworks for classroom observation and evaluation: Botel's (1977, 1979, 1981) Critical Experiences framework, Bartoli's (1989, 1990b) ecological framework, the Primary Language Record (Barrs et al., 1989), and Clay's (1979) New Zealand/Reading Recovery approach. They then went out to the field to observe, gather data, and learn about learning to read from the students, teachers, and parents in their practicum classrooms.

This accumulation of data has both confirmed and expanded my original conception of the ecology of learning to read, rooted in the longitudinal case studies begun in 1981 (Bartoli, 1986b). The interrelated systems of child, family, school, and community are still, I believe, vitally important to understand at a deeper level for the purposes of both valid diagnosis and meaningful intervention. But in addition, I believe we need to focus on the social interactional, personal meaning-making, communication, and relationship dynamics in learning to read, and in particular on the perceptions, beliefs, values, assumptions, biases, and definitions of all those who inhabit and interrelate in the ecology of the learner. We are dealing with a very complex, personal, human, and highly social process: humanity's ultimate quest for meaning. And the closer we can come to understanding these complex individual and social dynamics, the closer we will be to a more literate and a more humane society.

Over the past decade, in the process of observing, reflecting upon, and writing about the issues and themes of this book, I have discovered some of my own biases, "prejudgments," blame placing, and lack of understanding of others. I have moved from anger over the inequities I observed for 10 years in one school's labeling and tracking practices, to continued anger and blaming of people in schools for inequities in an inner-city school, to discouragement over finding similar problems and practices in many other suburban, urban, and rural schools, to a realization that I too was taking a narrow view. Instead of taking the ecological view that I believed in, I too was removing learning to read and schooling in general from the historical, economic, political, and social context that give them meaning. It took me many years to see that deficit thinking and prejudice—biased, stereotypical views of those who differ from us in color, or language, or cultural values and beliefs, or social and economic class, or behavior, or ways of knowing and learning—can be neither blamed on any one group or person, nor corrected with anything short of transforming our society.

ORGANIZATION OF THIS BOOK

Chapter 1 begins our exploration of the ecology of inequity with an overview of some of the enduring assumptions and myths about learning to read. Some common sense about what should be a natural process of learning to read broadens the definition of reading to one that is consistent with the research and theory building of the past 2 decades.

Chapter 2 describes what is meant by the use of the term *ecology* as it relates to the reading and learning processes. From nearly every field and discipline the call is for more integration, a more holistic approach, a broader and more inclusive view—a view that can include the multiple interrelated and interconnected aspects of complex human systems in their naturally occurring contexts, including family, school, and community systems as well as the historical, social, cultural, political, and economic factors that define them—a view that can lead us to deeper understanding and knowledge as teachers, parents, administrators, policy makers, and human beings.

After an examination of these issues, we move to the two case studies in Chapters 3 and 4 for an in-depth look at the perceptions, values, beliefs, and assumptions of those who make up these two very different (one is suburban and the other is urban), yet surprisingly similar, ecologies. Readers who would like a less interpretive view of the case studies are encouraged to read Chapters 3 and 4 before Chapters 1 and 2. I have attempted to allow the case studies to "speak for themselves," reserving most of the interpretation, analyses, and applications for other chapters in the book. Chapter 5 analyzes and compares what we can learn from the case studies, linking them with a broader view of the learning/nonlearning processes and issues.

Chapters 6 and 7 attempt to build a framework for second-order change of the system. Chapter 6 explores a Vygotskian interactive social systems theory of learning that suggests ways that children might learn because of, rather than in spite of, the ways that they are taught and evaluated in school. Chapter 7 adds a historical perspective and a systems lens, attempting also to answer some frequently asked questions about this integrative, "noniatrogenic" approach to learning to read and learning to learn—questions related to heterogeneous classrooms, inclusion of students in classrooms, and the new role of the specialist.

Chapters 8 and 9 bring us to transforming the ecology of inequity. Stories of ongoing change in schools are detailed in Chapter 8, along with examples of student and teacher growth and renewal. Several models for parent and community empowerment are described, including our "Smalltown" oral history project and other successful community-based efforts. Examples of preservice teacher development at Elizabethtown College further document the possibilities for change.

Chapter 9 includes two models for transforming schools. The first is a university–school building model for school reform and change that Morton Botel and I have been refining over the past 5 years. The second is a college–school partnership model for the professional development of both preservice and in-service teachers. This model was created in collaboration with the superintendent and faculty. And finally, we conclude with a revaluing of our vital human resources and our traditional American values of both individual freedom and community responsibility.

A GLIMPSE OF THE STORIES TO FOLLOW

Randall Bauer, who presently directs Pennsylvania's Division of Early Childhood and Family Education, frequently comments on the rather appalling fact that we have a need for a Children's Defense Fund in the United States. Connie Delmuth, the director of Children's Services for the Pennsylvania State Office of Mental Health and Mental Retardation, and Beth Beh, the Governor's Advisor on Child Care, are similarly dismayed at the statistics that cite the United States as having the poorest children, the most underfunded child and family care system, and the highest infant mortality rate of all the industrialized nations in the world. As a country, we have contributed for years to "Save the Children" efforts for starving and dying children from third world countries; it now appears that similar efforts need to be directed to our own children.

A young man from Ireland was brought recently to this country by a parish priest to work in what he described as third world conditions in a poor section of a neighboring city. He views his job as similar to Peace Corps work. Sister Miriam, who visits the families in the nearby housing projects of the same city, has been the sole provider of crisis counseling, social services, health care, economic relief, language translation, and basic human compassion and support for the past several years, with no help in sight. She tells me that her job was supposed to be helping people with their spiritual life, but she has all these other human needs to try to meet instead.

In a small northeastern town, a bright 20-year-old man ("James"), whom I have observed since fourth grade and have grown to care about like one of my own sons, has been judged by school personnel and community members to be part of the 70% of the young African American men caught in a tragic cycle of school failure, teenage parenthood, unemployment, poverty, despair, drugs, crime, prison, or death.

His "good" suburban school is experiencing serious racial problems, which the administration can no longer deny. And his "nice" middle-class, predominantly white town is finally beginning to see the need for a social/racial justice coalition to address the needs of this essentially segregated town—a town in which a dead bird and a white glove were placed on the altar of one of the four separate African American churches, one of which marks the spot where the underground railroad came through; a town whose historical museum holds little of the rich history of its own African American community; a town that recently had a cross burning on the lawn of an African American family that moved to a white neighborhood.

One of the lowest achieving schools in a major metropolitan city is within a Latino community. In this school, an entire first-grade class was retained recently, and only four of 35 second-grade students were passed. Current research has documented unquestionably the uselessness of grade retention as well as the high percentage of future dead ends for retained students; so the course may be set for the students you will meet in this inner-city story. In a school with a population of 1,000 students, 85% of whom are Latino, there is only one bilingual teacher valiantly trying to bridge huge cultural and linguistic misunderstandings and miscommunications. Bewildered children, badly in need of social interaction and understanding, are told to speak only English when they try to talk with a friend in the hallway.

Similarly, in another urban school where the African American population is 50%, there is only one African American teacher, and there are only white school board members, town council members, and administrators. Although there are no students of color in the gifted class, they are over-represented in special education, learning support, remedial, and behavior problem classes.

Fortunately, there are also some less tragic stories to share: stories of collaborative efforts to transform these ecologies. A group of colleagues in social work, communications, political science, education, business, religious studies, and music therapy departments at our small liberal arts college have been discussing a broad ecological approach to meeting the needs of poor and minority children and families in a nearby urban school district, while at the same time developing a variety of pre-professionals to address these needs in the future. We have begun to develop a college–school partnership that we hope to build as a model for other college/university–school partnerships.

The past and present superintendents of this district, Timothy Lafferty and Kenneth Kitch, have been working very hard to support the professionalism of the faculty, the school board, and the community. Using a Deweyan democratic model of reflective participation (Gibboney, 1984; Lafferty,

1988), they have facilitated an important shift toward responsible action in a culture previously dominated by hopelessness and passive acceptance. And they are collaborating with our college in the development of future teachers as well as grant proposals to establish a professional development site in their school district (see Chapter 9 for this model).

Two university researchers and professors, Morton Botel and Lynne Putnam, who collaborated in our first partnership project, have themselves directed broadly based major research and intervention efforts in inner-city schools in Philadelphia and Washington D.C. They provide both inspiration and consultation to our research and development projects. In addition, Morton Botel continues to work closely with inner-city schools, as well as more than 75 other school districts that are linked with his Penn Literacy Network in a process of renewal and reform (Botel, 1993a). For the past 14 years David Sambolin has worked tirelessly as a community legal services lawyer to advocate for inner-city children and families. His most recent successful interventions include the promise of $17 million from the school district to build a badly needed middle school and $1 million for a music center in the inner city.

A sociology professor at another small liberal arts college, Susan Rose, directed her independent and field study students, in collaboration with those of a high school English teacher, Andrea Fishman, to gather an oral history of the African American community in "Smalltown," U.S.A. (Palmer, Esolen, Rose, Fishman, & Bartoli, 1991). In that same town a retired principal, William Spraglin, has worked in his own community to better understand the needs of his fellow African Americans and to support efforts toward change and equity. He also lends ongoing support to a previous community action center leader with outstanding organizational ability, Curtis Thompson, who, in collaboration with Rita Smith Wade-El, has brought about the beginning stages of teacher sensitivity training and multicultural inclusiveness in the "Smalltown" School District.

In short, the situation is not hopeless. But it must be said that the process of transformation is incredibly demanding and highly ambitious in scope. We need each other as collaborating professionals and colleagues across all disciplines, agencies, departments, and institutions. And even this is not enough. We also need to learn from the children, families, and teachers who inhabit the ecologies that we hope to transform.

If real second-order change, beyond more-of-the-same first-order change, is ever to occur, we need to have the insiders teach us what we need to know to understand the problems at a deep human level, and we need to learn from them the ways that we can work together as colleagues in what can be a richly rewarding endeavor.

I believe that this is human research at its best, combining deeper levels of understanding and knowledge with democratic community service. Only in this way can we begin to realize the very ideals and values upon which our uniquely American education system was begun.

A note on the use of language regarding race:

I use African American, Black American, and Black interchangeably throughout this text. Some of my colleagues and friends have preferences regarding the use of Black over African American, and some prefer the reverse; so I have chosen to respect this in my writing, with apologies to readers who find it confusing. Similarly, a number of my colleagues from Puerto Rico prefer Latino to Hispanic, so I have chosen to use Latino in this text.

PART I

The Ecology of Learning to Read

Common Assumptions and Common Sense About Learning to Read

There is a common assumption among many United States citizens that we learn to read because of the way we are taught to read in school. After over a decade of carefully observing the way that reading is taught in schools in over 200 suburban, rural, and urban classrooms, and after much research on other classrooms and previous decades as well, I can say with confidence that this is not usually the case. Nor is it usually the case in learning disability or Chapter 1 classrooms, attention deficit disorder or behavior adjustment programs, alternative learning classrooms, or any variety of other special or remedial programs, resource rooms, or mobile learning resource units or vans.

Those who do learn to read successfully more often learn in *spite* of the system by which they are taught (Bartoli, 1990b), a process we will return to later in this chapter. And those who do not learn to read very well more often appear to learn exactly (and only) the fragmented lower level skills they are taught and tested on in school. The predominance of linear skill sequenced approaches to reading in most classrooms in the U.S. (despite all the research, dialogue, conference presentations, workshops, books, and courses about whole language, literature-based approaches and integrated learning), suggests the need for a fundamental transformation in schooling that will free teachers to create their own student-centered curriculum and evaluation methods rooted in a defensible theory and research base.

This is not to blame teachers for children's reading failures, or to deny their incalculable influence on children's motivation and success, or to suggest that teachers are not the intelligent, hard-working, dedicated professionals that they are. This is to suggest that, after decades of research, writing, and successful experiments with student-centered teaching and evaluating, most teachers are still constrained by district and state tests that drive the curriculum and reduce the quality of teaching, learning, and evaluating in far too many classrooms. And this, combined with misassumptions and myths about reading and learning, as well as children and families of color, has created not only an ecology of inequity for poor and minority students, but also an ecology of minimal learning for all students.

15

A second common assumption among many people is that our teachers are less well informed, less dedicated to teaching children, and less caring than teachers of previous eras. Having had the opportunity to work with hundreds of teachers and reading/learning specialists both in and out of their classrooms, I can say again with confidence that this also is not usually true.

Many of the teachers that I have come to know over the past decade are taking graduate level courses after school, in the evenings, and in the summers to enrich their knowledge of how children learn. They are attending and presenting at professional conferences and workshops, and they are developing and experimenting with their own curriculum and evaluation methods rooted in sound, defensible theory and research. Teacher-led and teacher-created schools like Pat Carini's Prospect School in Bennington, Vermont, Deborah Meier's Central Park East and the River East School in Harlem, and a host of other small, successful, experimental public and private schools are testimony to the competence, care, and persistence of teachers despite the odds. Like most other misassumptions, these two are rooted in untested beliefs and popular media myths rather than in any close, careful observation in actual classrooms.

A third common assumption about learning to read, most often made by people who have not studied current research on children's natural language learning processes, is that beginning readers need a steady diet of very short, linguistically controlled texts (e.g., "Nan has a pan. The pan is tan." Or "Look, look. See Spot sit.") The same people assume that children must memorize the letters and sounds of the alphabet before they can attempt to read or write at all. Hence, most preschool, kindergarten, and first-grade classrooms are filled with "letter people" (Aunt Apple, Mr. Yawn, etc.), letter songs, and letter crafts, accompanied by countless dittos or worksheets on letter and sound matching with uninspiring stories that would make even Aunt Apple yawn.

Hence, too, we see department stores and even grocery stores littered with phonics workbooks and games devoid of personal, human, social, or literary meaning or sense. And we are bombarded with commercials for "Hooked on Phonics" and similar narrowly conceived "reading" materials in book, kit, audio- and videotape, and computer forms. Concerned parents and grandparents across the country are given false information from powerful, profit-focused companies, many of whom have been exposed as fraudulent by the less powerful and nonprofit International Reading Association (IRA) and the National Council of Teachers of English (NCTE). Professional education associations have a long way to go to develop the needed power and influence vital to getting truthful and valid information about children's learning to the public. Closer collaboration with state and federal policy makers and more inclusion of the expertise and research of our national education associations in political decision making would be a good beginning. The example of Randall Bauer, Pennsylvania's Director of Early Childhood and Family Education, is instructive. He uses the National Association for the Education of Young Children (NAEYC) policies and program recommendations as the foundation for his division's policy making.

MISASSUMPTIONS ABOUT THE NATURAL READING PROCESS

Contrary to common assumptions, we learn to read in a literate society such as ours the same way that we learn to talk, walk, draw, and sing: by seeing and hearing reading modeled skillfully for us, by noticing and understanding that this is an interesting and useful thing to do, by being invited to join in the process with those who can do it better than we can, by being allowed to try it for ourselves when we desire to (occasionally with a little help from our friends), and by being allowed to learn unself-consciously from our own mistakes. In most other basic human activities we are allowed to go through this natural learning process, from learning to use a spoon and potty to learning to walk, rather than crawl, across the floor. It would be thought rather bizarre to expect 2-year-olds to eat, talk, walk, or wipe their bottoms like adults before they have had ample time and experience— at least a few years—with eating, talking, walking, and wiping like a child.

Not so with reading and writing. In far too many classrooms there is the expectation that children should decode and encode letters precisely like an experienced adult reader and writer would, long before they have had ample experience with reading and writing like a child. Children begin reading signs and other environmental print (Jello and cereal boxes, McDonald's signs, milk cartons, noodle soup cans, toothpaste tubes) on their own when they find it useful or interesting to do so. If you can stand the pressure, take any 3-year-old to the grocery store, and you will quickly see what they are capable of reading.

Children are willing and able to tackle words like *tyrannosaurus rex, ankylosaurus, Saturn,* and *Neptune* at age 3 or 4; and they can remember incredible details about a good story that interests them, the planets in the solar system, and the life and habits of dozens of dinosaurs. Anyone who has been asked by a 4-year-old to write "Michelangelo" or "Raphael" on a drawing (or has been enlisted to help write "Teenage Mutant Ninja Turtle") knows that young children do not shy away from big words.

So we have this paradox. Children love to try on adult words in their reading, writing, and speaking; and they love to play with adult language. But they are still children, and they need to be able to do it like children until they grow naturally into adult reading and writing. Despite this rather commonsensical need, parents and schools traditionally demand that they read and write like adults from the start. We are more inclined to let them proceed naturally in walking and talking (although we are seeing quite a few diagnosed speech "problems") than we are to let them proceed naturally in reading and writing. And our beginning reading vocabulary lists, pre-primer and primer texts, and accompanying worksheets and tests very rarely include *Leonardo, Mercury,* or *brontosaurus.*

Perhaps the problem is mainly an adult fear of children's "mistakes" leading to "bad habits," which is part of our Puritan heritage. If we adults can overcome our own fears and learn to trust children, recalling that, in fact, they do learn to walk and talk rather well if we let them do it their own way in their own good time (and remembering the ear-grating, yet somehow lovely, and certainly never "corrected" sounds of our children's early violin, piano, and trumpet songs), perhaps we can begin to advance to higher rates of literacy.

Trusting children to learn, along with trusting teachers to teach, will release us from the misguided dependency on narrow measures of account-ability and testing in schools. Through standardized testing, both students and teachers are being held accountable for meaningless isolated subskills—testable bits of trivia—that constrain and limit the construction of a curriculum for more meaningful learning. We need to trust teachers and their students to take responsibility for the whole reading, learning, and teaching process; and we need to support the professional development of teachers while they do this.

On a personal note, since I have never felt completely confident about my spelling of dinosaur names, I once asked my 6-year-old son Patrick to see if I spelled *ankylosaurus* and *tyrannosaurus* right. He immediately went to one of his favorite books and pointed out the correct spelling for me. And I noticed first-grade students in the River East School in New York City's Spanish Harlem solving their own hermit crab research problems in the same way. That told me something about what all emergent readers are capable of if they are provided with a literate environment at school (regardless of whether they have many books at home), and when we capture their interest and encourage their experimentation with reading, writing, and talking throughout the school day.

MISASSUMPTIONS ABOUT TEACHERS

Another false assumption is rather widespread and politically popular, particularly in these teacher-bashing days of recession and teacher strikes:

that is, that teachers either do not know enough or do not care enough to do anything about this unfortunate state of affairs. And, it is further assumed, these teachers should be tested, be weeded out if they score and perform poorly, or at least be better controlled (much like the system works for our defenseless children) so there will be more "excellence" in the classrooms. We have only to look at the less than inspiring record of children's test scores on critical thinking over the past few decades (especially in inner-city schools), or perhaps at those of the army where the whole testing game got its unfortunate start (Gould, 1981), to see that more tests are certainly not the answer.

The fallacy in testing teaching is, of course, the same as the fallacy in testing reading and writing processes with one-right-answer, multiple choice, standardized tests: We are testing only shallow, isolated variables and lower level skills out of their naturally occurring contexts. The actual process of teaching or reading or writing cannot be captured and measured by such superficial methods. Observation of teachers' and students' orchestration of multiple, complex, interrelated strategies and skills in the process of teaching and learning; samples of their work collected over time; self and peer evaluations of the quality of the teaching and learning experiences; and other ecologically valid methods are necessary for useful evaluation of both teaching and learning processes.

Good teachers, like good parents, have always known a great deal about how children learn best. And the fact that you and I are here together talking across this text is evidence that some teachers and parents did a good job with us. But many school, community, cultural, bureaucratic, legalistic, political, economic, and historical factors have mitigated against what good teachers and parents know and wish to do in their classrooms and homes. And it is these broader contexts that we will explore in Chapters 3 and 4 to better understand how to save the learning environment for our nation's children, and the ecology of equality for our nation as a whole.

COMMON SENSE ABOUT LEARNING TO READ

One of the strengths of early childhood education at its best is its fresh and innovative approaches, illustrating some of the major issues that are important in truly educating children. Having been less swept away by the number, naming, testing fever, early childhood educators have often retained more fidelity to a child-centered curriculum. Observation and curiosity are more often described as "the basics," and knowing how to go about finding *an* answer is held to be more important than giving back to a teacher the one *right* answer. Too much control, behavior management/modification, reward and punishment mechanisms, teacher-directed memorization activities, and rote learning (reciting the alphabet and memorizing phonics rules) are not a part of the developmentally appropriate curriculum endorsed by the NAEYC (Bredekamp, 1987; Bredekamp & Rosegrant, 1992).

The changes that have come about (or perhaps I should say the basics that have remained in early childhood education) are rooted in research on children's actual learning processes that reveals the complex, social interactional, imaginative ways in which young children learn. According to child development and learning theorist Vivian Gussin Paley (1983), what children learn in school can be broken down into a story. She suggests that if you allow children to talk about the little worlds they have created in school, they soon will be able to take on everything.

What does that mean for optimal early childhood curricula? It means that we allow children to talk about, construct, and write their own stories in their own ways. Then we celebrate and support their own invented spellings, their own drawings, their own pretend reading (which is less "pretend" than it is rather sophisticated practice in successive approximation or "trying on" of the reading process), and their own sense-making both in life and in language. We do this in much the same way that we as parents and grandparents celebrated the development of their ability to talk, or walk, or ride a bike.

Rather than limiting children's emergent writing to copying text, or correcting their "errors" and expecting (or coercing) them to do the adult, correct, perfected version initially, we celebrate their successive approximations, we tolerate their slips, slides, and circles backward (because human learning is recursive, not linear), and we let them learn in their own way and in their own good time. And it is noteworthy that we rarely have children who are talking disabled, walking disabled, or bike riding disordered.

John Dewey (1899, 1910) knew this at the turn of the twentieth century when he talked about student-centered learning. But many things happened over the course of this century to turn our thoughts away from a focus on active, continually learning children emerging as readers and writers of their own lives in a multitude of complex, imaginative, and interactive ways. The field of psychology began to focus more narrowly on behavior and control factors, developing easily testable methods to calculate who was to be labeled as intelligent or "able." We bet on the wrong horse, as Frank Smith once commented, following Thorndike's quantitative measures instead of Dewey's pragmatic good sense: We are a number-happy nation with escalating numbers of unhappy children.

TESTING AND OTHER WRONG HORSES

The field of education followed the lead of psychology and began focusing on similarly narrow, measurable parts and pieces of learning. So, as reading, English, and writing teachers we were taught to both teach and correct spelling, punctuation, vocabulary, and grammar as separate, testable skills. We incorrectly assumed that we had no other "measurable," valid, or reliable ways of determining good thinking and good writing except these isolated skill tests. In reading we used similarly isolated skill tests of phonics, spelling, grammar, and vocabulary, even though both research and common sense told us that proficient reading was the orchestration of all of these and a host of other complex cognitive, social, personal, biological, and motivational processes and strategies (i.e., sense-making within context, re-reading to find the meaning, linking with personal experience, mediation and scaffolding, integrating old and new knowledge, taking risks, problem-solving, making educated guesses, and using one's imagination).

What was missing in all of the numbers was the child as a whole—a complex, thinking, feeling human being with interests, motivation, emotions, important personal relationships, cultural values, and a wealth of meaningful experiences to bring to the task of learning. So what we ended up with was a system of schooling that was devoid of the fullness and depth of human experience, knowledge, and imagination. Early reading and writing programs focused on decontextualized skill building rather than on developing skillful readers and writers engaged in purposeful, meaningful reading and writing.

What does this tell us about how to teach children to read and write? It means that the stories of their own lives, and their personal meaning-making when they hear good stories read to them, should be the heart of the literacy program. Children, like we older human beings, are daily reading and writing the stories of their own lives. And, if given encouragement and opportunities, they will continue to refine and revise their own reading and writing, develop increasingly sophisticated strategies for doing this, and ultimately emerge as competent readers and writers. As Smith (1987) puts it, they will become members of the literacy club. This is a true multicultural curriculum without clichés, misrepresentations, tokenism, and distortion—where children truly see themselves, their worlds, and their own sense-making in the language arts program.

On the part of teachers this demands trust and faith in the capacities of children and their families to surprise and amaze us with their abilities and their potentials. On the part of parents it means the same trust and faith in their own children as well as in the teachers who are embracing what may appear to be a rather new and risky way of teaching and evaluating. Americans have been schooled for decades to trust only isolated skill knowledge and the tests that measure it. But it will take Erickson's (1987) notion of "trust at the edge of risk" along with much collaboration and cooperation on the part of teachers, administrators, policy makers, and parents to turn the tide back to the real basics: a focus on children in the process of actual meaning-making.

LEARNING IN SPITE OF THE SYSTEM

A common question frequently emerges in conversations about the teaching of reading and writing: How come I learned to read and write okay with these skill teaching and testing methods if they're so bad? The answer is that more students learn to read and write in spite of these methods and tests than because of them. Spelling tests, grammar and punctuation exercises, and memorizing phonics rules never made anyone a better writer or reader. Actual writing and reading, much of which students do outside the classroom, make them better writers and readers, just as talking and practice in riding a bike or playing soccer make children better speakers, bike riders, and soccer players. The skill drills can help to refine some points after children know the game, but they cannot improve in a truly meaningful way unless they actually put it all together and play the whole game— and play it often.

In addition, we need a new set of assumptions that are grounded in research and theory to support a fuller, richer, broader view of the process of learning to read. Drawing on the social science fields of both regular and special education, sociology and sociolinguistics, anthropology and educational ethnography, human ecology, social psychology and family systems psychiatry, social work, and philosophy, we can begin to create this definition of learning to read and learning to learn. A beginning formulation of this definition follows.

TOWARD DEFINING THE PROCESS OF LEARNING

Although we had some very excellent definitions of the learning process in the early part of this century, most notably those of John Dewey and Lev Vygotsky, we were swept away in both education and psychology by the more "scientific," empirically tested definitions of behaviorists like B. F. Skinner. To use the example of reading, the process of learning to read became less of an integrated growth process experienced by all human beings in their natural learning contexts, and more of a decontextualized set of skills that psychologists removed from this process, tested in laboratories with rats and pigeons, and sequenced in "appropriate" ways for teachers, the assumption being that the unscientific teachers needed this skill sequencing to teach better.

It is uncertain whether anyone actually asked children or teachers if they, in fact, needed or wanted this set of sequenced skills or the veritable mountain of drills and tests that accompanied them in basal readers and workbooks, programmed learning kits, and standardized testing companies that have profited immeasurably from this narrow definition of learning to read (Harman, 1991). Children, however, have not profited much, since they are not pigeons, but are instead active, growing human beings embedded in their unique sociocultural ecosystems.

Let us suppose that we had not narrowed our view, and instead embraced a larger vision of the learning process—one that included a deeper understanding of active, developing learners in interaction with their own and each other's ecologies as they struggle to make meaning in life and, symbolically, in language. What would be the important concepts in this broader definition of learning? I would like to propose five themes that have emerged from the literature and research in language learning over the past few decades that have the potential to broaden our vision of learning, teaching, and evaluating; themes that, most important, contain within them the power to help us provide every child in our country with a meaningful education.

It should be stressed that this is but a humble beginning in an attempt to begin to pool the great wealth of interdisciplinary resources that should be integrated for an ecologically valid definition of learning in which we could root our very best understanding of learners and our most meaningful and helpful diagnoses and interventions. Many of the ideas to follow come from the diverse fields of philosophy, psychology, sociology, psychiatry, ecology, regular and special education, sociolinguistics, and ethnography/anthropology—social sciences that have unfortunately become too fragmented from each other to engage in continuous fertile dialogue. With the additional dialogue and critical thinking of talented professionals in special education who care very much about people and learning, and whose experience with a wide variety of learning and behavior problems gives them a special competence, our more well-grounded definitions may yet lead the field ahead to "escape the current constraints on our thinking and creativity" (Adelman, 1989).

CRITICAL THEMES IN THE LEARNING PROCESSES

Examining the research and theory that have evolved over the past 2 decades on the reading and writing processes, we see five recurrent themes that hold great promise for an ecologically valid definition of learning in general, and for the process of learning to read in particular. (By ecologically valid, I mean situated in the broadest, most comprehensive context and inclusive of the interactions and interconnections of all parts to the whole. This automatically rules out narrow definitions that remove cognition from affect, skills from meaningful context and content, and behavior from relationships and social context.) These themes are *social* interaction, *personal* reflection and response, *integration* of interrelated competencies, *transformation* and growth, and *ecological* fit (SPITE): reminding us of the need to transform schooling so students learn *because* of, rather than in *spite* of, the system.

Social Interaction

The crucial importance of social interaction in the process of learning can be seen throughout the literature on the reading and writing processes. The early works of Lev Vygotsky (1934, 1962, 1978) in the 1920s and 1930s suggest a definition of learning that demands authentic dialogue, real human communication, and a reciprocal relationship between learner and teacher rooted in equality, respect, and trust. Vygotsky describes the supportive interpersonal mediation that is needed for the learner to progress: The teacher leads students ahead in the "zone of proximal [potential] development," which is a level just ahead of that which students can handle on their own. Bruner (1973, 1984, 1986) describes a similar type of mediation or scaffolding in learning, in which the teacher interacts to build supports that lead students ahead toward better learning.

This social interactional approach is not new to students of John Dewey (1899, 1916), who nearly a century ago described learning as requiring not only subject matter, but also a relationship of collaboration and partnership in an environment conducive to learning. Dewey saw the teacher as a catalytic agent—a liberator of the learner; and his metaphor for mechanistic, decontextualized teaching—like inscribing records on passive discs to be given back when the button (the test) is pushed—is as apt today as we approach the twenty-first century as it was at the turn of the twentieth century. Michael Apple's (1980, 1988) critiques of the mechanization of teaching suggest that it is even more important today. So much for progress.

Personal Reflection and Response

A second critical theme in broader definitions of the learning processes is the active, personal response and reflection of the student in interaction with the teacher, the text, the task, and the social contexts. This affective, emotional, feeling level of response that is vital to the learning process has been addressed by a wide variety of authors, most notably Louise Rosenblatt (1978, 1980) in the reader response literature and Sylvia Ashton-Warner (1963) in her classic book, *Teacher.* Dewey (1938) also described the importance of intrinsic motivation—the deep human level of interest, need, and goals—in the learning process.

In the sociolinguistic literature, Halliday (1978) describes the process of learning to read, or "learning to mean," as rooted in the functional needs and purposes of the individual learner: It is an active, personal, deeply human, and highly social process fueled by intrinsic motivation. Behavior modification advocates and other extrinsic reward and punishment proponents have narrowed their vision to exclude this critical aspect of learning; but the persistent failure and disability labeling rates suggest that neither this piece nor any other part of the ecology can be extracted without throwing the entire system into a muddle.

Integration of Interrelated Competencies

A third critical theme in the learning and teaching literature is the integration of the many complex and interrelated competencies that are a part of the learning process. Marie Clay (1979) writes about the importance of orchestrating the multitude of strategies involved in the reading process within the context of real, authentic reading—an integrative process that appears to be working very well in her native New Zealand, which has one of the highest literacy rates in the world. Morton Botel (1977, 1979, 1981) likewise describes this wide variety of interrelated strategies in the reading and writing processes, such as linking with prior experience and knowledge, self-monitoring, reflecting, and questioning. Like Vygotsky, Bateson, and Dewey (and unlike Piaget and Bloom), he describes these processes as non-linear and recursive rather than a stage developmental progression.

Transformation and Growth

A fourth critical theme in the best of current learning and reading literature is transformation. The learning process, at its best and most meaningful, involves change and growth leading to a new level of understanding. It is a personal renewal, an enlargement of thinking, a new sense of potential and awareness, an unleashing of energy and creativity. Paulo Freire (1980, 1983) describes this aspect of the learning process as liberating people to be independent thinkers who can look critically at their own culture and create it anew. By reflecting upon their own words and world they can rewrite that world, transforming themselves and their society. Freire's success in large-scale literacy campaigns in third world countries suggests the power of a transformational view of the learning process.

Although tragically few in number, the success stories of some of our inner-city schools owe much to their focus on the transformation of negative self-fulfilling prophesies of failure to belief in the potential of each child. But faith is not enough: This change in expectations needs to be backed by supportive mediation until the students themselves have faith in their ability to transform their own lives and make changes in their own communities (Ada, 1988; Bartoli, 1990a; Bartoli & Botel, 1989; Comer, 1988; Cummins, 1986). And they cannot achieve this without local, state, and national political, social, and economic commitments to truly make something happen for the students as well as their families.

James Britton (1970, 1988) also describes the process of learning to read as one that involves meaningful human growth and change, suggesting that learning, growing, and living are alternative words for the same process. So we begin to envision a growthful process of learning that evolves in a classroom community of readers and writers, much like Dewey described, focused on real student needs and purposes, yet linked with and critically conscious of the outside community that it works to both understand and transform. With such a Deweyan/Freirean linking of consciousness, reflection, and practice, we have the critical basis for a participatory democracy and a more humane society.

Ecological Fit

Such a delicately balanced and intricately interactive classroom ecology illustrates the fifth theme that appears in a variety of forms in the research and literature on the learning processes: ecology—the interaction of many systems and subsystems in the ecology of every learner, the interaction of biology and culture within each individual, the interrelationships between and among the learner, family, school, community, and culture, and the way all of this fits together to make up an interconnected whole.

The overwhelming complexity of the seemingly unending array of biological, environmental, social, emotional, familial, cognitive, linguistic, cultural, historical, economic, and political factors and relationships that make up the wider ecology of the learner threatens to defeat even the most organized and persistent ecological researchers. And yet there are many who continue to go "where angels fear" (Bateson & Bateson, 1987) and look for the illusive Batesonian "pattern that connects": the unifying thread that connects meaning throughout the ecology and helps to explain meaning within.

We have tried to separate cognition from emotions, intrinsic motivation from extrinsic rewards, learners from authentic learning contexts, and parts and pieces of learning from the interactive and interconnected process of learning, only to find that, in fact, the whole is different from and even greater than the sum of its parts. In reading, for example, we have discovered that children who score well on tests of fragmented reading skills and subskills ("skills," incidentally, that the IRA and the NCTE do not support in either definition or hierarchy) are not necessarily our most thoughtful, analytic, critical thinkers and readers. In writing we have found that students who score well in tests of writing skills (which are usually mere editing skills—not the fundamental, crucial processes of thinking, prewriting, drafting, and organizing that precede the final product that all writers edit) are not necessarily good writers.

In working with families, therapists frequently have noticed that, when a problem with one member is finally resolved (perhaps a reading problem), suddenly another problem (perhaps a math or behavior problem) presents itself—or another family member experiences problems. It seems that the family as a whole system has a life of its own, and attempting to treat the problems of individual members apart from a larger understanding of the family ecology is nonproductive. So we see across disciplines the search for the broader view—the wisdom to put it all together, to understand the whole more deeply, and ultimately to be able to use the knowledge in a way that is meaningful and conducive to growth to help those who are having problems.

Gregory Bateson (1972, 1979) was one of the early theorists who described the broader ecological picture in human communication and human relationships. He was also an early opponent of "chopping up the ecology" and thereby losing the more meaningful whole and of creating false dualities—simplistic either–or dichotomies like biology or culture (rather than an interaction between the two) and cognition or emotion (as if the mind could be split in two). In both reading and special education such dualities live on in the form of the current debates over phonics or whole language (as though good teaching does not demand both) and the full inclusion initiative/mainstreaming or pull-out programs (rather than an integration of the best of both approaches).

Solutions for children's problems that are rooted in a narrow view of the wider ecology of the child will always result in more problems—possibly worse ones than they started with. Bateson's advice for avoiding such problematic solutions is to understand the larger ecology—to see how it all fits together and works as an interactive whole. Fortunately, this advice greatly expands our repertoire for intervening in and solving problems in a way that promotes growth and transformational change—what Bateson and his colleagues (Watzlawick, Weakland, & Fisch, 1974) call second-order change as opposed to first-order, more-of-the-same change (see also Feuerstein, 1979; Feuerstein & Rand, 1988).

Some activities that are not so very helpful (to learning) have been taking place in classrooms across the country in the name of reading. Children have been more engaged in skill work than they have been given opportunities to play the game. Transforming this will take all of us working together to confront commonly asked and misinformed questions like, "Why aren't they testing/teaching more phonics and spelling in school?" We could answer such a question with (1) "They already are" and (2) "Would you judge a Pavarotti or Price (substituting a favorite singer) by the ability to tell you the names of the notes on sheet music, or would you instead listen to the performer sing the song?" And how do you suppose they became such good singers? Through reciting the names of notes, or through singing?

CHAPTER 2

The Fragile Ecology of Equality

Making well-thought out changes in living systems is a dangerous business. Fixing one part, on the one side, is likely to produce new and worse pathological events miles away on the other. . . . The most dangerous of all courses is to begin doing things without even recognizing the existence of a system, and in this case a system in which all people . . . are working parts. (Thomas, 1992, p. 82)

As a nation about to enter the twenty-first century, we need to carefully consider the increasingly fragile condition of the ecology of what traditionally has been called our most precious resource—our children. We have sometimes expended more effort and had more success in dealing with polluted air, streams and lakes, the ozone layer, acid rain, dying banks, ground pollution, and endangered animals than we have with preserving our most vulnerable children's environment for optimal learning and development. Millions of poor and minority children and youth across the country, along with a sizable number of their middle-class peers, fail to learn on a daily basis in our schools. For too many this begins a lifetime of failure and hopelessness that leads to devastating social consequences.

Over the past decade in American education the number of students given labels[1] of reading and learning disability or deficiency (e.g., LD, ADD, remedial, Chapter 1) has tripled, and the number of those failing or at risk for failure who eventually drop out of school has risen sharply as well. Kozol (1985) describes our literacy rate as 49th in the 150 nations of the United Nations. But most important, for a nation founded on democracy and the freedom of every individual to have equal access to educational and economic opportunity, those who have consistently been found on the bottom of the educational, social, and economic heap have been African American, Latino, Mexican American, and Native American people. So we have the additional problem of preserving the ecology of equality, particularly in learning opportunities for all of our nation's children.

The parallels in some alarming learning failure trends suggest two dimensions of the inequity problem. The first is that the proportion of students of color projected for the twenty-first century is one-third of our school population, with many inner-city schools having well over 50% minority populations. At the same time, combined rates of retention, dropout, and those labeled as at risk for failure will reach at least one-third, particularly in the inner city where failure rates may be 50% or more.

Second, the projected rate of disability/deficiency labeling for the next century, if it continues to escalate at present rates, is one out of four students. Coincidentally, the number of children living below the poverty level in our country is also one out of every four children (one out of two for African American children, who are disproportionately found in Chapter 1, remedial groups, and other low reader/slow learner groups). Even when schools do not use special categories for removing children from the mainstream classroom (the current trend is toward full inclusion),[2] the classroom teacher frequently informally divides or groups children into high, middle, and low groups based on "ability." So again we are left with one-third of the children in every classroom assumed to be deficient or below average.

Poor and functionally illiterate children and families, particularly if they are African American, Latino, or Native American, are in much greater danger of falling victim to a host of interrelated social ills: school failure and dropout, juvenile delinquency and crime, drug and alcohol abuse, teenage pregnancy, depression, poor health, and suicidal despair. The urgency of this ecological crisis cannot be overstated. If a nation can be evaluated on the basis of its ability to care for all its children, the dramatic increases in childhood poverty rates, infant mortality rates, childhood and adolescent depression, addiction, and suicide, and the alienation and despair of too many of our youth suggest that we are indeed "a nation at risk." And when the democratic and egalitarian principles on which our country was founded seem inaccessible to a third of the population, we have cause for alarm (Kozol, 1991).

Researchers and theorists have tended to view many of these social issues and problems in isolation from the larger interactive ecology in which they occur. In doing so, they have narrowed their vision and omitted from view the broader interactions and relationships that create and sustain the very problems they seek to understand. The major contribution of an ecological perspective for research in human learning and development is a broad view of the issues and problems, including perceptions and interrelationships throughout the ecology of the learner—an ecology that includes the school, the family, the community, and the larger culture as interactive and interconnected systems.

WHY USE THE TERM ECOLOGY?

I have chosen to use the term *ecology* for several reasons, some of which are practical and some of which are metaphorical. One of the practical reasons is that I could not find another term to include all of the data that I had collected between 1982 and 1986 for longitudinal case studies of low progress readers. I wanted to include the total environment as well as the interrelationships and interconnections among the various systems of child, school, and community/culture; and the variety and complexity of the data that I collected demanded the broadest framework I could find. It demanded one that included the notion of interdependent systems working as a whole, like individual family members in a family system.

There is an inclusive connotation to the word *ecology* that suggests the depth of study necessary to understand more fully the behavior of human beings in their natural social environments. We get the sense that we can never quite get it all, but that what will be learned in the attempt will be far richer than if we had never tried at all. I am reminded of the theme of the 1963 National Science Fair that I participated in as a teenager: Ah, but our reach should exceed our grasp, else what is a heaven for?

In addition to the more usual connection with environmental issues in field biology and interrelated complex systems in family therapy, ecology suggests a holistic perspective that takes into consideration multiple environmental and cultural influences as well as internal biological and emotional factors. It suggests a view that is context based, broadly conceived, inclusive of interdependencies and recursiveness, and richly descriptive of the infinite complexities of the human species.

Colleagues have suggested using *environment* as a substitute for ecology, and *ethnography* as a better term for this kind of broad and "thick" descriptive research. Although there are many similarities between environmental studies and what I have chosen to call ecological studies, I believe there are also many complex human systems dynamics explored by Bateson, Sarason, Rhodes, Ogbu, and Bronfenbrenner (see section to follow) that go beyond traditional conceptions of environment. And although good ethnography can describe the complex personal, social, and cultural influences that shape and constrain human behavior, there are additional interpersonal, intrapersonal, biological, and emotional factors along with broader political, economic, and historical issues that are sometimes omitted in ethnographic descriptions.

My use of ecology suggests the need for a more interdisciplinary view of human beings learning in their natural social environments—a view that can bring us closer to understanding each other and improving the life conditions of all human beings. Much in the same way that the development of sociolinguistics has increased our understanding of language use and language learning by connecting sociology, anthropology, and linguistics, I believe that an ecology of learning perspective might encourage collaborative research and development across the fields of sociology, social work, anthropology, biology, social psychology, family systems psychiatry, communication, sociolinguistics, philosophy, and education.

The work of Urie Bronfenbrenner, Gregory Bateson, and Lewis Thomas illustrates the advantages in developing an interdisciplinary field that focuses on human ecological systems in contemporary society. For instance, in describing the interconnected problems of overpopulation, disease, poverty, and malnutrition (I would add illiteracy), Thomas (1992) suggests that "overpopulation is, in part, the result of the disease, poverty, and malnutrition. . . . It is not one problem, it is a system of problems" (p. 82). And his warning about the danger of a narrow view that omits complex interrelationships begins this chapter.

Another reason for my choice of ecology is the metaphoric value of the inherent ideas of inclusiveness, wholeness, and infinite complexity—ideas that as researchers we should stand humbly before, recognizing the constraints and fallibility of our inevitably narrow thinking, the tentativeness of even our best conclusions, our need for interdisciplinary collaboration, and the long way we have to go in our quest for understanding and knowledge. To counter our problematic tendencies to separate and fragment, I am suggesting a collaborative dialogue across many fields, recognizing that we all need each other's perspectives if we are to solve immensely complex, and seemingly intractable, human problems. Perhaps this dialogue will take us beyond the fragmentation (chopping up the ecology), linear thinking, and dualities that Bateson (1972, 1979) so abhorred, beyond the objectivism and relativism that Bernstein (1983) described, to construct what Geertz (1973) called "a concept of human nature that, more than a statistical shadow and less than a primitive dream, has both substance and truth" (p. 52).

What is the hope for this? Thomas (1992) suggests that, although human beings are still a juvenile (and fragile) species, and although we fumble quite a bit, we will amaze ourselves by what we can become as a species.

> We may be all going through a kind of childhood in the evolution of our kind of animal . . . having only begun to master the one gift that distinguishes us from all other creatures, it should perhaps not be surprising that we fumble so much. We have not yet begun to grow up. (p. 81)

And, although historically in our attempts to improve education in the U.S.A. we have perhaps caused more problems than we have solved, Sarason

(1971) likewise is hopeful, if we can expand our ways of looking and thinking: "If at least part of the problem has been a consequence of the ways we have been thinking, one is not justified in concluding that we are dealing with a hopeless situation" (p. 230).

PRECEDENTS FOR STUDYING THE ECOLOGY OF HUMAN LEARNING

In this section I will explore some of the precedents in anthropology, psychology, sociology, and family therapy for an ecological view of human learning and growth. Research on the ecology of contemporary human beings is supported by the work of Bateson (1972, 1979) and Bateson & Ruesch (1951), who explored the ecology of mind and human communication; Bronfenbrenner (1979, 1986, 1988), who described the ecology of human development; Sarason (1971, 1982), who detailed the ecology of the school; Hobbs (1975), who wrote about the ecosystem of the learner; and Rhodes (1967), who described the ecology of the "disturbing" child.

Concerning the ecology of the school, Goodlad (1987) wrote about the ecology of school renewal; more recently, Darling-Hammond, Lieberman, and Miller (1992) have written about systemic restructuring of schools. Both Ogbu (1980) and McDermott (1974) linked ethnography and ecology to describe the ecology of caste-like minorities in schools, and Rist and Harrell (1982) looked at the social ecology of labeling students.

A number of family systems researchers, including Haley (1981), Minuchin (1974), Hoffman (1981), Napier & Whitaker (1978), and Watzlawick, Weakland, and Fisch (1974), who viewed families as dynamic, interconnected, interdependent wholes, have provided us with a strong foundation for understanding the school as a system. See Chapter 2, "An Ecological Systems View," in Bartoli and Botel (1988a) for a description of this body of research.

The use of the term *ecology* is borrowed primarily from field biology, wherein it describes the interconnected and interdependent environments of living organisms in nature. Close, careful, long-term observation and data collection in naturally occurring contexts are demanded, along with analyses that include the multiple interrelated systems and subsystems that together make up the ecology of the organism. Stephen Gould (1980, 1981), Lewis Thomas (1974, 1992), and Gregory Bateson (1972, 1979) provide many excellent examples from field biology research.

In this view of multiple and complex causality and interacting systems, the whole appears to have an added life of its own. Perhaps this is part of the success of creating holistic literate environments in classrooms: Whole texts explored in interactive social contexts seem to have a powerful effect on learners that is unmatched by solitary examinations of the parts and pieces of language in workbooks, textbooks, and tests. And the multiple effects of an integrated approach provide us with an antidote to the kind of fragmentation that Bateson decried as anathema to deeper understanding of complex human systems and Rosenblatt (1980) viewed as resulting in raising emotional cripples.

Enlarging our view to attempt to include the entire ecology of the learner (e.g., classroom, school, family, community, culture) as well as multiple subsystems (e.g., peers, curriculum, teachers, siblings, values, economics, politics) and their interrelationships, complete with difficult-to-sort-out and even contradictory information, keeps us humbly aware of how little we really know. And hopefully this will lead us to even closer, more careful observation; more supportive and successful interaction with children in the process of learning, and fewer negative assumptions.[3]

MULTIDISCIPLINARY DEFINITIONS AND APPLICATIONS OF ECOLOGY

As previously noted, the ecological approach taken in the research described in this section comes from the combined fields and perspectives of field biology, sociology, ecological psychology, social systems research (particularly using a family systems approach and Batesonian communication theory), sociolinguistics, and educational ethnography using a social interaction (Vygotskian) theory base. The field biology definition of ecology is the interrelationship of organisms and their environments; I have used ecology to mean the totality or whole ecosystem of a student, including the pattern of relations between human learners and their environments for learning.

Ecology in sociology refers to the distribution of humans and material resources, and the consequent social and cultural patterns and interdependencies that are created and maintained. This provides a way of looking at the ecology of inequity in education from a socioeconomic and sociopolitical perspective: Who has access to money for better schooling or power to make changes and who does not? and Why it is that those who have the least continue to get the least (Kozol, 1991)?

The ecology of human development, articulated best by Bronfenbrenner (1979, 1986, 1988) and Hobbs (1975, 1978), refers to the multiple contexts within which the human being is embedded, the perspectives of those who live in each context, and the mutual accommodations of the developing person and the changing contexts. Central to ecological psychology, and to its usefulness in understanding the learning process, is the theory that learning and development in one setting are profoundly affected by conditions in the broader context in which the setting is embedded. This, for instance, underscores the importance of the family–school interface and of understanding the perspectives and concerns of the family and the community as we try to help children learn.

The contribution of social systems theory and research is most evident in the view of the family and school as interactive and interrelated systems that are greater than the sum of their parts. Family and school systems research looks at the relationships and communication patterns between members in a social system as well as the perspectives of individuals. The contribution of Bateson (1972) and his research group, including Watzlawick, Beavin, and Jackson (1967), to understanding the complexities of human communication patterns is enormous, as is his vision of a pattern that connects, suggesting the larger question, How does it all fit together to make up an interactive whole?

The sociolinguistic approach to understanding language learning stresses the importance of social functions and uses of language, cultural influences, and social interaction. In the study of this highly social language learning process, ethnography provides the observational method to more deeply describe and understand the process in the actual learning contexts of school, home, and community. The work of Heath (1982, 1983) and that of Labov (1972, 1982) are excellent examples of this kind of human understanding. Common themes inherent in all of these approaches include the importance of understanding human relationships and social interaction in context, the importance of individual perceptions and views, and the search for interdependencies, interrelationships, and patterns across the whole ecology (also called the ecosystem) of an individual.

THE ECOLOGY OF EQUALITY

A major theme in this book is the need to preserve the ecology of equality: educationally, economically, politically, and socially. We have regressed rather than progressed in our efforts and our ability to provide for all our children equal opportunity for a meaningful, democratic education rooted in our highest American ideals. The traditional ideals of individual freedom and liberty, democratic self-governance, meaningful work, a caring and mutually responsive community, dedication to the common good, and a critically educated citizenry have regressed too often into class and race divisions, self-seeking abuses of power, unquestioned obedience to authority, passive acceptance of failure, and victim-blaming (Grubb & Lazerson, 1982).

To begin to preserve the ecology of these values for our children, we need to look at the complex social context in which they occur, and begin to understand the social processes that create or deny such values as equality of educational opportunity and individual freedom of choice (Bellah, Madsen, Sullivan, Swidler, & Tipton, 1985). With this contextual level of understanding, perhaps we can begin to find more fruitful possibilities for intervention and change: change that can truly transform the lives of our failing children by creating environments for authentic learning and growth.

Without such understanding we will continue to create problematic solutions that result in regression rather than progression toward change. Such problematic solutions as more testing, more standardization of curriculum and pedagogy, more "ability" grouping and tracking, more labeling, and more specialists to remove students from the classroom when they fail the tests and earn the labels are ample testimony to the futility of narrow approaches to the process of human learning (Bartoli, 1985b; Bartoli & Botel, 1988a).

Inequity in American education has been well documented for decades, but still it persists. The case studies that follow ask the question, How does this inequity happen—despite the concerned and sincere efforts of well-meaning teachers and administrators, and despite the presence or absence of social and economic stability? The answer to this question takes the form of an ecological case study covering a decade of suburban schooling for one African American student (Chapter 3) and a comparative study of urban schooling for Latino students (Chapter 4), which together detail the ecology of inequity in two very different settings. Many similarities are found between the learning and nonlearning experiences of James in his "good," traditional, middle-class suburban school and the experiences of Latino students in a large, "poor" urban school.

Acceptance of continued inequality and lack of academic success for disproportionate numbers of poor and minority students pervaded both the suburban and inner-city school and community contexts, allowing failure to be individualized rather than viewed as part of the wider ecology of social and economic inequality. Overrepresentation of poor white and African American students in low reading groups, remedial or Chapter 1 reading classes, learning disability or learning support classes, and lower academic tracks (as well as their underrepresentation in gifted, accelerated, advanced placement, or honors classes) was tolerated in the suburban school in the same way that 50–75% failure rates for Latino students were accepted as inevitable or "understandable" in the inner-city school.

Close, critical reflection of the role of the school structure, management, curriculum, and evaluation methods was noticeably absent in both settings. Critical reflection on the role of teacher, counselor, specialist, and administrative assumptions and expectations as they interacted with the continued rise in failure and disability was likewise absent. What seemed to be missing throughout was a view of the perceptions, relationships, and interrelationships across school, family, and community contexts that shaped and constrained the opportunities for poor and minority students and their families to succeed. And most noticeably absent was an ecological view of school inequality linked with social and economic justice in the larger society.

A second question—What can we do about it?—is addressed through (1) a social interactional theory of learning to root more optimal teaching practice, (2) a restructuring of teacher education at both the preservice and in-service levels, and (3) a proposal for a school-based model for integrated learning that embraces both the theory and the restructuring. The chapters following the case studies will address each of these issues involved in an ecological change process. This is vital to moving our education system to one that truly provides equal opportunity for all students to learn.

THE PROBLEMS WITH NARROW VIEWS OF HUMAN BEINGS

My own earlier graduate school training, first as an English major in the late 1960s, and later as a reading specialist in the late 1970s, did little to prepare me for a complex view of human learning. Linear skill sequences and corresponding prescriptive skill diagnoses were the standard tools of the trade. This left teachers and students equally frustrated when the scientific/mechanistic cures for learning problems too often left students impaled upon primers, locked into low achieving groups, labeled, and stuck (fewer than 2% of the labeled students ever progressed beyond their labels) in separate programs. Represented disproportionately in all categories of learning difficulty were (and continue to be) African American, Latino, Mexican American, and Native American students.

Myths abound where there are narrow views, and the past half century has produced quite a few narrowly conceived myths about children, families, and learning. Schrag and Divoky (1975), Hobbs (1975), Granger and Granger (1986), Coles (1987), Bartoli and Botel (1988a), and Donovan and McIntyre (1990) describe the myths of the hyperactive child, the fit/unfit child, the dyslexic or learning disabled child, and the at-risk, disturbed, or broken child—myths that have led educators and clinicians essentially to blame children (and/or their parents) for their own learning problems, ignoring the broader educational, social, cultural, economic, historic, and political dynamics that are part of the problem. Myths and misunderstandings about welfare and the "underclass" further fuel societal prejudices and widen the gap between the haves and the have nots. Popular media myths continue to win out over the more reasoned voices of researchers like Marmor, Mashaw, and Harvey (1992), Jencks (1992), Sitkoff (1993), and Wilson (1987).

Narrow views of learning rooted largely in decontextualized and controlled experiments obscure the knowledge of human social interaction, human development, and human relationship building so vital to children's growth and learning. Scientific attempts to control and manipulate human behavior, both experimentally and educationally, have had a critical impact on experimenters as well as subjects (McNeil, 1986). Some experimenters, authors, test makers, and textbook publishers have deluded themselves into thinking that conclusions drawn from artificially controlled experiments are directly applicable to all human beings in diverse social contexts. The dangers in this kind of omnipotent thinking are unfathomable, even beyond the trail of destruction left by narrowly conceived behavior management schemes, reductionistic and sequentially controlled curricula, and the ecologically invalid tests that drive them both.

One consequence of subjects being controlled (by the school, by the test, by the job, by the society) is a loss of personal responsibility for one's own behavior as well as a loss of belief in the possibilities for one's own life (Bellah et al., 1985). It is important to note that, in addition to the heavy reliance on behavior management schemes and teacher/school-dictated rules for control that dominate much of American schooling, there are even more such control measures in the inner-city schools that serve poor and minority students (see the many examples of rules and control in the inner-city case study in Chapter 4 as well as in Taylor & Dorsey-Gaines, 1988).

In his 1966 book, *They Thought They Were Free,* Milton Mayer wrote about the kind of society that evolves from a lack of individual responsibility and control.

> What happened [in Nazi Germany] was the gradual habituation of the people . . . to being governed by surprise; to receiving decisions deliberated in secret; to believing that the situation was so complicated that the government had to act on information which the people could not understand. (cited in Gray, 1992, p. 40)

Aldous Huxley (1932) gave us similar warnings over half a century ago in *Brave New World.* In his new world order individual freedom, choice, critical thinking, and personal responsibility reside only in the antiquated past or in remote villages of "savages." People are methodically conditioned to accept their scientifically controlled caste and destiny.

Although he is hopeful about the fragile human species, Thomas (1992) notes that he would feel better about our prospects, and more confident for our future, if he thought we were going to solve the immediate problem of inequity. Alluding to a creeping societal sense of powerlessness and loss of control, he says:

> The greatest danger of all is in our response. Having let nature take its course, we may someday decide that the problem has become insoluble, that the people knocking at our doors with hands outstretched have become the enemies at our gates, who can only be coped with by the traditional method of killing them. (p. 83)

Our growing numbers of disabled, at-risk, and failing learners (not to mention our swelling prison populations, poor children, and homeless families) are testimony to the need for more thoughtful observation of human beings in the context of their complex natural learning environments. By contrast, New Zealand, where teacher observations and interventions have been child-focused for the past 30 years, has one of the highest literacy rates in the world. There appears to be much truth in the old adage: The children will teach us, if we but let them.

What is needed, I believe, along with more child-centered, context-based, observational research, is an integrated view of the range of possibilities within the human species; a healthy respect for the richness and resources of human diversity that have always been the great strength of our nation; a commitment to the values of choice, equal opportunity, democracy, and cooperation; renewed efforts toward collaborative, contextual, interdisciplinary research and reform; and a strong sense of humility about the limitations of our knowledge.

We are reminded by Thomas (1992) that we do not have a choice in this, unless we plan to give up being human. His final argument is the simplest.

> We *owe* it. We have an obligation to assure something like fairness and equity. . . . The idea that all men and women are brothers and sisters is not a transient cultural notion, not a slogan made up to make us feel warm and comfortable inside. It is a biological imperative. (p. 95)

NOTES

1. On definitions: On the basis of a rather comprehensive review of the literature on reading and learning disabilities as well as other special education categories (the "in vogue" or popular label at present is attention deficit disorder, which is fast replacing the earlier learning disability label, which replaced dyslexia, which replaced word blindness), particularly on the definitional issues that divide the fields

of regular and special education, I have chosen to use the terms *reading disability, learning disability, low progress reading/learning,* and *learning/reading difficulty* interchangeably throughout this book. The majority of cases deal with the same problem—learning to read—regardless of the label.

The adoption of one label over another is frequently linked to social, historical, political, and economic factors rather than to purely diagnostic ones unique to the learner (Allington & McGill-Franzen, 1989; Bartoli & Botel, 1988a; Skrtic, 1991). Even in the few cases where a valid psychoneurological problem is involved, authorities suggest a balanced program in reading (Duffy, 1987; Vellutino, 1987). Hence there is neither diagnostic nor prescriptive value in choosing and assigning specific labels, an insight shared by one of the major framers of PL 94–142 (Walker, 1987), the past Assistant Secretary of the Bureau of Special Education (Will, 1986), and other authorities in the field (Allington, 1991; Clay, 1985; Coles, 1987; Gartner & Lipsky, 1987; Hobbs, 1975; Johnston, McGill-Franzen, & Allington, 1985; Sarason & Doris, 1979; Ysseldyke, Thurlow, Graden, Wesson, Algozzine, & Deno, 1983).

2. In a sense, the laws of ecology are operating to correct the runaway growth of special education labeling and placement in separate classrooms. In the case of learning disability placement, when the percentage of diagnosed students moved from the original 2% cap to 8%, 12%, and then 15% and above (particularly in inner-city schools where it soared well above 20%, broadening to an "at-risk" label), the bank literally broke. There was not enough money to cover so many pulled-out children and specialists, so the movement had to reverse itself toward mainstreaming. The current mandate is for full inclusion using instructional support teams to meet the needs of all learners in the mainstream classroom.

3. It could fairly be argued that one of the dangers in focusing on the ecology of the learner might be the neglect of equally important individual dynamics (not unlike the argument that integrated approaches to reading may neglect phonics, spelling, or grammar). Indeed this can happen if one's view is shortsighted and noninclusive. Balance is, of course, needed in any perspective or approach. My personal view is that it is better to begin with the most holistic perspective (in life and in language) and then work toward particulars within that context, rather than beginning with the parts and trying to piece together the whole. I believe this because human beings think in complex wholes from very early ages on (Bruner, 1986; Donaldson, 1978; Smith, 1987; Vygotsky, 1962, 1978) and because the whole may be different from, and indeed more than, the sum of its parts (Haley, 1981; Hoffman, 1981; Minuchin, 1974).

PART II

Case Studies of Inequity

CHAPTER 3

James's Story

This case study, like the inner-city study that follows, attempts to represent the perspectives of students and families whose voices typically are not heard in the literature on school reform and renewal. In the spirit of the student-centered ethnographic work of Denny Taylor and Catherine Dorsey-Gaines (1988), Shirley Heath (1983), Michelle Fine (1991), and Jane Hansen (1987, 1994), I have tried to let James tell us what we need to know to better understand some of the complexities of learning to read the world and the word. I have shared James's story with members of the Smalltown community, as well as with African American friends from other communities, to see if this case study is representative of the experience of other African American students, and they have assured me that it is.

Colleagues from other school districts and towns have also commented that this sounds like their school or their town; so this story appears to be describing "Anytown" U.S.A. and any school, rather than one selected town and school. Mainstream townspeople and school faculty may see less in this story that appears familiar or comfortable. But it is my hope that, in hearing other voices and in taking different views, we may all grow together in our ability to understand each other. For only on this foundation can we build more equitable and democratic communities, both in and out of school, that celebrate the talent and rich resources of their own diversity.

FIELDWORK JOURNAL (SPRING 1993)

I just talked with James yesterday on the telephone. At 20 he is a father now and is working for a trucking company, unloading on the docks—a pretty tough job with even tougher hours. He is considering someday going back for his GED since he never graduated from Smalltown High School.

We talked about some of the problems with the schools he went to and was labeled by: first remedial reader, then learning disabled, then learning and adjustment (previously labeled socially and emotionally disturbed) with oppositional behavior. And I shared with both him and his mother some of the data I have collected over the past decade concerning his school and community, asking for their thoughts as they looked back on what happened with James's schooling. I shared these data with the school administration as well.

Unlike the less positive administrators, James and his mother told me they thought that what I wrote reflected what they experienced. I wanted to know if they thought I had missed something or had somehow misrepresented their experience, and I was at once comforted in having gotten it right, and saddened that the problems were the difficult ones that I thought I was beginning to understand.

In a May 1993 interview, James reflected on his own story of learning and nonlearning in school, helping me to better understand some of the enduring problems that we face in the education of African American students in particular and students labeled as low achievers in general. Without the opportunity to interview and observe closely over time in James's classrooms, schools, and community, and without the opportunity to talk with and learn from James, his family, and the Black Community in Smalltown, I doubt that I would have come to better understand the larger context of learning to read.

I was not fully prepared for their messages or meanings when I first heard them, just as some of my college students—students who will be teachers tomorrow—are not prepared today. This case study, for which I thank James, his mother, his grandfather, his community, and all his teachers, principals, counselors, and specialists, is an attempt to help all of us to take a different view, to understand more fully from another perspective, and to broaden our understanding of what it means to both learn and not learn to read in the U.S.A.

NOTES ON THE CASE STUDY

The case study that follows [from a longitudinal study using participant observation (Agar, 1980; Spradley, 1980) story-taking (Sutton-Smith, 1982), ethnographic interviews (Spradley, 1979), dialogue journals (Kreeft, 1984), oral history (McLeod, 1987) and reading protocols (Lytle, 1982)] begins to answer the question of what schooling is like for an African American student growing up in a traditional suburban school district. With the historical data gathered from his early years in elementary school, a 2-year, follow-up study in middle and high school, an interview at age 20, and comparative interviews of other African American students in Smalltown, it is possible to describe over a decade of schooling for this student who was labeled as reading and learning disabled.

It has been known for a long time that African American, Latino, Native American, Mexican American, and poor students of all races have been overrepresented in such at-risk-for-failure categories as reading disability, low reading group, low academic track, learning disability, and other special education categories (ADD, EMR, SED, L&A). Yet educational researchers have rarely taken a long, close, careful look at the nature of the wider ecology of these students over time. In addition to the longitudinal contribution that this case study makes, the further reflective contributions of James, his peers, his family, and his community are significant for our understanding of their perception of how this inequity process works.

James's 1993 interview at age 20, reflecting over his school years, a 1990 interview with one of his peers (Shanell) at age 16, and a 1989 interview of a Smalltown resident (Rachel) at age 95 are interwoven into the case study to provide an interpretation from their current and historical perspectives. Their interview data will be followed by their pseudonyms for easier identification of the speaker. Their voices and experiences have taught me, as both a teacher and a teacher educator, how very much we need to learn from our students and their families if we hope to help them to learn to read.

In transcribing interviews, narratives, and protocols I have attempted to be faithful to the actual speech patterns of the participants. Such conversational expressions as *gonna* (going to), *doin'* (doing), and *wanna* (want to) do not denote poor grammar or lack of linguistic competence. They reflect informal conversational speech patterns typically found in this particular context.

James's case study illustrates the wealth of understanding that can come from an ecological exploration. In many ways James tells his own story, particularly through his own interviews and narratives, and we are led to agree with Freire (1980), who said:

> Intellectualist prejudices and above all class prejudices are responsible for the naive and unfounded notions that the people cannot write their own texts, or that a tape of their conversations is valueless since their conversations are impoverished of meaning. (p. 380)

THE SCHOOL SYSTEM

The worst thing about Smalltown is the schools. I think there's a lot of prejudice and there's a lack of caring for young people. There's a tendency to turn the other cheek and wait for something to go away. If there's a problem, they'll just try to wait it out. It's not gonna get better, it's gonna get worse.

—Shanell

The Smalltown School District, a "good" suburban district of medium size (5,000 students) in a Mid-Atlantic state, might best be described as a conservatively progressive reflection of is small town community of 20,000 people. Less kindly, one teacher commented, "The school system has been stagnant for the past decade." One previous school superintendent was the assistant to the superintendent in office during the 1960s and 1970s, who also was reported to be conservative and traditional, and another was a previous principal in the district. One rather liberal and progressive (change-oriented) superintendent had a short term before the present superintendent, but he was dismissed by the school board, and mystery still shrouds the reason for his dismissal.

A comment printed in the Smalltown newspaper serves as a metaphor for the school system's attitude toward change and renewal. It was made by an ascending superintendent from a nearby school district, who had been the assistant for the previous 15 years: "If the school district expects any great changes when I take over the job of superintendent, they've picked the wrong person." He intended to maintain the "same fine school system" that his predecessor maintained.

So we have a system that has operated in essentially the same way for decades in its overall structure, organization, and philosophy: not much change and not many risks taken. Many area teachers came through the Smalltown school system, studied at the area state colleges or state university (equally conservative and traditional), then returned to teach in the district.

There is a more liberal faction in the school district that runs counter, although sometimes (paradoxically) parallel, to the conservative group. This faction includes professionals (there is an exceptionally large number of doctors and lawyers in this small town), college faculty, and local business executives. It is this group that is very visible at PTA meetings, school advisory board meetings, the school board, and various school functions such as science fairs, music programs, and parent education workshops. Many support gifted education programs, standardized testing, academic tracking, rules and discipline, and more learning disability classes. They demand measurable "excellence" of the schools (i.e., high Stanford and SAT scores), and they are highly critical of teachers and administrators who they feel are not promoting such numerical accountability.

Likewise, they exert pressure on their children to produce, achieve, compete, and excel. These parents often demand that their children be placed in either the top academic sections or a gifted class, despite the supposedly objective criteria (test scores) that are said to qualify or disqualify students. Others demand that the proper "help" (usually LD or ADD labeling) be provided if the student is not producing as expected or on schedule with peers.

A 10-YEAR HISTORY OF JAMES'S SCHOOLING

> They put me in the slower class and that was my downfall from there. I knew I didn't belong in that class, cause I knew far more than what they were teaching us—far more.
>
> —James

James's Elementary School Experience

James began kindergarten at Carver, one of Smalltown's seven elementary schools. Carver was located near the segregated Black Community in Smalltown, and it had the largest population of Black and poor students in the district. James's kindergarten teacher could not remember him, but she described the Carver students in general as having problems with their home lives. She said they were mostly Black, low income, one-parent families in which the mother worked and the children had little stimulation. She described the parents as economically deprived and possibly too tired to read to their children, or she thought perhaps they did not care.

This teacher noted the "night and day" difference between the kindergarten children in her present school, which is populated by white children from business and professional homes, and the Carver children. Whereas she now has some children reading before first grade, she said she was not into that with the Carver children: They were "not capable" so she felt they were "not ready for it."

In first grade James had two teachers. The first teacher, whom I could not locate, left halfway through the year. According to the second teacher, the first teacher did not provide enough structure for the class. As a result of this, and the additional factor of the class having had a number of substitutes, she said the class had some "group problems." Specifically, she saw behavior problems from very active children who did not know their limits. She could not specifically remember James.

This first-grade teacher was placed in the Carver School for the half-year job only, never having taught there before or after; she described the children as "more worldly" and often from broken homes with working parents. She, like the kindergarten teacher, felt that these parents did not have time or were too tired to read to their children, that they probably did not have blocks for the children to play with, and that their family lives were "unstructured." She said that these children "responded to structure and to knowing what their limits were." James got unsatisfactory grades in reading, English, and writing from this teacher (the teacher from the first half of the year had given him satisfactory grades), so he was retained in first grade for the next year.

When James was in first grade for the second year, the two first-grade teachers decided to group the children homogeneously because, they said, the "spread was so great [between the high and low groups] and we thought we could better serve the children." One teacher took the upper reading group and the lower math group, and the other teacher took the lower reading group and the upper math group. The teachers thought this separation of the top half from the bottom half would help the children feel better about themselves.

James's first-grade reading teacher said she thought of James as academically average, and she put him in the middle reading group. She said that he was street-wise and always testing; but he was also a charmer with whom she felt she needed to set up a relationship. In addition, she mentioned that he did not have a great home situation (no father); and although he kept up academically, she felt he had emotional and social problems.

James's first-grade math teacher remembered James as being frustrated with learning new things, as struggling with math, and as having difficulty with thinking skills. He thought James was retained in first grade because of math, not reading; and he did not remember James being a behavior problem. When I asked why James was put in the remedial reading program after he repeated first grade (even though he had been put in the middle reading group and did not have any reading problems at that time), he said that the district automatically put children in remedial reading when they repeated first grade. A similar process occurred for children transferred from Carver to other schools in the district: They were automatically assumed to be deficient in reading and therefore put in remedial classes.

After his second year in first grade at Carver, James was transferred to Kunkle Elementary School because of a move to a new apartment and babysitting arrangements, according to the reading teacher. The second-grade teacher at Kunkle said James's personality switched to disruptive. She said he was below the bottom reading group, so she gave him a special education book. According to her, the psychologist said James should not have been taken out of Carver, and that the adjustment to a new school was causing the problems. One teacher described Carver as a close-knit neighborhood school where teachers and students had good, supportive relationships with each other.

James's third-grade teacher kept a lengthy journal on James's behavior in class. She found his behavior so much of a problem that she recommended James for SED (socially and emotionally disturbed) placement, and she gave her journal to the counselor as evidence. When I asked for her permission to examine the journal for this case study, she declined. I found samples from her journal, however, in the permanent record file to which I had access because of parental permission to do the study. The behavior she documented was similar to what I observed in the LD classroom. The difference was in the degree to which the teacher was disturbed by it: There is a frequent use in her notes of the words "disturbed" and "disturbing."

James's fourth-grade teacher had him for only half of that year; then he was placed in the LD classroom at her recommendation. Both James and his mother commented that he did not like his fourth-grade teacher. This teacher reported that James wanted a lot of attention, and he would do things just to get it.

JILL (JB): When you look back on it, can you think of why you got in trouble?

JAMES: Basically it was boredom, I think. It felt like they're just teaching everybody else, and they're not worried about my problems, so. . . .

JB: You were thinking, well they're not paying any attention to me, so I might as well do whatever I want?

JAMES: That's exactly how I felt. But when you're doing it at that age, you don't think that's what you're doing. Now that I look back, I was foolin' around because, you know, they weren't teaching me, so I might as well make them notice me somehow.

For 3 days each week both the fourth-grade teacher and the principal tutored James after school. This principal (the only Black principal in the school district) had previously recommended a tutor who had a long-standing reputation in Smalltown for dealing with problem students. But James stopped going to the tutor because he said he did not like the way the tutor pressured him. The fourth-grade teacher said that James thought the after school tutoring was a punishment, and she thought James felt pressured because the principal was also Black and James did not want him to know how far behind James was. This teacher said also that James would say, "I'm dumb," and she thought his tough guy act was a cover-up for his insecurity.

All through elementary school I had Mr. C. as a Black principal. And he was there for—he was there for everybody, but he was there for the Black people even more because he knew where we were comin' from, and he just knew what was goin' on.

—James

The LD classroom. James's fourth- and fifth-grade LD teacher, who had him for all subjects except math, said that James's problems began in third grade (where he was viewed as "disturbing" and "disturbed") when nothing was expected of him. She said the previous teacher had James reading on a first-grade level when he came to her class. By the time he left at the end of fifth-grade, she said he was reading at a late third- or beginning fourth-grade level.

The relationship that the LD teacher established with James was one in which he felt free to talk about his feelings, particularly during the group counseling sessions that occurred almost every day. The sessions lasted for 20 minutes to an hour, depending on how much the students wanted to talk. It was not unusual for James to take up 10 or 15 minutes, often talking about personal problems as many of the other students did (see Bartoli and Botel, 1988a, and Bartoli, 1986b, for samples of these sessions).

Both the LD teacher and the elementary counselor said that James had no learning disabilities—that his problems were emotional and related mostly to his family. The LD teacher said that James resented his mother's work schedule (when she worked nights he never saw her) and that he blamed his problems on this. She said he also complained about his grandfather, who called him "dumb," was mean to him, and would shut him up in a room for 3 hours to read. And he talked about how mean his brother was to him, calling him names (sped ed, stupid) and fighting with him. Thus, she said, James was belligerent and angry when he came into her LD class, because of the grief he got from his brother and grandfather about it.

This teacher thought that the grandparents had taken over the parent function in James's family. She said the family valued education but had given up on James. She felt that James wanted to be a good student and was hurt when his family would not accept his LD placement. So, she said, he covered up this hurt and fear of failure with misbehavior.

They took me out of my regular classes and put me in Miss D's. I didn't know why. They just took me out of my regular class because I was a problem kid—I used to get in trouble. No matter how good I did in class, they would not take me out of there [the slower class], cause they felt that I was a behavior problem, and that's where they put all their behavior kids.

—James

James's mother, according to the LD teacher, was a very tough disciplinarian, although other teachers felt she was lacking in discipline. She relayed paddling incidents that occurred once after a conference and once when she was called in by the teacher. The LD teacher said, "She beat the hell out of him, and then she threatened to do it in front of the whole class and the whole school the next time." This teacher implied that the SED placement recommended by the third-grade teacher might have been more appropriate for James's emotional problems, but she said the principal prevented that by insisting that James did not need SED placement.

James's Middle School Experience

James's sixth-grade social studies teacher said that James could grasp more than he let on, but he did not pay attention and he "often times has a little behavior problem—to get attention." But she said, "He has gotten away from that somewhat now because of the relationship I've tried to develop with him through confidential talks." She said that because of this she had less trouble with James than did some of the other teachers. She also attended the same church that James attended with his grandmother, and she said she talked with him about the Black experience, Martin Luther King, sports, and current events.

> She knew how to talk to people. She knew that you weren't just foolin' around. She could come to you and say, "I know you're going through some problems maybe," and just actually *listen* to you. A lot of teachers don't want to hear what you have to say. They just want to do their job and go home.
>
> —James

James was not a behavior problem for this teacher on the day that I observed. She called on him three times when he did not have his hand raised (she called on other students only when they had their hand raised), and she moved to his desk to help him at one point, which she did not do with the other students. Throughout the period James was rather quiet and never disruptive or disrespectful. This teacher was the only Black teacher in the district at that time.

By contrast, James's sixth-grade science teacher described James as a "very low student—he's probably reading on a second-grade level, and his attention span is about one minute." He said James cannot take notes, and "his writing is maybe two sentences, maybe not even that much." Concerning behavior, he said James was "very disturbing—he'll come up to the door and slam it or pound on the walls." He said James craves attention:

"He'll sit there and sniffle, pretend he is sick or he's cold." On the day that I observed, James said he was cold several times (it was a cold damp day, his sneakers were wet from the morning rain, and the room was chilly). The teacher first told me, then James, that it was 72 degrees and not that cold.

The science teacher said that James was "just poor in all subjects," and that "you can give James a test and he'll just get a zero—just nothing on a paper." He felt James had a poor attitude: "As far as learning, he makes about a 30% effort, and that's giving him the benefit of the doubt."

> I'm not sayin' I'm smart, but I knew everything. But if they give up on you, you know—they think you're a bad kid, it's gonna be a rough ride.
>
> —James

On the day that I observed in the science classroom James talked out and interacted with his peers more, complained several times about being cold, and was reprimanded often by the teacher for not paying attention, making signals to another student, moving out of his seat, and talking. Another student was also "disturbing" in the classroom, but the teacher quietly pulled this student aside for a talk. Later the teacher excused this student's behavior with, "Joe was just doing that to get your attention. His behavior would be much better than James's. He's very cooperative ordinarily." Oddly enough, he said the same thing about James's behavior at the close of our interview: "I think he was definitely putting on a show for you today. He would be working better than that, I'm sure—but he was doing everything to get your attention." But the way he reacted to James in the classroom was vastly different from the way he reacted to Joe (non-Black), as were his expectations for the potential of James as a student.

This teacher suggested that James's learning problem might be either physical or emotional.

> There's something more than we know. Perhaps this might have gone back to an accident or something like that. It might be something physical. Maybe an automobile accident or something like that. The home, or not having a father, or, you know, he lives with his mother but he has no father. You know, there's more behind this than . . . you know.

He said James was typical of the low group and that "the class is about the same very year. They're just low—really low." He said this low group is really a problem because some of them have no home: "There's a pattern [in the low group]. Usually your discipline problems run with broken homes, divorces—things like that." James, he felt, was "just not ready for a group . . . he's just not prepared for sixth grade at all."

> They didn't even teach you in C level. You just sat around all day. And a lot of them knew they were doin' it. They were entirely too busy. Too worried about getting done with the lesson that they had planned instead of worrying about if they're teaching a lesson.
>
> —James

James's sixth-grade math teacher said that his mathematical ability was "probably in the middle to upper range. He grasps things we are covering—he's doing just about average work." He said that James's work depended on his mood.

> If he's in a good mood he does extremely well—he's alert to what he's doing. But if he's in a bad mood—if he's had to go to the office for some reason or if before he came into my room he was having problems with another teacher—he's not gonna have a good time in the class. His mind isn't gonna be on what it's supposed to be on.

Concerning James's behavior, the math teacher said:

> I've only had a couple bad incidents with him this year, where for some reason or another, when he wasn't doing the way he should have been—walking into a large group instruction area, maybe he was kind of loud, and you tell him to be quiet, or he gets out of his seat and starts wandering around, you tell him to sit down—couple times there he didn't like being reminded to do that, so he had something to say about it.
>
> But most of the time he and I have been getting along okay. He kind of shrugs his shoulders, kind of does his thing. He'll listen to you and go about doing as much of what you tell him to do as he feels he can.

James was quiet and working throughout the class period on the day I observed. His only talking occurred at the end of the period in response to the girl behind him who was also talking. A word from the teacher silenced him. That evening, the teacher described this scene as follows:

> Today I told him to turn around—he started to do that, but he didn't go all the way. It's like he's kind of telling you, "Well, you may be boss, but I'm gonna do what I wanna do. And don't push me any

farther than what you are right now, or else there's gonna be problems." That's kind of the way I'm reading him.

Middle School LD Classroom

JB: How did you feel about the material they gave you in middle school?
JAMES: By that time I felt that's what I was gonna be doing all through high
school. The other kids who were in that [LD resource] room didn't
know what we were doing. I felt like . . . really dumb in this class. I
knew everything they were doing. And there's nothing I could do. I
tried to get good grades and everything. They would not take you out
of there.

James's learning disability teacher at the middle school, who diagnosed
him as needing vocabulary development at the second-grade level, said that
James was a "very good student . . . very intelligent when he *wants* to be."
She described him as in the middle range academically, in the top range in
ability, but in the bottom range for behavior.

He can be nice, polite, and helpful, as long as you don't challenge him in any way. He takes any correction as attack, and he at-
tacks back. Often behaviors interfere—he can't concentrate long
enough because he has to be blaming someone for doing something.

The LD teacher described the previous week as the "worst of the year."

Last week he was very, very defensive. If you even looked at him
he was screaming at you—"I didn't do it!" Even without saying anything to him. It was like maybe he did do something and he was
afraid somebody was gonna find out about it—I don't know, and I
don't think he knows either.

The RP (a gang of Black boys) does the things they do because
they are angry at the people in the community for being accused of
things because they are Black—being accused of wild and crazy
things. When you constantly have someone saying "You did this, you
did that," it really makes you mad, because there's nothing you can do
or say to convince them. They're either gonna lie or make up stuff.
—Shanell

They don't say it, but you automatically know. They're not
gonna tolerate anything you did even if you didn't do anything.

They're not gonna tolerate you, cause you're a Black kid. They're just gonna set you aside.

—James

Fieldword Journal: High School

The high school principal told Mr. C. [James's principal from elementary school] about the many problems James had "caused" in school, told him that James could be given B track equivalent classes in SED [an absurd statement], and implied that James would get back in regular education after the "learning and adjustment" treatment. The "adjustment" will include Ritalin and behavior modification, and the "learning" will continue on a reduced level as has been the pattern for the past 6 years in LD placement, the basic effect of which has been to deprive him of a challenging education equal to his ability.

Mr. C., Linda [another colleague from the Black Community], and I spent an evening with James and his mother, Donna, talking about a plan to prevent the placement and keep James in regular education and in a B track. When Donna tried to arrange the meeting with the school (including all of us to back her) she met with resistance or more salesmanship that resulted in her comment, "I just want what's best for James." James said to me that his mother will not push for regular placement because she does not want to make waves—she isn't strong enough—she won't push against the system.

But I had documented the previous 8 years of her pushing against the school system, I witnessed the accompanying lack of respect that she was afforded by counselors, teachers, and principals, and I had interviewed other Black mothers who were treated with similar disrespect by the school system. So I knew, in part, why she was losing heart.

When we talked with Donna she was totally against both the Ritalin and the placement, but the school system had convinced her otherwise. She was also totally against the psychiatric exam that she said the school pushed her into ("They kept buggin' me—they kept calling me at home and at work—told me they had to pay for the exam whether we went to it or not."). They probably woke her up many times because they were not sensitive to her alternating shift schedule—they wore her down.

James said that the psychiatrist only asked a few questions—mostly about his mother and father, asked him to stand on one foot and hold up hand/finger. Donna said it couldn't have been more than

30 minutes. He then only talked with her for 15 minutes, and on this he based his judgment. I discovered later from the permanent records that the school staff met with the psychiatrist to "fill him in" before they met James and Donna—not what you would call a "blind review."

In March I met with both James and Donna to propose tutoring for James—I wanted to help him get ahead academically so he could get into a B track the next year. [Both he and his mother said he wanted to go to college, and I told them James would never be prepared for this in C track and disability classes.] They agreed to tutoring, but James never showed up the following week or the week after, although I called his mother and she assured me she would get him there.

James told me later (in June) that he didn't come because no one pushed him to. I wanted to allow him to take responsibility for coming—perhaps his mother did too? But he did not take the initiative.

Now in August I again have asked him to take the initiative and get a tutor for one of the two classes that he failed. I asked him to contact either Linda or Mr. C. for help. Will he do it? I told him that was our best wedge in the meeting on the 17th with school personnel to determine his placement. James told me his mother won't push for regular education placement because she is too easy—not pushy enough.

A WEEK WITH JAMES AT THE LAKE

In July 1988 I invited James to come with my family (my husband and children, then ages 15, 13, 11, 8, and 2) on our trip to a lake area where we sail, swim, hike, and windsurf each summer. The following excerpt from my journal describes that trip:

> James just seemed like a normal kid—kind of quiet at first and very sensitive to our family rules for behavior in the beginning due to not knowing us very well—a perfect gentleman—very sensitive to all of our kids, even correcting Stephen's [age 11] treatment of Patrick [age 2] as sometimes not careful/protective enough.
>
> All six of them laughed and played together during the week, the boys staying up late every night talking and laughing. They wrestled and clowned and kidded each other with less contention and disagreement than if James were not along with us. David [our oldest son, who is James's age] and James were in charge on Wednesday eve-

ning when my husband and I went out, and they did just fine with both the supper/kitchen work and child care [except that they didn't bother cleaning the cookie sheets from baking—but nobody's perfect].

On the way home from the lake we hit a traffic jam (it lasted over an hour-and-a-half), so our 3-1/2-hour trip home lasted over 5 hours. Amazingly, all six kids were terrific—even the baby. Anyone who can survive 5 hours in a car with five children between the ages of 15 and 2 plus two rather authoritarian adults does not need Ritalin for behavior control.

I asked the kids what they thought about the idea that James could be a troublemaker or might start fights in school, and they said he is not the type. He never hurt any of them even in the many tussles, games, horseplay, and play fights and disagreements they had during the week. He told them he tried not to fight with the kid in school, but the kid punched him first and all of James's friends were standing there—what else could he do?

James said most of the kids at school were okay except for the "hicks" (local definition: dirty, torn clothes, "poor white trash," slobs—throw food and eat like pigs). I was asking questions to find out about racism, Ku Klux Klan connections [he said the kid who picked the fight was not in KKK], and other evidence of prejudice.

Thoughts on diversity. Is part of the problem with the C track classes that, in addition to the Black students, they are inhabited by "hicks" who may be more prejudiced and less well educated? Would James, and all students, do better in less economically, socially, and racially segregated classes with more broadly educated students? How can we prevent the slotting of narrowly educated white students with minority students? What is there in such an arrangement to lead to an appreciation of cultural diversity? Would the elimination of tracking and the addition of more collaborative grouping within heterogeneous classes lead to more constructive social interaction, more sensitivity to and appreciation for the many benefits of cultural diversity?

Journal: August 24, 1988

Last Monday Donna received a call from the school canceling the meeting they set up with her the previous Friday (very quickly after our Wednesday, 17th meeting) to tour the L&A classroom. Mr. C. advised Donna to call back about it, and the Special Education Director said there was no room in the L&A and J would have to return to the intermediate high school. We don't know whether to be happy that they're giving J a chance, to suspect that they are waiting for him to fail, or to assume that there really is no room.

Journal: October 7, 1988

After I was told that the principal wanted to call another IEP meeting and that he asked Mr. C. to make arrangements with Donna to come in, I decided to observe in the classroom to get closer to what is happening in school. I called the principal to see what the problem was, and he told me about a police citation for J's misconduct at a varsity football game, prohibition for J to attend football games as a spectator, and J's "barely passing" scores in school (a week ago there were no interim reports and everything was okay).

I talked with the assistant principal for more details. He mentioned playful antics—nothing really bad, but an accumulation of little annoyances like a balloon brought in to school and bounced off the head of kids, loud laughing and playful name calling in the cafeteria, hallway behavior, and forgetting gym clothes.

JB: What happened that one semester that they let you get in the regular classes?

JAMES: After they took me out of those classes, the teachers knew where I was coming from—slower classes. And so they figured I didn't know what I was doin', I guess. And by then I was already a goof-off, you know. And I wasn't gonna change overnight. So I got in those classes, and I sat in the back, as usual.

I mean, they just went on with their lesson. They didn't, you know, come back and say, "This is where we've been and this how far we've gone" to catch me up. They just started their lesson, and I didn't know what was goin' on. So I sat in the back of the class and goofed off—by myself.

. . . They weren't teaching *me* anything. They were just teaching the kids who had already known what was going on. And any kid who slows down—even if he's just being quiet—they just let you alone.

The guidance counselor said J's behavior was "back and forth"— sometimes he dressed and acted like a student (almost preppie clothes and a briefcase) and other times like Mr. T (chains and flashy clothes along with accompanying behavior). She said he was having more difficulty in algebra and that she talked with him about his having missed so much school last year and having missed out on "skills" he needs this year. I asked if she talked with him about a solution—like maybe tutoring. She said she hesitated to suggest tutoring because of the expense, but that they were going to organize peer tutoring soon. I suggested a good peer tutor to begin with J right away. She checked his schedule and found a study hall in sync with J's, and I told her to go ahead.

I talked with James's English teacher in her planning room after the class I observed. She said James wasn't all that different from several other kids in the class, and that he was passing, which she felt was good considering his nonpreparation for the class in previous years. She said that if she hadn't been made aware of all of James's other previous problems, she would probably just treat him like one of her problems that she would find a way to deal with. But because of all she knows about him—his reputation—she is on the fence about him, not knowing whether he will be able to handle both the work and his behavior. She said he has not been a problem for her so far, and that when she confronts him openly, when necessary, in and out of class, he is not disrespectful.

JAMES: A lot of teachers would . . . if you had any kind of behavior problems, and you came to class, they wouldn't want you to disrupt their class. So they figured by allowing you to do anything you wanted, not doing your homework and things like that, that you wouldn't cause a problem.

But it really made it worse, because that made it easier on me to do anything I wanted to, and they were still putting me through school. It was just getting easier and easier. I thought, hey, I'm doin' good here—I'm goin' through high school, I'm never doin' homework. And all I gotta do is sit in class and don't do anything.

[One teacher] didn't even make me take tests—I'd be sittin' there—he wouldn't even pass me the papers back. And I figured, he's not worried about me—I'm not gonna complain. Most teenagers would not go to the principal and say, "He's not givin' me my work."

JB: Suppose you went back now—suppose you decided, "I'm gonna be a teacher and show them how this is done." How are you gonna teach one of those C level classes in eleventh grade?

JAMES: I'd teach to the point where, I'd make the students know that, if you did you work, and I saw that you knew what you were doin', I'd get you out of here. Because every kid in there didn't want to be there. You know, it was like, "Man, I feel like I'm a dumb thing."

And I'd make sure that they knew what they were doin'—set a
goal, cause you had no goals once you were put in the lower levels.
You think you're just there cause you're dumb.

JB: So you'd teach up rather than down?

JAMES: I would *teach*. Cause they don't teach at the high school. They—
you'd just go in there and sit in class, and kids would be walkin' around.
As long as you weren't loud and a troublemaker and starting fights and
things, you could go through high school and it'd be easy.

JAMES'S FAMILY

James's mother, Donna, married his father when she was 18. They
moved from Smalltown to a southern state and lived there for 5 years, during which time both James's older brother and James were born. Then the
marriage broke up, and the two boys and their mother returned to
Smalltown, where they have lived ever since.

Although their relationship has been filled with broken promises and
years of absence, Donna refrained from criticizing James's father except for
his showering the children with gifts when he saw them to try to "buy"
their love. When she described him to the psychologist she said he had been
a good provider and basically a nice guy. To me she spoke kindly of the
close relationship her husband had with James, who was named after his
father (although he was the second son born), and how much time they
spent together the first 2 years of James's life. She suggested that James's
storytelling ability might have been "inherited" from his father who, she
said, was quite a storyteller.

James's Mother

Donna has been the sole wage earner for the family, working an alternating shift of 7 a.m. to 3 p.m. and 3 p.m. to 11 p.m. every other week.
Living close to her parents has helped her with child care arrangements—
the boys spend their after school and evening time with their grandparents
when their mother works evenings.

School teachers and principals have described Donna as somewhat defensive and strict. They commented on the unusual tactic of her coming
into the school to paddle James in front of them and of her threatening to
do it in front of his classmates if he did not behave better in school. The
middle school principals told me that she would not allow them to discipline
James in school or give him after school detention, but that she wanted
them to tell her if there was a problem so she could handle it. I asked if that

was a typical way for a parent to handle behavior problems at school, and they said it was not.

Donna said that James's behavior problems began in third grade when he realized he was having trouble with reading. He began making noises in class, annoying others, and talking back to the teachers. Donna said that James will not try to get away with bad behavior with her. Although she has said at times that she does not know what to do with James (with regard to his behavior in school), she also said that when she came into the school those few times, his behavior improved. During her last meeting with the principals they agreed on a behavior contract for James, and she felt it worked because James had to bring a report home from each teacher for her to see each day.

When Donna and I met for an end-of-the-year interview after James's first year at the middle school, we talked about the possibility of James's bad behavior being related to his wish to see his dad or reunite his parents.

JB: Does he think if he is bad enough, there would be a change in his relationship with his dad?

D: That could be.

JB: What would he gain? Say if he says, "If I'm bad enough . . ."?

D: Maybe my mom will send me to my dad.

JB: Is that what he wants?

D: Yeah. I mean he don't want to go there and live, but he . . . See, when his dad does come around, he just gives him anything he—everything he wants to do is okay. You know, it's different with me. He can't do everything and get away with it. I can't afford to give him everything he wants. But when he's with him, you know, the sky's the limit. And he would really like to be with him. In fact he was looking forward to bein' with him this summer. I don't know what happened—I don't even know where he's at.

Donna and I also talked about her expectations for James, and she said that she would like to see her sons go to college and go on to become professional football players.

I expect them to go through school, go to college; and both my boys love football. And I expect them to go on to be professional football players. But I don't want them to be pushed through like some of them are, you know, instead of sayin', if you're a good ath-lete they'll give you any grade just to be able to get you out there to play football. But I would really like to see that for both my boys.

James's Grandparents

James was described by his grandmother as very active, stubborn, and more of a follower of his peers than his brother, who she said was more obedient. Donna also said that she had no problems with her older son, but that James could be mouthy and disruptive in school. Both Donna and her mother said that James was no problem at home, but his behavior was not always good in school.

One of James's teachers, who attends the same church as James's grandmother, said that James is a perfect gentleman when he is at church with his grandmother. She said you would never know it was the same person (as the misbehaved boy in school).

James's grandmother said that her husband really pushes reading. She said he reads a lot, and he has encouraged his family to read about Black history. James's mother confirmed this, telling me that two of her sisters were reading books about Black history. James's grandmother described the help that James's grandfather gave with reading. She said he was impatient with James and would force him to sit down with the newspaper and read orally under constant pressure. Alternatively, James's grandfather would shut James in a room for 3 hours with a book.

When I spoke with the grandfather he told me that he helped James with reading only when he was really fed up with his grandson. He considers James to be just lazy because he has problems with reading, and he sees no reason (besides laziness) that James cannot teach himself to read: "If you are normal, or even half normal, you can certainly teach yourself to read." According to him, children who do not read have the concept that they do not need it. He thinks that pride is missing today in young people and that they are "cry babies."

James's grandfather told me that Smalltown schools are no good for Blacks. He said that Smalltown was one of the last districts to desegregate, and that even after desegregation in 1955 the Blacks were second class citizens—that they would laugh at a Black student in a college preparatory section. According to him, 40 out of 50 teachers in Smalltown do not like Blacks, so there is no motivation or incentive to succeed—Blacks think, "What's the point?" He said that the school system caters to the white students, and that Black history is suppressed from them.

SHANELL: There's no education about Blacks to white students or to Black students for that matter. I mean Black students are just as ignorant about their culture as white students are ignorant about Black culture, because they were never taught.

RACHEL: Well, I went to school—at the Black school until eighth grade and then I went to the high school that technically was integrated. But we got a different diploma—with a different name for the school on it than the white kids got. Our diplomas were no good because there wasn't such a place as Lincoln High School. No one knew where it was.

JB: What could teachers and principals do [to motivate students]?

JAMES: Teach that person. Like myself, teach me more about the things we were learning in high school. They didn't teach me anything. They just wanted me to basically stop the Black kids who were always around me from fighting amongst the white kids. Not teach them to go to class and things like that—they weren't worried about me—us—learning. They were more worried about keeping a calm through the high school.

James's grandfather spoke angrily about racial prejudice and injustice that Blacks have experienced and about the denial of education to Blacks.

Throughout the slave states, the most cardinal sin—the one unpunishable sin that the White man could commit—was that he was caught teachin' a slave to read or write. That was a death sentence in some sections of this country. That was death, because as long as you take this man's culture and don't let him be able to educate himself to the point that he can look and see what you did . . .

He talked also about the rights he has been denied—rights he and his father fought for.

The Black man in this country (inaudible) says, "Hey, wait a minute—I fought for this country—I died for this country. You're gonna tell me you're gonna bring other people over here, because they're White or Caucasian they can go places and do the things that I can't do, and I was born and raised here."

You see the Constitution of the United States for the average Black man and me—it wasn't worth the paper it was wrote on. The Declaration of Independence? Statue of Liberty and all that stuff? That means nothin' to me. The Declaration of Independence—that all men are endowed—the men that wrote the damn thing, 95% of them were slave owners. Now how in the hell could they tell me on a piece of paper that everything is alright when they held slaves.

One of the injustices that James's grandfather described occurred when he returned from service in World War II. Interestingly, the daughter of the family who owns the restaurant in which the following incident occurred was James's third-grade teacher, who recommended him for SED placement.

> How can a man be happy when he knows he's a second class citizen. Here in Smalltown, when I came back from World War II, I got damn immigrants—just came from the old country, can't even speak English—but they can say enough to tell you, "Sorry, me no can serva you." Here a son-of-a-bitch is not even a naturalized citizen, and he's gonna tell me, and I fought for the country, and my father fought, and his father before him fought. He's gonna tell me—and it's through my blood and guts is how in the hell he got here.

THE SMALLTOWN COMMUNITY

Smalltown has a white, middle-class, protestant majority and a small (5%) Black minority. It has several medium-sized, thriving industrial plants and two small colleges in the vicinity. White residents describe the town as "a nice small town in which to raise a family," since there are a variety of organized sports (baseball, soccer, basketball, football, swimming) and clubs (scouts, church youth groups, YMCA activities) for the children to be involved in, along with a variety of adult groups for the parents (service and social groups, music and art clubs, civic and garden clubs, church groups). Smalltown is very much a middle-class town with little evidence of either a very rich upper class or a very poor lower class. This has not, however, prevented differentiation of groups along economic and social lines. There appears to be a rather marked stratification and isolation of certain groups, notably Blacks, poor whites, and the long-time resident group of upper-middle-class whites who own the town businesses and control the power in the town.

The town is somewhat isolated and self-contained, both in location and in general ambiance. It is several hours removed from major cities, with the exception of one small city (70,000) that is within half an hour's drive. But more important, the town retains its somewhat rural, conservative, traditional, and fundamentalist atmosphere despite the influx of fast food chains, shopping malls, movie theaters, and mobile families associated with the small industries and colleges.

A headline in the town paper is illustrative of the fundamentalist perspective: "PARENTS: SCHOOLS UNDERMINE VALUES." A principal is quoted as saying, "We need to push on to get a prayer bill passed for public schools."

There are local groups who oppose what they view as "humanistic" approaches in teaching; and recent controversies about the issue of values in outcome-based assessment have also highlighted the conservative stance, forcing the state to remove respect for diversity and appreciation of others' perspectives from its list of outcomes.

It is not unusual in Smalltown to be visited by representatives of various churches who appear at the door to proselytize, and citizens of the town say that there are as many churches as there are bars in Smalltown. In addition to the fundamentalist groups, there are Mennonite and Amish groups in the surrounding area who also value conservativism, Bible reading, and moderation in dress, speech, and behavior. Cleanliness is still next to godliness with many groups, as are respectability, discipline, hard work, and good manners.

Traditional, rural, and conservative qualities of the town are visible at the town square (compete with trees and benches), where parades march every Halloween, Christmas, Memorial Day, and Fourth of July and where citizens gather for community Christmas caroling, craft shows, sidewalk sale days, and a Fourth of July street dance during the Smalltown Summerfair. Formerly at the square, but now relocated to accommodate more people, is the Smalltown Farmers Market, where town and country people congregate each Friday to purchase fresh produce, meat, bread, cheese, and other farm products. Community people come to socialize as much as to shop, and backyard gardeners and a few novice farmers (businesspeople and professionals who have bought small farms near the town) come seeking guidance from the "real" farm people concerning their chickens, sheep, tomatoes, and corn.

On patriotic holidays members of the Kiwanis, Jaycees, Elks, Moose, VFW, and Lions Clubs (all-white memberships) join in the town parades along with the Girl Scouts, Boy Scouts, Smalltown Band, and area school bands. The town's large volunteer firefighters' group and ambulance corps also appear in the parades. The firefighters' group is also active in dances and suppers similar to those of the area church groups. Ham suppers, chicken barbecues, and spaghetti suppers are advertised frequently; one citizen of the town said he goes to some area group's supper (it is usually family style—all you can eat) nearly every week of the year.

The Black Community

When you walk downtown and see the beautiful old buildings, or you walk by the medical center and see the beautiful houses, then you look at the Black Community, it's like, something is wrong here.

There's nothing. I mean it's low income housing, it's like you're sardines.

—Shanell

According to James's grandfather, who reared six children in Smalltown, the idea that Smalltown is a nice, friendly community is a myth for Black families. He said that Smalltown wants to "show the whole world we're a beautiful town, and everybody's the same here—but that don't exist, that's just words." People are happy in Smalltown, he said, only if they are middle-class whites.

Smalltown is not a nice community—it's a nice community for middle-class Anglo-Saxons or an Anglo-Saxon that has a couple dollars, it's a very beautiful community. But it can't be for no one else— how can it be beautiful? How can a man be happy when he knows he's a second class citizen?

I'd describe the general relationship between the white and Black communities in Smalltown as being fake. There's this fake front that everything's perfect and everything's all nice and neat—tied up in a little bow: The whites are trying to help the Blacks and the Blacks are trying to help the whites, and there's a great cultural exchange. But actually there's not. All you have to do is observe things.

—Shanell

In response to the question, "What was it like growing up in Smalltown?" Rachel, born in 1895, replied:

Bad! Just like putting a chicken in a bear's cave, cuz of course you just couldn't get along with the whites and I guess they felt the same way about us. Lots of times you wasn't doing anything to them and they would start something.

It wasn't a sweet life. I wouldn't call it a sweet life because you had lots to contend with you know. You know you—the white people—I hate to say this, but the white people caused a lot of trouble because you could be sitting at your own door, standing at your own door, not even bothering them and they'd go and holler "*Nigger!*" and when they said "*Nigger!*" that meant *Fight!* That was all there was to it and then of course they were never bothering you, it was always you bothering them.

James's grandfather does not feel that Blacks are accepted in Smalltown "as an individual that is for the benefit of the community." He spoke of the insignificance of traditional Smalltown events.

> The Memorial Day ceremonies—they mean nothin' to me. A man in the military even now that's willing to die for this country, if his face is other than white, all he's doin' is gettin' a paycheck and a couple meals from the government. He has no country. There's no Black or no Latino, or no Indian livin' in the United States right now that has a country—he don't have nothin'.

It is commonly assumed and accepted among the white population of Smalltown that the Blacks in the town have no motivation for advancement or success in the school system or in the work system. Many teachers who noted the absence of Blacks in the top academic tracks attribute this to the "unstimulating, unmotivated, and deprived environments" from which the Black children come. They assume that their parents, like the poor white parents, either do not care or do not know how to help their children toward advancement. And these assumptions are left unchallenged because the Black parents, keenly sensitive to these disrespectful assumptions of deficiency, rarely come to Back-to-School Night, PTA meetings, Parent Advisory Counsel meetings, and unrequired conferences with the teacher.

> Don't ever assume something. You can't *assume* about people. That's just something that isn't possible, because your assumptions when it comes to people are most all of the time wrong.
>
> —Shanell

Both James's family and his mother's family have chosen to live apart from the Black Community in the town. Both of Donna's apartments have been in predominantly white, middle-class neighborhoods. Her parents' home is removed even farther from the downtown and Black district of Smalltown, and is also in a predominantly white, blue collar neighborhood. Donna has made sure that James was cared for by relatives when she was at work. But this did not prevent school personnel from commenting that James's home life was not very good or that his environment was unstimulating, disadvantaged, unmotivating, or insecure. And it was not uncommon for his reading problems to be attributed to the poverty of his family environment, particularly with respect to his "broken home" and his "working mother."

When I get older, if I have children I never want my kids to have to go through being stereotyped, being judged before they're known, being called something that you're totally opposite from. I just want everybody to give my kids a chance before you judge them—get to know them.

—Shanell

Work in the Black Community. James's grandfather told me that there are no jobs for Blacks in Smalltown and that Blacks have no incentive because of this.

You don't acquire good jobs in Smalltown, so how can you make a barely living wage . . . [and] send your child to college?

Go into your courthouse—you don't see no Blacks in there working. Go out to your county home [public retirement home]—no Blacks workin'. Marion County—I'll bet they don't employ five Blacks—in the whole county.

I asked him where Blacks from Smalltown do get jobs, and he said:

Federal government—or travel to Watertown [closest city, 20 miles away]. The factories [in Smalltown] won't hire you. They hire the poor white whose crowning issue is the fact that, as long as I don't have to work with none of them [Blacks], he'll work. Danner [local factory owner] has them in slavery too—they don't have nothin'.

He said you get a "token job here and there," but in general there is nothing in Smalltown for Blacks. This is what kills motivation for the Blacks in Smalltown, according to him, and it is the reason that long-range goals are impossible.

Certainly that kills the motivation in a lot of cases. What's the point? . . . Any poor man, he cannot get a long-range goal—only get the fact that, I thank God for the fact that for this day the things that I needed He obtained for me. That's it. Life is only today—life is not tomorrow.

What if a Black kid had a goal in mind to become the president of the United States? That'll never happen. So what the hell is a goal? When I was a kid, if I was to decide all of a sudden I wanted to be a fireman, you know there was no Black firemen. Those long-range goals mean nothin'.

According to James's grandfather the schools gear poor families toward work in the local factories.

> The local high school in Smalltown for years has been geared to the fact that after high school you go into Danners or Quaker Tools [town factories] or various places like that, if you're blue collar or a poor family. That's the only thing you had whether you were white or Black. Well the Blacks couldn't work in Danners or Quaker Tools, so as a result you had nothing. The girls was geared to the fact to come into some white person's kitchen and cook and clean for them, see. The guys was geared to diggin' ditches.
>
> After high school, there wasn't anywheres for you to climb. There was nothing for you to do—what I mean no pick—you had to work as they the expression "in a white folks' kitchen." You had to be a cook or a waitress or a maid. Sometimes you could get a job nursing you know and that kept you out in the street pushing this baby up and down. You couldn't find much to do. No polished jobs.
>
> —Rachel

James's mother has a factory job with a company outside of Smalltown. She has had a difficult split shift since James has been in school. Another mother, who also has a factory job with a 3 to 11 p.m. shift, told me that it is very hard to change shifts. According to her, it would have to be something very severe like lots of home problems or a medical doctor's excuse for the company to consider allowing a shift change. And if you do change, she said, you take a big cut in pay and are moved down several levels. So both she and James's mother have kept the same shift for years, even though it is difficult for them as parents.

Community Values

James has been judged by conservative, traditional community values, particularly with respect to his "broken home" and his working mother. Although I did not hear him directly referred to as a "latch-key" child, several of the middle school teachers said they thought he was "pretty much on this own" and that they did not think he got much help from home. Some elementary teachers assumed his environment was deprived of stimulation, or at least deficient in the type of direct parental stimulation they saw as vital to success in reading. The kindergarten teacher, for example, noted the "night and day" difference in her classes at the more "advantaged" upper-middle-class school where she now teaches and the Carver School wherein she had James. The Carver children, she said, were not as "capable" due to their family backgrounds.

Smalltown is very much a churchgoing sort of town, with many citizens affiliated with the multitude of churches in the surrounding area. But according to James's grandfather, it is the churches that help to promote racism and prejudice. When I asked him about the possibilities for change in the plight of the Blacks in Smalltown, especially with respect to education in the schools, he replied:

> You cannot change your heart, my lady. A heart that is taught hatred . . . you see, a great lot of the white man's hatred comes from, of all places, the church. There are a lot of white people that have this concept that their holy Bible indicates that [the Black man should be hated]. Your first place of teaching hatred is the home and the church—that's where it's taught—the home and the church.

There are, in fact, many fundamentalist sects in the Smalltown area that appear to have their own private interpretation of the Bible, generally excluding from "salvation" any group that is different from their own small sect. For instance, as recently as 40 years ago Catholics in the community suffered severe discrimination in Smalltown, and even at the present time fundamentalists who proselytize from door to door have no doubt that Catholics, Jews, Muslims, and Mormons will never get to heaven.

The vast majority of the churches in Smalltown have all-white memberships, with only a rare Black family included in the congregation. One of the more liberal protestant churches in the town had one Black family for a few years. But they were an upper-middle-class family who had moved in from another state—they were not from the Black Community in Smalltown. The church with the largest single membership in the town, the Catholic church, has only a few Black families. Few of them have children who still attend, and two are older couples who have attended for years. No new Black families have joined. There are four Black churches in the town, all of which are much smaller than most of the white churches, and they are not a part of Smalltown's interdenominational council of churches.

Town Politics

There have only been two Black Community members in elected offices in Smalltown's history. No Blacks hold positions of power in Smalltown businesses, and only recently has there been a Black doctor. He moved to Smalltown a few years ago from a large city; he was originally associated with a nearby college and later decided to set up a private practice. His wife and social circle, however, are not from the Black Community.

Over the past 10 years there have been two school issues involving the Black Community, and in both of those it appeared that James's grandfather's viewpoint was valid—the Black Community had no unity or power. The first of these issues concerned the closing of the Carver School. This school was located near the Black Community, and many former teachers (one of whom was Black) felt that the school was very much a community school with a particularly close and supportive relationship among staff, children, and families. When the administration of the school system decided to close the school, ostensibly for financial reasons, they handed the decision down from above and asked for no input from school personnel or the community.

Teachers reported that the sudden closing was very difficult: Families were upset; children were tense, anxious, and insecure about going to a new school; and teachers were angry. They felt the superintendent did not give them the straight story and that he just used his power to do what he wanted without any justification for the school closing.

One teacher commented that Carver was an easy target for a school closing because "there is no power in the Black Community." She talked about the difference between the Carver situation and what would happen if they tried to close the white middle-class school where she is now: Parents would stick together, protest, and use their influence and power to fight for the school. But, she said, there are no influential Blacks: "Look at the adult community—you see no Blacks in professions in town." She said the one Black school board member does not speak for the Black Community or align with them.

The second issue was similar to the first. The superintendent made a decision to change principals around in the schools. One such move involved the Black principal at the Kunkle School. A teacher said that several Black parents protested the move, saying that the principal was a good role model for the children, but there was not a united effort. In addition, the Black school board member would not voice support for the principal.

Black and white politics enter the real estate market, according to a Black resident who works for a federal employment service in town. She said that for several years she left Smalltown and lived in the Caribbean. When she made plans to return to Smalltown, she contacted a local real estate agent to find a home. The agent found a small farm for her, but when she came to town to look at the property, and the agent discovered that she was a previous Black resident, the property suddenly came off the market. Afterward, she said, she was shown only property in the Black districts of the town.

Concerning the judicial system in Smalltown, one Black resident re-layed the story of her protests against false accusations against Black youth, who, she said, were often convicted of crimes committed by the whites in Smalltown. Last year she joined with a lawyer and several other citizens and proved the innocence of two Black youths who were falsely accused and "set up" by whites from the town. They succeeded with that case, but she said her own children felt the repercussions of her efforts. Her son was to be assigned to a low track section the following year, and the school also suggested remedial reading classes for her daughter. Both children were good readers and had previously been achieving well academically.

There have been only a few Black police officers over the past several years in Smalltown, some of whom have been state police rather than local police. One of these men came from the military and is still on the force. Another, a Smalltown resident, was thrown off the force because of an "un-lawful delivery of drugs" charge. A white state policewoman, who was act-ing as an undercover drug agent, approached this man and convinced him to obtain marijuana for her. She then turned him in. Interestingly, she did not approach anyone else on the force.

> The police always assume the worst—they don't give kids the
> benefit of the doubt. The solution is just to send them away.
> —Shanell

The expelled policeman is considering initiating entrapment charges against the woman, but it is uncertain how well he will fare in the local court system. As a former Smalltown probation officer said, "I'd rather be white than Black if I went through the local court system." He said a Black tried to get a job on the probation staff, but this was opposed by the local judge. The former probation officer is convinced that a Black will never get a job there. After watching favoritism doled out for 20 years by the same resident judge, who dominated the town's judicial system for 30 years, this man quit his job in disgust. When he had been approached earlier by the state education department concerning how they could help him in his work with juveniles, his reply was, "Teach these kids to read."

Wilbert Rideau, an African American who has been imprisoned since 1962 at the Louisiana State Penitentiary, also suggested an educational solu-tion to crime—one that focuses on improving people rather than punishing or controlling them.

I'd like to see more efforts aimed at really improving people. Crime is a social problem, and education is the only real deterrent. Look at all of us in prison: We were all truants and dropouts, a failure of the education system. Look at your truancy problem, and you're looking at your future prisoners. Put your money there. (Woodbury, 1993)

JB: How many Black students are feeling the same kind of anger and frustration from their parents and grandparents when they come into a system that hasn't changed in the past century?

JAMES: Oh, a lot of Black students—almost maybe all of them. I really wasn't raised in the inner-town area. But it was just the way it seemed like it's been forever.

I would say that a lot of anger is directed against people in the white community. There's the Smalltown community, and there's the Smalltown Black Community. There's a couple families that are scattered, but basically the Blacks live in one area.

I still think it all stems from the fact that there's nothing [for teenagers] to do, and the fact that Blacks are isolated from the whites in the community. If you grew up with a group of people, you're not gonna have prejudices against them because they're someone you know better. I think prejudice is from fear and ignorance.

I think Smalltown could be an ideal town, because we have some very ideal people. I think they just need to come together. I hope someday there is not a Black Community nor a white community—just the Smalltown community.

—Shanell

CHAPTER 4

An Inner-City Comparison

The project described in this chapter resulted from a university–school collaborative effort to try out the theory and methods developed in *Reading/ Learning Disability: An Ecological Approach* (Bartoli & Botel, 1988a) to reduce the number of learners labeled as disabled by the school system. Following the plan of the book, teachers and specialists were asked to take a broader view of the processes of learning and nonlearning, to develop a more integrated plan for heterogeneous classroom learning, and to collaborate as colleagues to build optimal classroom environments for all students, regardless of their previous labels, test levels, or rates of progress. In addition, we planned to link the family and community with the school in meaningful ways to support student learning.

One of the lowest achieving elementary schools in a large inner-city school district was chosen to conduct a year-long, on-site faculty seminar to work toward the goals of the project. What follows is a description of the project and a beginning description of the wider ecology of an inner-city elementary school as it relates to learning to learn and learning to fail. Rather than focusing on one student, as in the previous case study of James, I have focused more broadly on the environment for learning, both in the school and in the community.

THE FIRST YEAR: STEPS TOWARD AN ECOLOGICAL DESCRIPTION OF AN INNER-CITY ELEMENTARY SCHOOL PROJECT

The first-year report begins to scratch the surface of (1) perspectives, assumptions, and expectations of various participants (teachers, administrators, parents, and outside observers), and (2) how the school functions as an interactive and interconnected system in the wider ecology of the student (family, community, culture). As in the previous case study, I have attempted to give a voice to the underrepresented perspective of the students and families.

Although the administration and school faculty may perceive this report to be critical and unreflective of the many positives in the school, the perception of the Latino colleagues with whom I shared the study is that this is the reality they experienced. So, with my respectful apologies to those who may feel uncomfortable with this report, I share it as yet another opportunity to take a different view and learn from it.

The limitations of this study are twofold. First, it was only a one-year study, and little of the long-term change process in the following years could be documented. This longer change process over the course of 5 years has been documented partly in Bryan (1992) and Feinberg (1993). Second, researchers are human, enmeshed in their own deeply held values and beliefs; these biases can and did get in the way during observation, staff development, project planning, data analysis, and reporting of findings.

The particular biases that I carried with me into the field concerning meaning versus mechanics in texts, autonomy versus control of students in the school, and the importance of theory to support practice came into direct conflict with the more traditional beliefs and practices of the school. Not only were there problems with a mismatch of deeply held values, but there was the additional tendency to perceive them dualistically as opposing views, rather than as varying points along a continuum. So communication did not flow smoothly during the first year, in part because of competing value systems, in part because of dualistic blame placing, and in part because of the normal disequilibrium common to any serious change effort.

As a researcher I learned two major lessons from this piece of research. First, qualitative research and evaluation of schools should be done in full collaboration with the school faculty, following their lead and engaging them in the research and evaluation process. This collaboration should include formulation of the questions to be asked as well as participation in the data collection and analysis (see the second project in Chapter 9 for an example of this). Not only does this increase the usefulness and value of the ongoing research and evaluation process, build the professionalism of the faculty, and increase ownership and responsibility; it also decreases the very real danger of creating feelings of distrust and betrayal too often incurred in qualitative research.

Second, research on the process of school reform and renewal should be long term, preferably 5 to 7 years. Michael Fullan (1991) suggests 10 years as a minimum for meaningful change. If such long-term collaborative relationships can be sustained, the research will be useful to the school and to others interested in the long-term process of school reform and renewal. And most important, long-term collaborations have the best chance for truly making a difference in the lives of children and families.

PROJECT DESCRIPTION

The project was a university–school collaborative effort to more fully understand, support, and document the development of learning potential for students as well as teachers in an inner-city elementary school. The ecological approach views high failure, retention, disability labeling, and dropout rates in the inner city to be interrelated and interconnected in the wider ecology of the student: an ecology that is too often complicated by poverty, family distress, low expectations and strained relationships in school, teenage pregnancy, joblessness, drugs, and crime. Thus the model includes intervention and documentation in all parts of the ecology of the student—the school, the family, and the community.

The four-part plan to develop the potential of inner-city students included (1) staff development centered on an integrative, collaborative, comprehensive curriculum and evaluation plan for building optimal classroom learning environments; (2) linking with the family through parent meetings, visits, workshops, and a proposed in-school family and child counseling center with social work outreach to build trusting, respectful, and supportive relationships between the school and the home/community, to support families in crisis, and to support better home learning; (3) collaborative teaching, consulting, observing, and learning (teachers and specialists, university and school, students and peers) that makes the best use of resources for developing the potential of all individuals; and (4) ecological research and continual collegial problem solving and refining of plans with university faculty integrated into the school improvement team.

Working through a shared governance process with the principal, school faculty, parents, and community, our university team made a commitment to develop student potential through collaboratively building, refining, and documenting an ecologically valid model for renewing better education and strengthening families in the inner city. We made links with other resources, so that this work could be connected with and supported by a variety of agencies and supporting groups. And we attempted to both model and extend the kind of networking and alliance/partnership building that is vital to the renewal of inner-city schools and communities.

PROJECT SITE

The inner-city school site was chosen as a research site for three major reasons: the school integrated labeled (learning/reading disabled) students into the regular classroom and put teachers and specialists in the classroom together, the leadership appeared open to change, and there were many critical needs in both the school and community. The principal was recommended as an energetic and innovative administrator who was committed to school improvement and better learning for the students of his school. When approached about a school–university partnership that would support his goals, he was enthusiastic about the possibilities.

Need was established partly on the basis of the school's low rank in the city school system: The school was ranked 171 out of 176 schools in the city on achievement tests. Like other schools in this district, the at-risk, failure, and retention rates were nearly 50%; and the percentage of families living below the poverty level was quite high, with over 85% of the children at the school receiving free lunches. Other factors that contributed to need included high unemployment rates, drug problems, and racial tension in the community. In addition, bilingual education and greater cultural understanding and communication were both needs and problems in the school and the community.

In the first year we worked with a principal and faculty who were committed to school improvement in the basic skills, reducing absenteeism, and encouraging more reading. They brought to that commitment a high level of energy and involvement as collaborators in meeting their goals. The principal had a philosophy of shared governance, and the faculty was open to experimentation. During the first year they worked on more integrative approaches to linking language and learning, and they explored forms of evaluation that could reduce what they saw as too much time taken from teaching to test their students. The goal we hoped to share as partner/collaborator as well as researcher/documenter was the development of the potential of all of their students.

What follows is a report of the observations from the first year of the project from the perspective of various participants in the ecology of the learner in an attempt to sketch the environment for learning in this inner-city school. The first section includes analyses of observations and interviews of teachers, specialists, and administrators. The second section includes perspectives of families, and the third section is a brief family case study illustrating some of the complex and challenging dynamics in the family, community, and school.

SECTION ONE: PERCEPTIONS IN THE SCHOOL SYSTEM

Teacher Perceptions

During the first staff development seminar, participants were asked to respond to a personal teaching philosophy questionnaire. I wanted to better understand their views on learning to read and write, causes of student failure and success, evaluation, and expectations of parents and administration. Teachers viewed success with reading as more heavily dependent on school and learner factors. Conversely, they viewed failure with reading as more dependent on family and learner factors, which are less controllable by the school.

In response to "learning to read involves . . . " and "student success is caused by . . . ," many of the teachers viewed success in learning to read as dependent on specific skills (decoding, oral reading, attention), much experience and practice with reading, and interest and desire on the part of the student. The suggested school factors to be provided included decoding, word attack skills, easy reading material "on their level," and lots of practice. Learner factors involved such personal characteristics as motivation, interest, and background; and student abilities such as attention span, memory, comprehension, expression, and oral reading skills. The one reference to the contribution of the family in learning to read was the suggestion that everyone, both at home and at school, should be actively involved.

Many of the teachers viewed failure with reading as dependent on student and/or parent deficits such as lack of motivation, interest, experience, or poor self-image in the student; and lack of involvement, caring, support, background, or discipline from the parents as well as lack of knowledge and use of English. The few references to the school's contribution to failure in reading included past failure, lack of previous skills that might promote future failure, programs that were too structured, and a lack of opportunity to feel successful and worthwhile. The lion's share of attributions for failure, however, rested with the family and the learner. There was the implicit assumption that the school methods and approach should work for all children, and those who do not fit in are failures due to their own inherent deficiencies.

When individual teachers discussed the families of their students, they frequently referred to such problems as young, unmarried mothers who were on drugs; poor mothers with large families living on welfare; families that move back and forth to Puerto Rico; and parents who do not consistently get their children to school or visit the school themselves. Several teachers surveyed other faculty members to see what they thought were the major communication problems between the home and school. Teachers viewed the problems as: no interest on the part of the parents, no telephone, or notes not getting through to parents. The discussions at staff meetings concerning home and school communication focused on how to ensure that the notes get to the parents: teacher techniques for when (time of day or day of the week) and where (attached to homework or test, in separate envelope) to put the notes. Again, the attributions for failure—this time with communication—appeared to be beyond the control of the teachers and the school.

Perceptions of Specialists and Administration

When the principal first came to the school 3 years ago, he said his first job was to "calm the place down." He described the disorder and chaos in the hallways before, during, and after school, with too many people coming in and out of the building in a disorderly manner. Thus he began the policies of students lining up before and after school with their teachers to enter and leave the building, of proceeding through the school hallways with the teacher in lines with stopping points along the way, of lining up to move from one classroom to another and to lunch or recess, and of having parents wait outside the building in the school yard both before and after school.

The rules for behavior both while in line to move about the school and in the classroom are frequently reviewed, sometimes before school in the school yard, during morning announcements, during class periods, or during the "Rules Week" held before the second report period. During the lunch period, if there is too much noise the principal or other person in charge may give a hands up signal, whereupon the students are to respond with their hand up and their mouth closed. This same signal was used during an evening performance for the families in May to reduce the noise level when the children were performing on the stage. The focus in this system of behavior management is on keeping an orderly, quiet, and disciplined school.

A second major effort led by the principal was a focus on more reading. There were a variety of incentives and activities focusing on reading: reading campaigns, books used as awards for various events, the principal's personal interest in reading as conveyed in announcements and suggestions before, during, and after school, a special evening program focused on literature, and a book fair. The principal also supported and personally attended the Literacy Network Seminars, which focused on more reading, writing, and talking across the whole school curriculum; and he personally organized additional reading through literature workshops for the faculty.

The perception of the counselor, reading teacher, and administrative assistant concerning the families of the school seemed to be focused on the deficits of the parents and the community. The reading teacher described the families as "environment poor" and needing to be "fed." The counselor described the families as "dysfunctional families" who do not support their members and do not have much strength, bonding, or stability. Neither the reading teacher nor the counselor visited the homes to confirm their opinions, however.

During a problem-solving meeting the reading teacher described the students as blank tablets starting off with nothing.

> They are coming to us, I call it with no imprinting at all. Not what we would do in our own home with our own children—they know nothing. It's almost like a blank sheet of paper and we have to start from the very, very beginning. (11/1/88)

Both of the administrators described their efforts to get the parents to come into the school for Back-to-School-Night, parent–teacher conferences, reading to the students in the classroom, or helping at the school in other ways; but they have been disappointed with the small response to these suggestions and events. They said there was a better turnout for school events in which the children perform and when they serve food, such as Literature Night and Family Day in May.

The counselor and the reading teacher planned a parent workshop to model a better parent–child communication method—one that avoids yelling at or hitting the child. They feel that more workshops should be given to teach the parents how to be parents. At an April meeting that included the Children's Services Director for the city and the Director of Special Programs from the neighboring Child Psychiatry Center, the school nurse discussed the many incidents of child abuse reported to her informally by students in the school. Again, home visits were not made to inquire about either the validity of these reports or the need for family support.

One of the content area specialists expressed her feeling of isolation in the school system. She said she never got to plan activities or units with the teachers, because when she comes into their classrooms, they go out. She said she would like to do more collaborative planning and teaching, perhaps focusing on thematic units; but there is no time during the day to plan and co-teach. She is what the district calls a prep specialist, whose job is to relieve regular classroom teachers for their class preparation period.

Due to the scheduling problem and the teachers union regulations surrounding prep specialists/prep periods, the classroom curriculum is fragmented both in content (unintegrated with the rest of the day/week's plan) and in management (a different teacher with a different management style disconnected from the regular teacher). Since the prep specialist has few opportunities to talk, plan, or teach with the regular classroom teacher, she cannot benefit from the classroom teacher's understanding of individual student needs, interests, or strengths. This further fragments the learning environment in the classroom for both teacher and students.

SECTION TWO: PERSPECTIVES OF THE FAMILY

Although many of the school personnel assume that parents are not interested in their children's school progress, the school–community coordinator (M) and the home and school association president (A) reported in one of our problem-solving meetings that parents are quite concerned.

> A: Everytime you talk to them about something like this—to help their kids—they're all for it—they never say no to help. They would like more help. (11/22/88)

> M: People are interested, because everytime I communicate with the parent—either I make a home visit or I call—they sound enthusiastic about it. And they are very thankful that I call, because they say, "I didn't know anything about it . . . I didn't receive anything—my child didn't give me anything." They're very responsive about that. (11/22/88)

When I visited families with the school–community coordinator in the fall and winter, parents were quite concerned about the school progress and behavior of their children. They also seemed anxious to discuss the behavior they observed at home with someone from the school, hoping to find resources for help. Parents were particularly appreciative of teachers who had taken an interest in their child, sent notes and newsletters home, and otherwise kept them informed about what was happening in school. They were disappointed with teachers who did not tell them anything or who made their child fearful in class.

Parents were very concerned about teachers waiting so long before telling them that their child was having problems in school. They said they would like to know immediately if the child was struggling or failing, yet the first scheduled parent–teacher conference and report card did not come until December 13. One parent commented:

> Yesterday I was really depressed when I got my kid's report card. I said, "Why are you going to wait 3 months to let me know my child is failing? Why not let me know ahead of time if he is misbehaving or being bad?" A lot of parents were there and they got aggravated and mad.

Parents said they would like to know even the first week of school if the child was misbehaving, and they felt that the lack of communication from the school indicated little concern or respect for them.

I felt like I shouldn't be down so low where a parent has to know 3 months later—it should be right away. A lot of parents agree with that too. . . . If a child is giving you a problem at the beginning of the year—right there the first week he's misbehaved already—let them know right away. 'Cause we like to know.

The tradition in Puerto Rico, where many of the parents came from, is for the parents to bring the children to their classroom each morning, chat informally with the teacher about their children, and then leave when they see the children sitting quietly at their desks. The school–community coordinator explained:

When Hispanic parents have a problem with a child, they want to know how the child is doing in school, and they just come straight to the teacher. . . . They were used to just going into the room and talking with the teacher, and they liked that. (10/11/88)

This open door policy is quite different from the more formal constraints of most U.S. schools. Parents are not permitted into the school building in the morning to accompany their children to class, and a specific appointment time is required to talk with the teacher. The coordinator explained:

But over here they cannot do that—they have to come to the office first, and ask for permission, and most of the time, the time is not appropriate to see the teacher because she is giving a lesson. (10/11/88)

This difference in traditions has caused misunderstandings and negative feelings between some parents and the school, because parents sometimes feel excluded rather than welcome in the school.

The fact that most of the teachers do not speak Spanish is an additional barrier to impromptu, informal conversations between parents and teachers. The coordinator tries to arrange meetings between parents and teachers during the teacher's preparation time; but if she cannot be there, either someone else must be found to translate for the parent or the meeting must be canceled. In addition, preparation times are often used for other school meetings or for class coverage for an absent or sick teacher (the school has only one substitute teacher).

School personnel have reprimanded parents for bringing their children into school, just as they have reprimanded the children for not using English in the hallways. Such interactions lead parents to feel less than welcome and uncomfortable about speaking their own language in the school. A teacher relayed the following incident in a problem-solving meeting:

> I put two mothers down this morning that walked those kids up to second grade. And I've been arguing this point and arguing this point at this school. You *have* to say good-bye to those children in the school yard, and *not* walk them up the steps. You *must* say good-bye. (11/22/88)

This teacher said she delivered the same message in a kindergarten workshop for parents: "We said to them, 'You must leave them go, mommas, you must leave them go.'"

During the problem-solving meeting at the beginning of November, the home and school association president and school–community coordinator explained that parents are often afraid to come to the school and talk with the teacher, which presents a further barrier to communication.

> M: They feel that since the teacher has more education, they are going to be embarrassed by the teacher or they won't know what the teacher is saying.
> A: A lot of times the parents are scared to come . . . they don't understand and they get scared that they won't understand the teachers.

The language issue is complicated by the shortage of bilingual teachers in the school and in the district in general. Over the past 8 years there has been a movement away from bilingual education in favor of English immersion (all English in the school) or the use of ESOL (English for speakers of other languages) teachers. Hence there are fewer bilingual teachers hired for even largely Spanish speaking populations such as in this school. The result is more failure and retention for students new to English; more disappointment, confusion, frustration, and anger for parents, students, teachers, specialists, and administrators; and more strained relationships devoid of trust. One parent explained the situation like this.

> When they get the homework, they can't understand what is going on because they can't even read it in English. . . . Therefore the child comes back to the school without their homework done. Or the child tries by himself—it's hard because he might not be able to read it. So this is a big problem.
> A lot of times the child is not going at the same pace and he has

to be retained—a lot of parents don't like that. They think that the teacher is prejudiced or something. (11/1/88)

This ongoing relationship problem reached a crisis point when 10 bilingual students were moved out of their bilingual class into a regular classroom due to overcrowding. Eight of these students failed throughout the year, and their parents asked for help from Community Legal Services to require the school to hire another bilingual teacher. Some of the parents viewed the school as insensitive to the needs and desires of the Spanish speaking children and families. They were frustrated and angry because their children were allowed to fail throughout the year, and they felt that the school did not seem to respect either the desire of the parents for bilingual education for their children or the needs of the students who were trying (and failing) to cope with education in a foreign language.

The principal tried to find another bilingual teacher, but he was unsuccessful in his efforts. In addition to the critical shortage of minority teachers in the United States, there is a vast shortage of bilingual teachers.

Some Questions for Further Research

1. Is it possible that students may choose not to deliver notes and messages from the school to their families, fearing bad reports or possible repercussions? (Or is it possible that parents may not be able to read or fully understand notes sent home and that they may assume a negative report and therefore deny the existence of the note to cover their embarrassment or fear of negative judgments?) Both parents and teachers have complained that messages do not get through—parents are often uninformed, and teachers hear no response to notes and messages sent to parents.

2. Is it possible that students may at times capitalize on the lack of trusting relationships between families and the school by telling either parents or school personnel what the students think they want to hear? (Could students describe teachers to parents as more negative and unsupportive than they actually are, or could they describe parents to school personnel as less concerned or more neglectful than they really are, all in hopes of gaining more sympathy or support as one side plays against the other? Or might parents and teachers engage in similar interactions, scapegoating the child?) Are they all learning too well the lesson that "life is manipulation"?

3. What would happen if teachers and other school personnel sent more good reports home with children; and if they learned which parents do not speak and write English so they could make an effort to have some notes written in Spanish? Or if they began dialogue journals with parents or ongoing progress records and homework contracts that included the par-

ents as vital colleagues in the child's continued growth? (And what might help to ensure that the interactions were fully understood by the parents?)

4. Do students and their families view school rules for order and control (and/or the school curriculum and tests) as contributing to the personal and academic growth of children, or do they view them as primarily serving the system?

5. Would students view teachers and other school personnel as more supportive and worthy of trust and respect if their parents achieved a stronger, respectful, collaborative relationship with the school? (For instance, would students more easily follow school rules if their parents were a part of making up and enforcing the rules for order, devising ways to reduce absenteeism, or building a better curriculum for learning?)

6. Would students be helped to develop a deeper sense of pride and identity by having their families included in a school-wide effort to celebrate both their language and culture? (For example, could families work with teachers and specialists to develop a thematic unit on Puerto Rican art, history, and music? Or could families share favorite stories and songs in both Spanish and English to enrich the language learning of all the students in the school? Or could the art teacher include a cultural tradition such as mask making in her school-wide projects for the year?) Or could teachers request the help of bilingual parents and children to communicate better with Spanish speaking parents and children, both in and out of the classroom?

SECTION THREE: A FAMILY CASE STUDY

The brief portrait of a family that follows combines data from participant observation during two home visits and a meeting with the INTERACT group at the school; (INTERACT is a city-based institute focused on understanding complex sets of interacting problems and opportunities in social systems, members of whom graciously volunteered to be a resource to the school for community self-development); data from subsequent conversations with school personnel and the family; and comparative data from several Puerto Rican families in the United States and in Puerto Rico. This case study can provide only a glimpse of some of the possible family dynamics in the ecology of the learners at our inner-city school, the majority of whom are Puerto Rican.

A note on the ecological view: The purpose of this case study is to illustrate the interrelatedness of school, family, and community issues and problems, and to show how these interrelationships affect learning for the student. Throughout, the reader should search for avenues for intervention and change rather than labeling pathology or placing blame. As always, names have been changed and exact dates withheld for confidentiality.

A Glimpse of the Family System

In December 1988 I went with the school–community coordinator to visit the home of 12-year-old Juan, whose third-grade teacher reported that he had been out of school for a month. We were greeted cordially by Juan's grandmother and 4-year-old sister, and told that Juan was with his mother, Maria, at a psychiatric appointment. Juan's grandmother described his "nervous" condition—screaming uncontrollably sometimes, breaking out in hives, withdrawing at other times—and she said he was afraid of the teacher because she threw an eraser at him.

After we spoke for a short time in the family's living room, Juan's grandmother tearfully told us the story of her daughter's struggle with drugs and alcohol. Now 29 years old, Maria has been involved with drugs for 16 years (we later found out she is using crack). She said Maria was using drugs when Juan was born and she continues to disappear into a nearby bar or to go with "bad" friends for several days at a time. Juan has said that he wanted to go into the bar, drag his mother out, and bring her home. But his grandmother told him he could not do that because he was under age and the police would come. Juan has also said he was not going to school because he was worried about his mother leaving for the bar.

There are three other children in the family, ages 4, 9, and 11. The grandmother is staying with the family because she is afraid Maria will drink and take drugs and not care for the children. She said her daughter does not want her to stay, but she fears Maria will have parties with her "bad" friends and the children will be sitting in the corners of the room, afraid and bewildered. She is also afraid that Maria will ask the father of the two younger children, who she said sometimes hits Juan, to come and live with them because she is lonely and wants a husband.

Juan's grandmother said that Maria has expressed an interest in going back to school to finish her education (she only went to sixth grade), so she appreciated the suggestion that Maria might begin a GED course. As we were discussing this, Maria returned with Juan, and we talked further about Juan's difficulty with school. We suggested that Maria come to the school to talk with the teacher about how sensitive Juan is, and that she talk with the counselor as well, hoping that she might confide her own problems to him.

The openness of the family to the visit by the school–community coordinator, even accompanied by an unknown outsider such as myself, and their sincere interest and concern about their children were typical of the other families whom I had the opportunity to visit. We were always invited to sit down and talk, usually in the family's living room. In the one home where there was no furniture to sit on, the mother apologized for not having a place for us to sit. (The room contained a small bassinet with a baby she was caring for until the mother could return, and a rocking chair occupied by a rather heavy teenage boy who was quiet and unresponsive.)

The parents we visited at the request of either the teachers or the principal carried many heavy personal and family burdens, and they seemed grateful to have someone from the school who was as concerned about their children as they were. The tone of these informal home visits was courteous and respectful, as well as inquiring and searching as we explored together ideas and suggestions to better meet the needs of their child as well as their own personal needs.

Mothers and grandmothers were particularly open to the school–community coordinator, who is a warm and nonjudgmental listener, and is herself Puerto Rican and Spanish speaking. They felt comfortable confiding their personal problems to her, and they listened politely as she made suggestions or explained what their child was doing (or not doing) in school. An example of the honesty in this relationship involved a mother of six children who told the coordinator sadly, as she leaned wearily over the broom she was using to sweep the living room floor, that the reason her oldest son had not been in school for several weeks was that he had to be home to care for his brothers and sisters while she was in the hospital having a baby. In addition, she said he was absent other times to serve as a translator for doctors' appointments. There was no one else, she said, to help her. Her 11-year-old son added that he liked school and he would like to be there.

A Mother Reaches for Help

In January 1989 I invited Maria to come to a meeting at the school with INTERACT to discuss the problems in the community and talk about possibilities for change. She came to the office early and said she did not think she could stay due to an appointment in the afternoon. I told her how much we needed her thoughts on the needs and problems of the community, especially since no other parents had shown up for the meeting. I said that INTERACT wanted to help, but they needed her help to come up with ways to begin a homework club, to find other ways to assist children such as hers with learning problems, and to understand what might work or not work. She reluctantly agreed to stay, and we held the meeting in the school–community coordinator's office with three members of INTERACT (Dr. Alan Barstow, Dr. Herman Wrice, and Jason Magidson), Maria and her 4-year-old daughter, the school–community coordinator, Penny Bryan (a researcher from Penn), and, later, the administrative assistant.

When we talked about the problem of drugs and fear in the community, Maria said that was the "number one thing." Excerpts from the meeting follow:

JILL (JB): [to Maria] I liked what you said before about safety and fear in the community. We should get your input on this. Is this a safe community? Are the parents afraid for their children to go out in the community? How do they feel about this community?

MARIA: Sometimes they are afraid, because there are problems (inaudible).

JB: Then they would be afraid to let their children out for after school activities? If they started an after school club, would parents be afraid to let their children walk over to the school?

MARIA: Well yes, they should be concerned. Afraid, yes. Something might happen to them. Somebody could (inaudible). If I am not there my mother walks the kids to school.

JB: What are the biggest fears and problems that mothers like you see?

MARISSA (school–community coordinator): What are parents afraid of in the community for their kids?

MARIA: Drugs are the number one thing.

MARISSA: We've had accidental deaths because of drug dealings. There was a child killed a couple years ago, and recently a girl was shot. I think it was drug related—they were going to shoot her brother.

JB: [to Dr. Herman Wrice] What successful ways have you found to deal with these problems that you could transpose here?

DR. WRICE: One is working from the community into the school. There have to be people in the area who are willing to accept that [drugs are] the number one problem, and then start with that as a working base. You find the hardest thing to do is find enough people to really stand up and face that issue, because if you don't do something with the drugs, then none of the other things happen—homework won't happen, free play won't happen, people won't want to come out and volunteer. We found that getting the parents involved and standing up against the problem—not saying how bad it is—we know how bad it is—but what are we going to do about the problem. Homework is the solution to in-school attitudes and marks, but the people that would flow from the antidrug movement will also be your tutors or help with the tutors. They'll be able to tell her [Maria] not to worry cause we're going to be out there on Tuesday. And they see her, and she sees them enough to know that they are for real.

DR. ALAN BARSTOW: That's why it's important to link up whatever we're doing with other groups and activities. So they can say we're going to an after school activity and we can walk home in groups of kids to certain neighborhoods. It's got to be a change from somebody saying, "It's a bad situation." to "We're going to do something about it."

JB: Who else is concerned about this? Who are the other people that could come together as the nucleus Herman was talking about—who would be concerned and get started? They can be a catalyst if people come together. [to Maria] Do you have neighbors and friends who would come with you also, and be as concerned about their children as you are?

MARIA: As a matter of fact, it's the opposite. I know so many parents—it's pitiful. I don't want to say anymore.

JB: You don't see enough parents who would be able to come in like you . . .

MARIA: It's the opposite. It's what they teach their kids, it's what their kids do, what their kids get into.

JB: The problem is some of the parents?

HERMAN: I think what she's saying is, some of the kids that are in these homes are doing it. We found that when we got to the bottom of it these weren't strangers from all over town. These were the kids two doors down and three doors over.

Maria was noticeably upset throughout the meeting, and she finally turned to me and asked to talk outside alone. When we were outside the office she said she felt as though everyone in the room was talking about her (part of the conversation had been about the problem of drugs in the community). She said tearfully that she was here at the school because she cared very much about her children, and I assured her that we knew and greatly appreciated that. She said that she was having many problems herself, and that surely everyone in the room could see that (she had been near tears several times during the meeting), and I told her that was all the more reason that we needed her help to plan for other mothers who are experiencing the same problems.

She then asked if she could speak alone with Dr. Wrice, the INTERACT member who was most knowledgeable about and experienced with drug problems, saying that she could not trust all those people in the room. So I returned to the meeting and asked Dr. Wrice if he would talk privately with Maria. When he returned to the meeting, he said he arranged to meet with Maria and some of her friends at her home later that week. It seemed a hopeful sign that she was asking for help and that she was willing to take the risk to reach out to someone for that help, not only for herself but for her children as well.

The following week Maria called the school to ask the home and school coordinator to come to her home. Two of her sons would not come to school and she didn't know what to do about it. I joined the visit, and we talked with both of the boys about how they felt about school. Juan said that he did not like reading—he found it hard—and he would like to be in his younger brother's class because he could handle the material better. He said he liked physical education, and he would like to be in the after school club that is held for fourth and fifth graders. His grandmother and mother said he was very good in art.

We said we would help Juan look into the physical education club, and I suggested that he might illustrate some of the books being used in either his own classroom or the classrooms of the faculty in the staff development seminar, and he could make "little books"—his own copies of fun and easy to read stories—to help him strengthen his reading. Before we left both of the boys agreed to come back to school.

Maria began coming into the school to visit with the school–community coordinator, talk about her problems as well as those of her children, and look for solutions. She planned to sign up for a GED course, and she began volunteering at the school library since she loved to read. In February Maria came into the school several times a week to help in the library and to talk with the school–community coordinator. At one point she was coming in every day, and she completed the application to take the GED course offered at the Lighthouse nearby.

But then things started falling apart for her. The school–community coordinator was out sick for a few days and couldn't see her, and Maria could not get in contact with Dr. Wrice. She began putting things in the wrong places in the library, and eventually she stopped coming into the library or the school. When I called her home in early March to invite Maria to a home and school meeting that a professor from Penn's School of Social Work would be attending, the grandmother said she had moved out. The grandmother came to the meeting and said that she was caring for the children, and Maria was back on drugs.

CHAPTER 5

Learning and Nonlearning in Suburban and Urban Schools

The striking parallels in the themes that emerge from my observations in two quite different settings—a majority white, middle-class suburban school and a majority Latino, poor inner-city school—underscore the larger cultural and societal issues that need to be considered. But first a caveat: These case studies are not meant to be viewed as a condemnation of teachers, administrators, parents, or communities. Blaming those in schools or selected communities for what is played out daily in our society is senseless, allowing us to both ignore the complexity of the issues and delay taking personal responsibility for what we can do about them. Sarason (1971) has suggested that, if part of the problem in school change efforts is our way of looking and thinking, we are not dealing with a hopeless situation. Chapters 3 and 4 attempt to fill in some of the gaps vital to a broader, more hopeful view.

Looking at the case studies in Chapters 3 and 4, there are several recurring themes and implications that emerge as significant to a deeper understanding of the complex issue of learning to read in the U.S.A. The most obvious theme throughout the case studies is the assumption of deficit reflected in racial, ethnic, and social class biases and stereotypes that pervade the ecologies of both African American and Latino children and families. Closely connected with this is a second theme: the lack of trusting, respectful communication and relationship building between the home and school that are a significant barrier to learning for these children and families.

A third common theme in both case studies involves the lack of integration within the school as well as in the larger community. Multiple forms of segregation and fragmentation result from the separation of mechanics from meaning, student experience and world knowledge from textbooks and tests, school curricula from student-centered evaluation, "abled" from "disabled" students, specialists from teachers, teachers from administrators, parents from the school, and poor and nonwhite families from nonpoor white families. Such pervasive fragmentation points to the need for more inclusive, integrative, mediational, ecologically supportive approaches to reading, learning, evaluation, and living.

The most salient implication from these case studies is that we may be looking for our explanations for reading and learning failure in the wrong places. Our ungrounded solutions to reading failure may, in fact, be a large part of the problem. The teachers, specialists, counselors, and principals who attempted to help either James or the Latino students looked at I.Q. and other test scores to find the students' cognitive and perceptual deficits; they looked at family backgrounds and environment for disadvantage and lack of motivation; and they looked at classroom behavior for differences that they found intolerable or unacceptable relative to their own values and norms.

Where they did *not* look was at the student's potential, language ability, competence, maturity, and strengths. They also did not look at the *real* family of the child behind the school and community assumptions and preconceptions, a view that could come only from an established relationship built on trust, meaningful communication, and genuine concern. They did not look at the culture of the classroom with its white middle-class norms and values of individual competition, "fitness" for the mainstream, and narrowly defined competence that allowed for very little diversity. Nor did they look closely at the fragmented and differentiated curriculum, its evaluation methods geared to maintaining the status quo, and the devastating results of the labeling and tracking procedures used by the school system. And finally, they did not look at their own history for the basis of their expectations and personal biases: They did not carefully examine their own community and cultural values and assumptions.

This chapter will explore some of the issues inherent in these themes and implications, which together point out the need for system-wide change. Chapters 6 and 7 will further develop the theoretical and conceptual framework necessary to future directions for improving teaching, learning, evaluation, and living in the context of our pluralistic democracy. Then Chapter 8 will detail some of the promising transformations that have occurred in both the suburban district and the inner-city school.

ASSUMPTIONS OF DEFICIT

James was assumed to be deficient by virtue of the community he came from, the race he belonged to, and the school he first attended. He was unjustifiably placed in a first-grade low reading group, and he was homogeneously grouped with other "low achievers" in a system that assumed such tracking and grouping practices to be beneficial. Due to her status as a single, Black, working mother, James's mother was alternatively assumed to be either too harsh or too lenient a disciplinarian, and she was often assumed to be either not interested in or not capable of helping James.

Stereotyping of inner-city Puerto Rican parents, especially young, single mothers, was similar to that found in the Smalltown Black Community. There were low expectations for their ability and competence as parents, their investment in their children, and the value they placed on education. It was assumed that many of "them" (quite a different sort from "us") would not have the language, values, or academic competence to help their children, even if they wanted to. Their desire to help was equally questioned, particularly when Spanish was spoken at home. In spite of everything that we know about the cognitive, linguistic, and cultural value of bilingualism, this was assumed to be a deficit.

We look to multicultural education, and in particular to an antibias curriculum (Derman-Sparks, 1989), as the way out of this destructive cycle of deficit assumptions, low expectations, and school failure. James Banks (1993) describes a major goal of multicultural education as the reform of schools "so that students from diverse racial, ethnic, and social-class groups will experience educational equality" (p. 3). He also describes the advantages of a systems approach to reforming schools, suggesting a broadly conceived and well-integrated program. In such a program, more democratic racial attitudes emerge for students in the process of understanding how knowledge is constructed from diverse ethnic and cultural perspectives.

Shanell had it right when she said:

> Don't ever assume something. You can't *assume* about people. That's just something that isn't possible, because your assumptions when it comes to people are most all of the time wrong.

The alternative to deficit assumptions and stereotypes is the time-consuming enterprise of getting to know people as individuals, and building respectful and enduring relationships with them based on that knowledge. This brings us to the second recurring theme, which is inextricably linked with the first.

COMMUNICATION AND RELATIONSHIP PROBLEMS

Teachers said they were surprised when James's mother showed up for school conferences or team meetings. And when she was there, like many other mothers from the Smalltown Black Community, she found herself more often talked at than respectfully talked with. At a middle school team meeting they didn't suggest a homework contract to her because they thought she would not follow up. The counselor in that school asked me privately after a meeting with James's mother if her name was the same as James's.

James's mother was virtually ignored in the faculty meeting when all of James's high school teachers listed their complaints. At one point she tried to get them to think about why James had respect for his previous principal, but they ignored the question. Other parents who later formed Smalltown's Concerned African-American Parents group (see Chapter 8) also felt a lack of respect from the school.

Similar feelings on the part of the inner-city Latino parents were expressed. Commenting on the school's failure to inform them of their children's failure or problems until it was too late, the PTA president said, "Why should I have to be so low." Comments about the inner-city parents by teachers, specialists, and the counselor were rarely filled with respect, and there was very little in their infrequent interactions with parents that could serve as a basis for trust and meaningful relationship building.

The views of Puerto Rican parents concerning time and participation in school were not well understood or respected within the school. "Puerto Rican time," which places a high priority on interpersonal relationships and family needs, sometimes came into conflict with the more impersonal and precise Anglo concept of promptness for school appointments (Toro-Lopez, 1992). Similarly, the Puerto Rican tradition of coming into the school in the morning, chatting informally with the teacher in the classroom, and then letting the teacher take charge of the child's schooling was misinterpreted as intrusive and overprotective (in the mornings when parents wanted to bring their children into the classroom) and neglectful (since parents were not used to volunteering in the school). Little basis can be found in these miscommunications for building trusting, respectful relationships.

When trust and communication are at a minimum, the common response of traditional U.S. educational administration has been tighter control of students and teachers. This leads often to an adversarial climate, with more time, energy, and money spent on resisting and enforcing authority. Steven Goldberg (1993) suggests that, if we are to permanently move beyond the cycle of failure and violence in schools, traditional notions of control must give way to building a community where individual responsibility and trust are the guiding principles.

In agreement with Linda McNeil's (1986) research on the contradictions of a control and management orientation, this new approach would seek less to keep parents at a distance and keep students and teachers in line, and seek instead to develop trusting, respectful, collegial relationships among students, teachers, parents, administration, and the community.

Teachers would take charge of their classrooms within a framework of trust, equitable relationships, and cultural understanding; but they would not seek to condescendingly control or take individual responsibility away from parents or students.

The conflicts surrounding bilingual education for the Latino community, Black history for the Black Community, and multicultural education in general are symbolic of the need for more trust, respect, and appreciation of others. Attempts to create more respectful communication and equality through these educational solutions are often met with built-in historic, social, political, racial, and economic barriers that are neither addressed seriously nor given priority in the school system, the community, or society in general.

Resolving these conflicts will require developing relationships among teachers, parents, students, administrators, and community members rooted in equality and mutual respect. And from these collaborative relationships a Deweyan democratic system of participation and planning, goal setting and strategy development, and conflict resolution can emerge. Just as this ongoing, recursive community learning process of collaboratively planning and working together formed the basis of our democracy in the eighteenth century, so can it be the basis for our renewed pluralistic society in the twenty-first century.

INTEGRATION PROBLEMS

James and the Latino students were overdosed on skill work to the neglect of integrated reading, writing, and talking across the curriculum. The teachers' definitions of reading reflected a linear, skill-focused approach, particularly with students who were considered poor readers. Thus, the very students who needed more opportunities to make sense in meaningful contexts had fewer opportunities to do so. Those who needed more integrated reading, writing, and talking across the curriculum got less. And those who most needed to be evaluated with congruent, process-oriented, student-centered methods that put value in their progression and strengths, were devalued instead by isolated skill tests devoid of meaningful context or sense.

Students who most needed to develop confidence in their own abilities, to be surrounded by motivated and capable peers, and to contribute in a community of learners, were instead segregated into lower level groups and tracks wherein motivation and self-confidence were sadly lacking. Teachers of the more "disabled" learners were similarly isolated, with few opportunities to collaborate with colleagues to problem-solve and build more meaningful learning environments for the students who most needed them.

The parents of low achieving students, disproportionately poor and nonwhite, were too often estranged or disenfranchised from the school due to past histories of failure and disrespect, or the present realities of miscommunication, distrust, and poor relationships. And in the wider community and society the parents were similarly unsuccessful in their quest for better jobs, decent housing, and affordable child care. Housing and child care, when available, were more often segregated by income and race, perpetuating the distancing, lack of communication, and misunderstanding among racial and socioeconomic groups.

Isolation and fragmentation are evident in the need of mothers to keep young children home from school to serve as interpreters or translators, or to help with child care. The social workers, helping agencies, and child care facilities in such inner-city areas as our site are severely overtaxed, with help available only to some of the many families in need. Families, often headed by women alone, come to the school–community coordinator and school administrators for help with problems concerning basic living conditions, knowing neither how to deal with the bureaucracy in housing, employment, welfare, or medical systems nor what agencies are there to help them. Services are so fragmented and scattered that it is impossible for city or school personnel to be as informed and helpful as they would like to be.

Individual families are often isolated from each other in what could surely be described as a hostile and dangerous community—drug, crime, and racial problems are not uncommon. Those who move into the neighborhood without friends and relatives to support and advise them, or to translate for them if necessary, are extremely isolated from sources of help. A single mother without friends or relatives who is shy about meeting people, such as the mother of six who had to rely only on her young children, is at a particular disadvantage not only for herself personally, but for her children as well. Yet such families may contribute to their own isolation because they are fearful of the bureaucracy, institutions, and government that traditionally have threatened their sense of self-worth, their identity, their language, and their culture.

Partly due to inner-city job shortages for unskilled workers and those without fluent English (combined with social and institutional inequities), there is a vast shortage of minority males who have jobs that will allow them to consider marriage and families (Wilson, 1987). This increases the number of single, female-headed families with strained resources for both children and mothers, who may have to turn to welfare for their very survival. With little or no affordable child care, mothers cannot leave their children and go to work themselves or educate themselves for better life options. In addition, mothers may view caring for their children as a higher priority than getting a low paying job. Continued school failure for the children adds to the perpetuation of the existing problems.

This self-perpetuating failure cycle is common for children who are labeled as learning/reading disabled, but who are actually disabled by their absences from school, the negative assumptions of school personnel (mother "doesn't care" or is "neglectful," child is "disadvantaged" or "disabled"), and the inability—or unwillingness—of the society to either view or support all of its members as equal in human value and potential.

Further isolation of families in the community may occur for physical protection. Racial aggression and violence are not uncommon in this community or in the city as a whole. Last spring when a Puerto Rican mother with two children attempted to buy a home on an all-white block near the area, she faced broken windows and threats that ended in her leaving the neighborhood. There have been incidents of Puerto Rican youths beaten and killed as well as whites killed in retaliation; so Puerto Rican, Black, and white groups tend to move as a block, with little mixing of races. In a recent study this city was cited as one of the seven worst cities for segregation in the country.

Some isolation is also perpetuated by language differences. The need to communicate with others at a deep human level draws together people whose mother tongue is the same. Speaking one's native language can counteract some of the adverse effects of isolation and difficult conditions in the inner city, but more than this it fulfills the basic human need to be understood—to fully express oneself to others.

A physician from Puerto Rico who studied in Boston explained the lack of belonging and lack of acceptance that may keep families from trying to learn English: They may wish to retreat to the circle of warmth and acceptance in their Spanish speaking community. Other cultural differences may keep Puerto Rican families apart from the mainstream of U.S. society, such as the importance to them of cooperation rather than competition at the expense of the group; or the value they place in the hometown concept in Puerto Rico, in close family and social relationships, and in the desire to return to Puerto Rico when they can earn enough money for their families to live there. These cultural values differ from the typical mainstream U.S. value or emphasis placed on individual competitiveness, promptness and pushing a time clock, and more interpersonal distance.

To Puerto Rican families who are used to much social interaction in a close hometown environment, and who maintained daily informal contacts with teachers when they brought their children to school in Puerto Rico, schools and families in the United States may appear lacking in personal warmth, acceptance, and social interaction. A logical suggestion offered by the above-mentioned physician, who is also a parent of young children, is to help the families to feel that they belong—that they are a part of the school, the community, and the society rather than being separated, isolated, or estranged. Otherwise their roots, their cultural values, and their language may remain unchanged even after many years in the United States. Unlike many immigrant populations who view coming to the United States as a one-way trip, these families are more likely to think that someday they will go back to Puerto Rico.

The school–community coordinator said also that some of the families coming to the school go back and forth between here and the island, making the population of the school less than stable. This may contribute to the frustration of school personnel and the negative assumptions of some about the families whom they view as unconcerned about the welfare and education of their children, unwilling to make commitments and invest time in school projects and events, and clinging to their own Spanish language (they need it when they return to Puerto Rico). This might also explain part of the weak response reported by the principal, counselor, and some teachers to school efforts to link with the parents.

FRAGMENTATION IN SCHOOLS

The interrelated problems of fragmented teaching, learning, and evaluating are certainly not new ones. A century ago John Dewey described the problems inherent in fragmented learning removed from authentic learning contexts; and Socrates opposed inadequate, piecemeal teaching and learning over a thousand years ago. Many other holistic, ecologically minded philosophers and educators across the centuries have done likewise.

What is new is the biological and social interactional research that verifies the vital necessity for integration and social interaction in human sensemaking. We learn because we can connect with the whole, because we can link with our past experiences, because we can work with and learn from each other, and because we see how it all fits sensibly together. Learning proceeds more from whole to part, and then back to the whole. It does not proceed primarily from part to whole, as the fragmented curriculum and evaluation approaches so pervasive in U.S. schools, textbooks, and tests suggest.

The particular problematic issues of fragmented curricula and evaluation methods and the labeling process are detailed in Bartoli & Botel (1988a). They have also been addressed by all of the major national education associations for the past 3 decades, as well as by countless authors in the field of education from John Dewey at the turn of the 20th century to John

Goodlad nearing the end. That they persist despite the well-documented research that has exposed their inadequacies is evidence of the challenging, committed, sustained, collaborative hard work needed for second-order transformational change of the system.

MOVING TOWARD TRANSFORMATION

When I asked James at age 20 about the needed changes in schools, and in particular what future teachers could do to eliminate some of the racial tension in schools, he suggested a change of view on the part of teachers.

> Basically, [that] the kid is not a troublemaker because he is Black. That's what a lot of teachers look at—he's a Black kid, oh man, I'm not gonna mess with him. I won't say anything to him. They're afraid that just because he is Black he's gonna get in trouble.

Of course, getting beyond these stereotypes and biases is not an easy task, as much of our social history in this country will show. Shanell suggested that the major problem was the separation of races in Smalltown.

> There's no really intermixing of the community at all. I mean it's like the Black Community is separate from the white community. . . . I think that prejudice is from fear and ignorance, and if you grow up with somebody and you are around somebody all of your life, you know them so you're not ignorant of them.

Segregation of African American and Latino children and families in the community was common in both the inner-city and small town sites. Low income children, many of whom are African American or Latino, are segregated as preschoolers into Head Start programs or other special programs (the Smalltown YWCA, for example, has a separate preschool program for poor children).

Reducing fragmentation and separation in all parts of the ecology would certainly be a good beginning point. Staff development programs like Penn's Literacy Network, which seeks to make connections among reading, writing, and talking across the curriculum in heterogeneous classrooms, and to connect teachers and specialists with each other both within and among schools and districts, attempt to reduce fragmentation across the ecology of the child. Beyond integration within and across our system of education, I believe that we need to become advocates for transforming both the education system and our society to ones that more closely reflect our professed national ideals of equality, democracy, and individual rights for all.

CHANGING THE SYSTEM

In the 1992 movie version of Aaron Sorkin's *A Few Good Men,* Corporal Dawson had to explain to Private Downey why their dishonorable discharge verdict made sense, even though they, in obeying a "code red" order that resulted in the death of a fellow soldier (Willy), were just doing what they were ordered to do. Like many officers and soldiers before them in other countries and in other times, they were faced with the moral and ethical choice of either obeying the orders of a system that did not uphold the highest ideals of humanity, or disobeying at their own peril. Dawson's explanation of the court's decision and of why they should have disobeyed was, "We were supposed to fight for people who couldn't fight for themselves. We were supposed to fight for Willy."

The trials of Nazi officers after World War II likewise upheld the higher moral duty of humanity to respond ethically and morally in response to others in need. Disobeying the system and trying to dismantle it, however, have few extrinsic rewards and many severe punishments in most camps. Dawson and Downey were damned if they did and damned if they didn't help Willy. The question was whether they, or anyone else, could respond beyond the level of their own safety and obeyance of the system, to the needs of their fellow human being. And perhaps this is one of the ultimate human dilemmas faced by us all—and part of the reason that there is more first-order change that leaves the system essentially unchanged.

The rewards for teachers and administrators who seek to transform the inequities in our system of education are not high either. As it is for soldiers, it is often a "Catch 22." The administrator who worked very hard toward system-wide change in the Smalltown School District was mysteriously dismissed. One teacher in the inner-city school confided her defiance of the district's prescriptive curriculum behind the classroom doors, but she also told me with tears in her eyes that she had to fail all but four of her 35 second-grade students because of district-mandated tests.

I have many poignant memories and many pages of transcripts from interviews of teachers, specialists, and administrators agonizing over the unfairness of testing, labeling, grouping, and tracking practices and the fragmented and mediocre learning environments that resulted for those most in need of help. As he reflected upon the letter that the Smalltown School District required him to send to middle school parents (telling them that their child was either above average, average, or below average and would be tracked accordingly), a principal told me that he had questioned that procedure, and he really worried about it when he first took the job. Discouraged about James's low track placement that went with his LD label, an LD specialist said, "It really shouldn't be this way, but the way the system works now, there really isn't any choice."

Over the past 10 years, having talked at length with well over 100 teachers in the privacy of their classrooms, I have yet to meet a teacher who has not agonized over the inequities of the system, the unfairness of testing and labeling practices, and the inadequacies of the environment for learning, particularly for those who need the most help. But teachers, like soldiers, are duty bound to uphold the system even when they know it is unfair and unjust. Too often their reward for pushing the system toward disequilibrium, which is a necessary part of all change and growth, is censure or expulsion from the system. Principals and superintendents share a similar fate. And faculty in college and university education departments are no exception to the "be a team player" rule—don't cause dissention.

I think Thoreau had it right in his essay "Civil Disobedience," and I believe that most of us in education believe in the ideals of equality, democracy, and individual opportunity for all. What is needed for the kind of systemic reform or transformation of the system to occur—a change that moves us toward both equity and excellence—is collaboration and networking at the level of the school, the community, the state, and the nation.

TAKING THE NEXT STEPS

> Becoming aware of our own "blind prejudices," learning that there is more to the "world" and to different forms of life than is captured by our own entrenched forms of life and genres, is only the beginning—not the end—of wisdom. (Bernstein, 1983, p. 106)

What needs to come next, after a deeper understanding of the broader ecology of inequity and an acceptance of our own biases and responsibility, is continued reflection and critical thinking, collaborative participation in the change process, and a renewed commitment to the values that traditionally have held us together as a nation. Critical thinking is enriched and strengthened by honestly and respectfully listening to, reflecting upon, and talking about diverse perspectives. Democratic participation has validity only when all voices can be heard equally. And renewed commitment to shared democratic values will come more surely in the process of building together a vision that avoids the problematic solutions of the past.

Teachers and administrators alone cannot change a system that is merely a microcosm of the larger society. Broader understanding of the way the system is working inequitably (outlined in Chapters 3 and 4) and of the foundation for a broader definition of human learning (addressed in Chapters 1, 6, and 7), coupled with consistent and committed support for second-order change (described in Chapters 8 and 9), will need to come from policy makers, community members, institutions of higher education, and the nation as a whole. We need leadership, now as never before in our country, with knowledge and understanding, commitment to our highest ideals, and a vision of what could be. Otherwise we risk losing the very ideals and values upon which our nation was founded.

PART III

A Framework for Second-Order Change

CHAPTER 6

Social Interaction and Constructing Meaning

Problematic solutions rooted in narrow views of learners and their learning processes have been characteristic of U.S. attempts to teach all children to read since before the turn of the 20th century. This chapter will address the problematic solutions we have created in the field of reading, and then it will examine nonproblematic alternatives for learning to read rooted in a broader notion of making meaning in the context of social interaction, individual needs and interests, and meaningful purposes. Congruent research in both family and school literary and language learning will illustrate some important connections that can be made across a wide range of research and theory.

Visitors to the United States as well as critics from within the country have noted what appears to be an American obsession with the issues of reading ability and reading/learning disability or deficiency. Our country can probably boast more blue ribbon commissions to examine the reading ability of its citizens, more critics delineating the horrors of our reading and learning problems, more high profile political campaigns to eradicate the plague of illiteracy, more standardized testing to calculate the acquisition of decoding skills, more widespread educational programs to remediate those who fail the tests, and more reading and learning specialists and supervisors per capita than any other country in the world.

Paradoxically, we also have a growing underclass of educationally, socially, emotionally, and economically disenfranchised children and youth who will make up one-third of the population in the 21st century. Nor can we say much about our inner-city school students, over half of whom fail to learn to read adequately. In an inner-city school in which I observed, one entire first-grade class was failed, and 60% of many other first- and second-grade classes were retained. And the number of students labeled as remedial, disabled, and at risk for failure or dropout continues to grow. All of this happens despite decades of the Elementary/Secondary Education Act, Right to Read, and Head Start, and the more recent Education for All Handicapped Children Act (PL 94–142). And it happens despite the help of an array of basic skills specialists from Chapter 1 programs, reading supervisors and specialists in every district and school, content area specialists (math, social studies, science) in many schools, learning disability or learning support specialists from special education, and the new crop of Instructional Support Teachers for our Pennsylvania state inclusion model.

So what is the problem? Systems thinkers would look to faulty definitions and problematic solutions, and indeed it appears that part of the problem with learning to read in the United States is rooted in the narrow definitions used for reading and learning, and the problematic solutions, assumptions, and expectations that accompany these definitions. And if such is the case, this suggests the need for both broader definitions and alternative solutions for teaching, learning, and evaluating that are not problematic.

Gregory Bateson and his colleagues (Watzlawick, Weakland, & Fisch, 1974) lend support to this approach of (1) beginning with a clear definition of the problem, (2) investigating the solutions maintaining the problem, and then (3) planning meaningful change (a transformation of the system versus "more of the same") aimed at the attempted solutions to avoid the problem–solution paradox. So we will look first at how we have been narrowing our vision, "chopping up the ecology," and creating false dualities (Bateson, 1972, 1979), before suggesting a plan for change.

PROBLEMATIC SOLUTIONS FROM A NARROW DEFINITION OF READING

Conventional notions of learning to read held by many educators, policy makers, and the general public suggest a prescriptive, linear, phonetic code learning sequence that can be taught rather mechanically with computer programs or individualized learning kits, and tested relatively easily— particularly with the advances in computerized testing and skill learning programs. But, as described in Chapter 1, it is a leap of faith to make the cause and effect assumption that children learn to read because of the skill sequenced method of decoding by which they were trained. Good intuitive teachers and clinicians have known for quite some time that many more children learn to read in spite of the conventional methods of teaching reading, as described in Chapter 1, than because of them (Bartoli, 1990b; Goodman, 1988; Smith, 1987).

Despite the growing body of research over the past several decades that substantially supports a much larger notion of the actual reading processes (Botel, 1977, 1979, 1981; Britton, 1970; Clay, 1985; Freire, 1980; Halliday, 1978; Lytle & Botel, 1990; Mellon, 1981; Purvis, 1981), the majority of classrooms and schools are still dominated by a narrow, fragmented, skill sequenced view of reading. So persistent is this view that, even when staff development efforts focused on more integrated approaches are conducted at a school site, most classroom teaching and testing remain skill oriented

(Bartoli, 1990a; Bryan, 1992). The dominance of this boring and reductionistic basal reader and workbook-driven approach has been well documented (Goodlad, 1984; Smith, 1987) and is evident in the financial success of basal reader and testing companies, which it turns out are often one and the same handful of powerful and lucrative businesses (Daniels, 1993; Harman, 1991).

The proliferation of whole language and writing process discussions in educational journals (see *Language Arts, The Reading Teacher,* and *Young Children,* for example), at conferences of the IRA, NCTE, and NAEYC, and in current texts (see Heinemann Educational Books, Teachers College Press, and Richard C. Owen Publishers) leads us to believe that a broader view of language learning is sweeping the country. This notion is fueled by the current debates and "silenced" dialogues over the efficacy of such approaches with minority students (Delpit, 1986, 1988) and the right-wing backlash that insists there are "holes" in "whole language" that will put American education even further behind in the world literacy race. (Does this suggest that our present ranking of forty-ninth out of the 150 United Nations countries is okay: or, If it ain't broke, why fix it?)

Despite the "whole language," writing process, and language experience movements, the reality in the majority of classrooms is what Smith calls "skill, drill, kill." The majority of classrooms and schools have changed very little over the past several decades in their basic approach to teaching and testing reading. Over the past 4 years my students at Elizabethtown College have observed in over 200 classrooms, and they have found very few of the Critical Experiences for learning (see Chapter 8 for an example of this) and surprisingly little of the integrated language approach that their college courses describe. This is not so much a problem for those socially and emotionally secure learners who come from highly literate, mainstream, middle-class environments, for they generally have the resources to learn regardless of the method taught in the classroom. But for those learners for whom school personnel have low expectations (who are not assumed to have the benefit of a strong family literacy background), for those who are not from the majority culture, and/or who are not economically, emotionally, or socially secure, the result of fragmented, abstract skill teaching can be, and often is, failure to learn to read. That is, they learn exactly—and only—what is taught.

Other cultural, emotional, social, economic, and political factors can make the picture even more complex. However, the present system of teaching reading appears to be driven mainly by three major problematic solutions—all of which are rooted in the same narrow definition of what reading really is. These are described elsewhere in detail (Bartoli, 1985b, 1986b), but briefly they are (1) standardized and minimal competency testing as evaluative solutions; (2) fragmented, subskill-oriented curricula as accompanying pedagogical solutions; and (3) special remedial and disability programs as organizational solutions to the problems created by the first two "solutions." To illustrate, consider how in Chapters 3 and 4 the definition of reading instruction as subskill teaching created a fragmented curriculum with tests to match. Similarly, consider how defining evaluation of reading (as well as math, science, writing, and social studies) as one-right-answer responses on standardized multiple choice tests was a social prescription for trivial education, segregated students, and disabled readers.

The results of these problematic solutions have been documented by other researchers for several decades in terms of a "caste system" (McDermott, 1974; Rist, 1970), a sorting and labeling process perpetuating the cultural status quo (Bart, 1984; Bartoli, 1986b; Cummins, 1986; Hobbs, 1975), and "iatrogenic retardation" (Sarason & Doris, 1979), which suggests that children are "disadvantaged" by the system of schooling.

> . . . just as the administration of certain medications in the treatment of physical disease can cause the appearance of new disease related to the nature of the medication and the patient's idiopathic response to it, . . . so, in like manner, a considerable part of the problem of educably retarded children derives from the way in which we have devised our educational system. (p. 154)

Data from our present college–urban school partnership as well as data from the inner-city project site in Chapter 4 give ample testimony to a continuation of more of the same definitional, pedagogical, and evaluative solutions that perpetuate massive educational failure in the inner city. The case study of James in Chapter 3 (along with recent observations in many other suburban schools) suggests that the same problems exist in suburban schools.

Clearly we need a new definition of learning to read that will not result in such tragic loss of human potential: a definition that goes beyond decoding the written word to the socially interactive meanings, purposes, and processes that are orchestrated during the act of reading. Within this larger notion of reading as meaning construction in social interaction, we can root practice that leads to a transformation of the system and an unleashing of the potential of all individual learners.

DEFINING READING WITHIN SOCIAL INTERACTION THEORY

Much of the current work in reading using a social interactional view of language learning and development has its roots in the theories of Lev Vygotsky (1934, 1962, 1978), particularly his view of the social process of language learning. Three of Vygotsky's concepts are of particular importance to teachers and researchers in language and learning: (1) the dialectical unity of biological and cultural factors in the learning process, (2) the zone of proximal development as it relates to language learning, and (3) the development of higher order cognitive processes through social interaction.

Dialectical Unity

Vygotsky's concept of the dialectical unity of biological and cultural factors is not an artificial duality between natural and cultural factors, but rather a way of describing a very complex human process. While the dialectical approach admits the influence of nature on humans, it also asserts that humans affect nature, creating new conditions for existence. Human development for Vygotsky is "a complex dialectical process, characterized by periodicity, unevenness in the development of different functions, metamorphosis or qualitative transformation of one form into another, intertwining of external and internal factors, and adaptive processes" (Vygotsky, 1978). His emphasis is on the interaction between changing social conditions and the biological substrata of development, and he insists that "an experimenter must study both components and the laws which govern their interlacement at each stage of a child's development" (p. 123).

As it is for Dewey (1910), contextual research is a must in Vygotsky's view. And a broader-based ecological approach, not unlike Bateson's (1972, 1979), also seems consonant with what Vygotsky describes as "interaction" and "intertwining." This interactional view contrasts sharply with linear stages of development and conventional "readiness" concepts that too often deny learning opportunities to the "disadvantaged" underclass. Vygotskian research, as well as teaching, would instead search for strengths to build upon in the wider ecology of the learner (family, school, and community), as in the work of Michael Cole and others at the Laboratory of Comparative Human Cognition.

Zone of Proximal Development

Vygotsky (1978) describes the second concept—the "zone of proximal development"—as

> the distance between the actual development level as determined by independent problem solving and the level of potential development as determined through problem solving under adult guidance or in collaboration with more capable peers. (p. 86)

The zone of proximal development defines those functions that are currently in a state of formation, and it was Vygotsky's position that the state of a child's mental development could be determined only by taking both the present developmental level and the zone of proximal development into account. Learning, in this view, must lead development.

> What the child can do in co-operation today he can do alone tomorrow. Therefore the only good kind of instruction is that which marches ahead of development and leads it. (1962)

Here we see the dynamic, interactive nature of Vygotsky's theory. Rather than determining a child's development by static tests (yesterday's development, which "fossilizes" human potential), Vygotsky proposes mediation, focusing on learning that is in advance of development. This prevents the conventional practice of allowing tests to dictate the reading level of a child, restricting or sabotaging the natural learning process—"impaling a child on a primer." The 50% inner-city retention and at-risk rates are ample testimony to the fallacy of such test score-driven practice. Additional testimony can be found in the research, theory, and practice of Clay (1985) and Johnston (1989, 1992).

The idea of mediation to lead the learner ahead is as significant in family literacy as in school literacy. Much inequity in education and society is justified with test results that dictate a level, a label, a track, a high school program, or a career choice. School personnel may advise parents early on that they are not to expect too much of their children, rather than suggesting the need for even more intensive mediation in the zone of proximal development. And parents can be convinced by the "experts" that their child has a "miswired brain," a "block," a "disability," or a "disorder" that cannot be helped by their personal mediation. The promises of individual attention and special programs are added incentives to accept the verdict of experts armed with tests, scientific labels, and drug prescriptions. For the teacher, the promise is that someone else—a specialist—will take the responsibility, own the problem, and solve it.

Higher Order Processes

Vygotsky's fundamental hypothesis, one that is supported by current brain research as well as anthropological data, is that the higher mental functions are socially formed and culturally transmitted. A child's cognitive development is shaped by this social and historical interaction to the extent that "if one changes the tools of thinking available to a child, his mind will have a radically different structure" (Vygotsky, 1978, p. 126). Elsasser and

John-Steiner (1977) describe the importance of this interactional process of language growth and cognition.

> Language is extraordinarily important in the growing cognitive sophistication of children, as well as in their increasing social affectiveness, because language is the means by which children (and adults) systematize their perceptions. Through words human beings formulate generalizations, abstractions, and other forms of mediated thinking. (p. 355)

Furthermore, these words are "sociohistorically determined and therefore shaped, limited, or expanded through individual and collective experience" (p. 355).

Language learning, in short, is a profoundly social process; and the burden of proof lies with the system of schooling and the society that it reflects, not the student, when massive failure occurs. Ample research testifies that such practices as placing students in low reading groups, tracks, and separate remedial or disability placements have dire consequences resulting from the fact that the tools of thinking are not available to the students (Allington, 1983; Bartoli, 1989; Cazden, 1981; Goodlad, 1984; Mehan, 1980; Oakes, 1985), along with the low expectations that create a self-fulfilling prophesy for failure.

A COMPARISON OF MODELS

The importance of a social interactional theory to understanding language development and learning perhaps can be more clearly described by comparing it with the stage development or medical model that currently dominates the field of education. Piaget's stage development model, for instance, posits inherent cognitive structures as the vehicle for knowledge. The child assimilates and accommodates to the environment, which nurtures the growth of mental structures emanating from the child's biology (Coles, 1983). There are universal stages of development through which the child presumably progresses linearly in a steady upward progression toward language competence.

In Vygotsky's social interactional model, the child engages in meaningful interaction with others, and through this interaction inner language unfolds. There is a dynamic relationship between the child's biology and culture, as mental processes develop through individual social relationships. And it is in part these relationships—the cultural tools with which the student is provided—that lead ahead, or retard, learning. Progression through the zone of proximal development is a complex dialectical process characterized by periodicity, recursiveness, unevenness, and, ultimately, transformation. No universal stages can represent this dynamic relationship, which is unique to the ecology of each child.

Educational researchers in the United States, using both behaviorist and Piagetian models, have studied cognition separately from emotions, motivations, history, prior learning, and social relationships. Perception, sequencing, attention, impulsivity, perceptual processing, and other factors are studied as though they were separate phenomena existing independently of the real and full lives of persons. Psychometric tests, which purport to describe mental processes, are assumed to explain them as a product of the person's neurology (Coles, 1978, 1987; Donovan & McIntyre, 1990).

Researchers using the social interaction model explore the child's activity in the classroom, among peers, and in the family to understand cognitive functioning. Mental processes are studied as part of activity, but are never extracted from it; as Coles (1983) explains, in an integrative, Deweyan manner, "cognitive function would make little sense if seen as separate from the totality of the individual" (p. 622). In Vygotsky's model, mental processes are both formed and studied in the context of the person's social activity. The researcher seeks therein to uncover the interactive relationships that influence the process of language development.

Learning dysfunction in the stage development/medical model is thought to be biological in nature—neurological dysfunction inherent in the individual child. The social interaction model looks instead to the interactions in the ecology of the child for the creation and maintenance of a problem. The medical model reduces interactive phenomena to a biological explanation: It blames the victim as the cause of the problem without regard for the interactions, social situations, and contexts that were a part of the creation or exacerbation of the problem (Bartoli & Botel, 1988a; Coles, 1987).

With regard to remediation of language dysfunction, in the medical/ stage development model, following the path of its psychometric tests, one teaches the same isolated subskills of language that are thought to be deficient. Language subskills are sequenced in a linear order and taught as though they were prerequisites for higher level thinking skills. In addition, the thrust of the remediation is toward—or below—the child's tested level (yesterday's level in Vygotsky's model). By contrast, Vygotsky's model, using the concept of the zone of proximal development, suggests teaching beyond the children's present level and mediating or coaching them to rise to that potential level on their own (Feuerstein, 1979; Palincsar & Brown, 1984). Vygotsky assures us that what children can do in cooperation with us today, they can do alone tomorrow.

A broad sociohistorical and sociocultural perspective reveals the medical model as ultimately maintaining the status quo. The present learning disabilities field is representative of the medical model's creation of stationary categories and a stationary social order that operates essentially to maintain the status quo of the professional and social systems (Bart, 1984; Hobbs, 1975). The social interaction model, by contrast, would seek to transform the child, the school, and the society to unlock the potential of each learner.

Freire, in his description of the act of reading as part of a wider process of growth based on understanding one's own experiences and the social world, gives us an example of the importance of the social interaction theory as it relates to family literacy. Along with Feuerstein and Britton, he stresses the vital importance of meaningful verbal interaction both in the family and in the school. It is full human communication, first with family members then later with teachers and peers, that builds within the child the capacity to learn, and this is the precursor to cognitive growth. The child learns to make meaning in interaction with the family, providing the base of family literacy without which school literacy cannot develop.

Family literacy defined in this way encourages us to design programs that celebrate the language and culture of the home, programs that validate child and family narratives, programs that respect the unique contributions that all families make to the literacy development of their children, programs that respectfully ask parents to be colleagues in both design and implementation. Ada's (1988) Pajaro Valley project wherein families write and share their own stories, thereby attaining literacy for the whole family, as well as our Smalltown oral history project (see Chapter 8) that sought to collaborate with the Black Community in telling their own history, are examples of more respectful family literacy programs.

As professionals we are not only called on to be colleagues with parents, as we learn from them, and facilitators, building upon their strengths; we are also called to a role of advocacy for families and children who are, in dramatically increasing numbers, living in poverty and hopelessness. Over 85% of the 1,000 children at the inner-city site in Chapter 4 are eligible for the free lunch program, which means their families are below the poverty line. Unless we can go beyond programs that attempt to make their parents more like the white middle class, to programs that empower them to better understand and transform their own communities, their own lives, and the lives of their children, we will create victims in another problem–solution paradox.

We are not dealing with a trivial process when we speak of language learning in the sense of meaning-making or Halliday's (1978) "learning to mean." We are dealing with what gives shape, depth, and meaning to life— what makes it worth living. We are hearing too often that children and adolescents are finding life devoid of meaning, and that a sense of hopelessness is increasingly leading to school failure, dropout, drug and alcohol abuse, teenage pregnancy, adolescent crime, and teenage suicide. Postman (1980) has said that "it is an outrage that children who do not read well, or at all, are treated as if they are stupid" (p. 360). To this I would add that it is a tragedy of our society, of our parenting, and of our teaching that we have failed to help our youth to find and make meaning in life and in language. Are alienation, loneliness, and existential despair to replace the natural zest for naming and drive to explore with which a child begins language learning? Are we somehow encouraging nonlearning, nonliving, and nongrowing processes instead of their creative and meaningful counterparts?

Postman's (1980) answer to this requires schools to become learning centers where intelligence would be defined in a new way: "A student's ability to create an idea would be at least as important as his ability to classify and remember the ideas of others." And schools might also be places for "helping young people to resolve some of their more wrenching emotional problems" (p. 361). At our inner-city site, we are proposing an in-school family and child counseling center with social worker outreach for just this purpose. And Feuerstein (1984) likewise suggests more mediated learning wherein "a caring adult interposes herself or himself between a child and the world" (p. 20). Mediation for Feuerstein involves "guidance in emotion, motivation and learning: it is how culture is transmitted" (p. 20).

There is much urgently needed work to be done by all of us connected with or concerned about education and equity for all children and youth. In the school system we need to build a curriculum for meaningful learning and critical thinking that does not accept failure labels or tests that freeze potential. Botel's Critical Experiences plan is an excellent model for this, particularly when combined with a collaborative plan to include specialists and parents in the learning process (Bartoli & Botel, 1988a).

We also need to find more ways to link with the family system to build respectful relationships that can establish the trust needed to make learning possible. The Pajaro Valley project (Ada, 1988) and Auerbach's (1989) social-contextual model are consistent with this goal. And in the community and society, we need to put action to Freire's assertion that education is a political activity.

Grubb and Lazerson (1982) provide insightful policy suggestions for the interrelated problems of transforming economic, political, social, and educational institutions. The central issue for them (and us) is

> whether it is possible to reform children's institutions in ways that conform to our deepest ideals for children, and whether we can resurrect uncorrupted versions of the principles on which the United States was founded. (p. 307)

Data from our inner-city projects suggest that, if we can work collaboratively toward a deeper understanding of and sensitivity to the pressing needs of others in our society, toward an appreciation and celebration of cultural and language differences, and toward advocacy and aid for the growing number of families and children who are living in poverty, we will be able to avoid the problem–solution paradox.

The crucible in which higher cognitive skills develop includes the family, the community, and the school wherein the child continues language learning through social interaction with teachers and peers, hopefully in an environment that is open to the child's potential. The picture of learning that emerges is uneven, sporadic, and recursive as the developing child interacts with a changing environment, at times seeming to regress but eventually leaping to automaticity in reading. Freire (1980) describes the pedagogical contribution to this process as an authentic dialogue between the teacher and the learner: the use of dialogue to synthesize (mediate) the educator's knowledge and the learner's knowing, ultimately leading to the awareness of learners of their right and capacity as human beings to transform reality.

> Becoming literate means far more than learning to decode the written representation of a sound system. It is truly an act of knowing, through which a person is able to look critically at the culture which has shaped him, and to move toward reflection and positive action upon his world. (p. 363)

Herein we have the essence of the power of a social interactional view of learning to read and learning to learn: interactive meaning-making that can educate to transform the lives of people and their worlds.

CHAPTER 7

Community, Diversity, and Change

In Aldous Huxley's (1932) *Brave New World* the utopian World State motto is "Community, Identity, Stability." As we take a look at our own history of dealing with diversity in schools and society, and as we attempt to build a framework for transforming an inequitable system of schooling, Huxley's "utopia" of behavior modification and control, standardization of human beings, pacification through drugs and continual amusement, and devaluing of committed and respectful relationships provides an interesting metaphoric comparison.

Similarly, Waldrop's *Complexity* (1992) provides us with an intriguing metaphor for the inherent instability of systems and the need for a new framework for the 21st century that includes chaos and complexity. Following constructivist learning theory (Saunders, 1992) as well as family systems theory (Hoffman, 1981), disorder, disequilibrium, and even chaos are described as vital to higher level thinking, complex learning, and second-order change. Waldrop suggests that linear and reductionist thinking, which has dominated science since Newton, has now "gone about as far as it can go in addressing the problems of our modern world" (p. 13). The new framework will need to be about change, forming and dissolving of patterns, complexity, surprise, and transformation.

This chapter will address three major questions while linking with the utopia and systems metaphors.

1. How can a historical perspective on schooling help us to understand where we have come from, where we are going, and where we need to go?
2. How can an ecological systems lens help us to reframe the problems and transform the system?
3. What would the professionals in a renewed democratic society look like, and how could they lead us toward a vision of empowered individuals collaborating to build a democratic community?

In Part IV, Chapters 8 and 9 will provide glimpses of current examples of transformations as well as future plans for restructuring and reform of teaching, learning, and evaluation.

A BRIEF HISTORY OF DIVERSITY IN U.S. SCHOOLS

Before the compulsory school laws (1852–1918) forced immigrant populations in America to come under the social control of the white, Anglo-Saxon majority, public schools and classrooms were rarely divided into separate groups of students, and most U.S. students were exposed to roughly the same curriculum. But swelling classrooms and the consequent demands of educating a growing, culturally diverse society brought schools face to face with the problem of meeting the educational needs of a widely diverse population. Critics at that time accused schools of teaching to the middle and ignoring individual differences, the major complaint being that the high progress students might be bored and the low progress students might not catch up to the average group.

In actuality, good teachers found a variety of ways to educate a wide range of students, just as many do today in both private and public schools. Students help each other in small group and partnering activities; teacher scaffolding (framing, concept building, reading to students, strategy development) allows students at all levels of progress to participate in the classroom community of learners; a cooperative, supportive classroom climate is built by the teacher and students collaboratively; and students are allowed to explore additional individually chosen topics of interest, which they then share with their classmates. Morton Botel (1993b) refers to this kind of learning as a conversation or dialogue in which there is intellectual generosity of thought and a spirit of appreciation for the individual contributions of students.

Positivist science, however, entered the scene to solve the problem of meeting individual needs (along with the eugenics movement's attempts to "purify the deteriorating American stock"), giving us I.Q. scores and other standardized methods of rank ordering and slotting students into "ability" groups with predestined expectations for their success or nonsuccess. High, middle, and low reading groups in the elementary school and eventually high, middle, and low sections and tracks in the high school became commonplace and exist to this day. Across the United States there are differential curricula and differential expectations for the quality and quantity of learning that will occur in the different groups (Bartoli & Botel, 1988a; Goodlad, 1984; Oakes, 1985).

The tests were, of course, rooted in white, Anglo-Saxon, middle-class values, experiences, and knowledge, so that Black and poor white students tended to score below their middle-class white peers. So too did Native Americans, most of the immigrant populations who entered the country in the 1920s and 1930s, and the more recent Latino and Mexican American immigrants, due to their nonexposure to (or noncompliance with) the white, middle-class culture that shaped the tests. There was little protest against the cultural class replication that resulted in the schools due to this differentiation by I.Q. and other standardized tests, because the economic and political power lay in the hands of the white middle class that mainly populated the upper reading groups and upper academic tracks. The cultural status quo was thus replicated and maintained, and is to this day, in public schools across the country (Cummins, 1986; McDermott, 1974, 1987; Oakes, 1985).

"Matthew effects" (Bronfenbrenner, 1988; Stanovich, 1986; Walberg & Tsai, 1983) sustain the placement of those who are placed in the various groups and tracks: "Those who have, will get more until they grow rich, while those who have not, will lose even the little they have" (Matthew 25:29). Those perceived as good readers, writers, and thinkers are provided with increased opportunities to read, write, and think critically. Those designated as poor readers or disabled learners are given fewer opportunities to read, write, or think critically, as James's case study illustrates, because it is assumed that they are not ready to do what the "able" learners are doing. Along with this come fewer opportunities to develop the vocabulary, concepts, strategies, world knowledge, and sustained practice with meaningful literacy activities necessary for increased cognitive development and efficient reading and writing. Thus, the self-fulfilling and self-reinforcing expectations of educators with respect to the different groups interact to seal the doom for students like James.

Even further differentiation in the school system came in midcentury, the late 1950s and early 1960s, with the birth of special education (Bart, 1984; Gartner & Lipsky, 1987; Hobbs, 1975). Those who could not keep up in the low reading groups, and were judged to be less competent than the low group (often due to cultural differences), were placed in special education and given one of a variety of labels that were in vogue at the time: educably/mildly mentally retarded, word blind, slow learner, dyslexic, or, currently, learning disabled or attention deficit disorder (see Bartoli & Botel, 1988a, for details on the history of this movement).

It was assumed that, since these "special" students had difficulty with the regular classroom curriculum, they needed something different. Rather than taking a critical look at the tests and differential curriculum that helped to produce the failures, positivist science focused on the "difference" in the student. The prescription was generally a different classroom, teacher, test, text, or set of material. Popular "scientific" mythology and publicity suggested that there was greater quality of learning taking place in the special classroom, especially in learning disability or learning support classes.

But current research reports significantly less quantity and quality of literacy instruction actually occurring in both special and remedial classrooms (Allington, 1991; Bartoli & Botel, 1988a). In contrast with what we currently know is critical to the development of the reading and writing processes, there is significantly less real reading, writing, and talking; less concept and world knowledge building; and less of other vital forms of higher level critical thinking to be found in most remedial and special education classrooms. In addition, there is the problem of curricular coherence as students must move between two possibly conflicting views of teaching reading.

PROBLEMS WITH A FOCUS ON DIFFERENCE

As was clearly evident from the informal interview data in the case study of James, one has only to sit down and talk openly with teachers or administrators for a few hours about their understanding of the various "ability" levels in their classroom or school to hear the underlying assumptions and preconceptions that riddle their definitions of who should get placed where and why. What we have accepted for so long and assumed to be reasonable practice is clearly a highly subjective and scientifically unsound system of undemocratic differentiation for not only low progress learners, but for those labeled "gifted" as well. In addition to inequity, three other significant problems have been created by the problematic solution of focusing on supposed differences to meet the needs of the individual student.

1. A focus on difference results in the loss of a sense of community as classroom learners and as citizens in a democracy, since community requires equality and unity, whereas grouping by difference separates learners as competitors.
2. Grouping and labeling deny true individuality. The uniqueness and voice of the individual learner are lost beneath the voices of the psychologist, specialist, administrator, and teacher.
3. The positivist, quantitative theory behind differential ranking, testing, sorting, and labeling promotes more fragmentation within the school, between the family and school, and between the school and the community, creating adversarial relationships with little communication, understanding or trust.

Understanding individual differences and human diversity is vital to all learning. But the iatrogenic solutions offered for accommodating human differences have ignored the broader context of human commonalities, thereby subverting both community building and learning. We turn now to a closer look at each of these three problems.

Differences and Community

With an individual difference focus, we neglect to capitalize on the many similarities that all learners have in meaning-making, or making sense of their world. Basic human similarities in the reading, writing, and other learning processes make it possible to have meaningful discussions, debates, and reflections with all students on a variety of texts, concepts, themes, and ideas using heterogeneous groups of all sizes—from 2 to 42. And this provides the environment for Botel's concepts of conversation, intellectual generosity of thought, appreciation of others' contributions, and building a classroom community of learners.

A difference, deficit, gifted, disability, or ability focus in the classroom results in less heterogeneous grouping, particularly fewer whole class activities such as discussion, brainstorming, debate, reflection, or unstructured sharing of ideas and feelings. Fewer mixed "ability" or high/low progress learners work together in either partners or small groups, and the resources for understanding cultural diversity, learning to mediate, or providing scaffolding for a peer are thus denied to students. They are denied the experience of growing as concerned, culturally literate future citizens of a multicultural and multiracial democracy.

William Labov (1982) tells the story of a Chinese friend's explanation of how the problem of "poor readers" is handled in Chinese schools. He explained that, if a student in a Chinese classroom is having trouble with reading, others get together and help the student to learn. In many private U.S. schools there are no separate classes, categories, or labels for poor readers. James Coleman (1987) has attributed much of the success of Catholic schools to the supportive relationships they create and maintain both in and out of school. Teachers and students are linked with each other just as families are linked with the school. Students help each other in explaining reading assignments or math concepts, since often a peer can explain in a way that communicates better to a fellow student.

Piaget's notion of reflective abstraction reminds us that it is both of the students who benefit from peer tutoring: The peer teacher must reflect on the idea or concept at a higher level of abstraction to be able to teach it to another student. Similarly, Vygotsky's concept of the zone of proximal development affirms the power of peer mediation as well as teacher–student mediation and support. Students and teachers are linked together in supportive social interaction that continually leads to more advanced learning.

In the classroom, the school, and the society in general, the differentiation process results in a loss of community—the loss of a climate for the collaborative social interaction that is vital to learning, vital to building trusting, supportive relationships with other human beings, vital to establishing a caring community of learners who are free to take the risks necessary for true learning, and vital to a democratic society.

Erickson (1987) describes the link between trust and risk taking in the learning process.

> In pedagogy it is essential that the teacher and the students establish and maintain trust in each other at the edge of risk. To learn is to entertain risk since learning involves moving just past the level of competence, what is already mastered, to the nearest region of incompetence, what has not yet been mastered. (p. 344)

For learning to occur, Erickson says, a student must also trust in the good intentions of those who are exercising authority, and they must trust that their identity will be maintained positively. But in the traditional tracked or "ability" grouped classroom, instead of a climate of trust, collaboration, and mutual support, there is a climate of competition for individual achievement with little tolerance for those who are different and/or off-schedule.

The separated, fragmented, competing groups of students lose out in an understanding of human and cultural diversity and in a sense of community as well. An elitist group is developed in the top reading groups, top academic sections, and gifted classes that becomes progressively less tolerant, less understanding, and less concerned about those beneath them. An underclass is developed in the bottom reading groups, low academic sections, remedial classes, and special education classes (particularly EMR, LD, and SED—the names may change, but the stigma, low expectations, and low rate of return to regular education, unfortunately, remain the same). And the "average" students may be given short shrift compared with the top and bottom groups, who command more attention and resources.

Aldous Huxley's separate classes of people come to mind: Stability and a rigidly controlled community are maintained through segregation, differentiation, and schooling. Quoting the observations of a young man after the 1991 acquittals of the Los Angeles police officers in the Rodney King beating case, Rev. James Allen said, "It don't look too good" for the struggle for equality of all people. During Smalltown's 1994 community service commemorating Martin Luther King, Rev. James, the former director of Philadelphia's Human Relations Commission, noted that the rich in this country are still getting richer and the poor are still getting poorer. He suggested that the hope for a future with equality lies with three possibilities: (1) "We all ought to be able to recognize our individual particularities while recognizing our commonality." (2) "We need to learn how to love one another." and (3) "In this crisis, we can learn something about others and about God."

Differences and Individuality

Paradoxically, within an individual difference orientation, individual students are not allowed to develop their unique individuality, because tests and professional ("expert") judgment slot them into a prescribed group and give them a fixed label such as accelerated, gifted, remedial, learning disabled, low/high ability, slow/fast reader, creative/dull, worker/lazy, motivated/unmotivated, hopeful/hopeless. We appear closer to Huxley's uniformity, standardization, and stability than to a democracy that values and respects all individuals.

We have discovered that all learning involves social interaction, yet we often reduce the opportunities for that interaction with individualized workbook or computer skill programs for the "disabled" and the "gifted" wherein they receive less interaction with both the teacher and peers. Isolation and solitary tasks are common in the name of individualization. Mediation, collaborative learning, and cooperative tasks are rare in a differentiation model.

Too much pressure may be put on those slotted for success. In the midst of our individual pursuit of excellence and accountability, we are witnessing a parallel increase in suicide, along with other forms of escape, including drug and alcohol abuse, among very able, high progress students. Conversely, expectations for success among those slotted for failure may be so low that these and other forms of escape, like teenage pregnancy, delinquency, or dropping out (see Fine, 1991), may be used to achieve a sense of power, individuality, ownership, or meaning for one's own life—meaning that behavior modification techniques, mono-cultural textbooks, and prescribed, mechanical, programmed learning attempt to take away. A sense of boredom or apathy among those slotted as average may limit their chances to experience the joys of learning that come from challenging academic experiences and finding one's own voice in the learning process.

In *Brave New World* boredom and apathy, along with critical thinking, are tranquilized with the drug soma, with multiple pleasure-seeking opportunities, and with sophisticated entertainment media. Neil Postman's *Amusing Ourselves to Death* (1985) suggests some fascinating parallels in our present society. But even more frightening is the current increase of alienation of our nation's youth (Bronfenbrenner, 1986) and the concurrent lack of serious critical reflection in both our schools and society. For without a critically thinking citizenry, a democracy cannot survive.

Differences and Fragmentation

The positivist theory of science underlying notions of deficit, I.Q., one-right-answer basal readers and tests, and differential treatments for learners (different learning styles, modalities, competencies, deficiencies, giftedness, and ability groups) promotes fragmentation while it maintains the status quo. Allington (1991) reminds us that if we expect that a third of the class will cover all of the classroom material; a third of the class will cover most, but not all of it; and a third will master only a part of it, and not very well, then we are reinforcing a system that is slotting a third of the population for functional illiteracy. Further fragmentation includes curriculum and relationship problems as skills are fragmented from content, subjects are fragmented from concepts and connecting themes, and families are fragmented from the school.

Positivist science suggests linear notions of skill sequenced reading that are as fragmented from meaningful, functional content and context as they are from an ecologically valid theory of the reading process. Isolated skills, presumed to be prerequisite to real reading and writing, consequently constrain literacy. Subskills that students do not need, except for meaningless tests, are substituted for the actual reading, writing, and concept building that they do need.

Only commercial textbook, workbook, skill kit, and testing companies and unethical or narrowly educated "experts" profit from this fragmentation of teaching, learning, and evaluation. But their pollution of the learning environment extends beyond the skills and drills. Children are also taught at an early age to differentiate among their peers and, as in Huxley's utopia, to segregate themselves from others not like them.

> Delta Children wear khaki. Oh no, I don't want to play with Delta children. And Epsilons are still worse. They're too stupid to be able to read or write. Besides, they wear black, which is such a beastly colour. I'm *so* glad I'm a Beta. (Huxley, 1932, p. 18)

It embarrasses me to reflect that I hardly know the names of any of my high school classmates who were not in the college preparatory sections, and that I never got to know any African American people as friends until I was in graduate school. Nor can I remember many occasions in which we celebrated each other's differences or explored our human commonalities in school.

A SYSTEMS LENS FOR CHANGE

In opposition to reductionist, positivist thinking, Waldrop (1992) and other systems thinkers suggest the need for a new science that goes beyond simplistic linear thinking: one that is congruent with the kind of universe described by the second law of thermodynamics—a universe governed by an "inexorable tendency toward disorder, dissolution, and decay" (p. 10). The world is viewed in all its complex evolution, upheaval, and surprise. The irrationality, messiness, human frailty and passion are what life is all about—not the predictable, ordered, structured universe that humans attempt to reduce it to. And herein lies the potential for change—at the edge of chaos.

This balance point between order and chaos is where new ideas and innovations are

> nibbling away at the edges of the status quo . . . where life has enough stability to sustain itself and enough creativity to deserve the name of life. . . . The edge of chaos is the constantly shifting battle zone between stagnation and anarchy, the one place where a complex system can be spontaneous, adaptive, and alive. (p. 12)

The examples that Waldrop gives for transformational systems change include 70 years of Soviet communism giving way to political turmoil, and centuries of slavery and segregation giving way to the civil rights movement in the 1960s.

Where do we look for change in reading and learning? The systems lens provides us with an answer that has exciting possibilities. In this view a reading "disability" is considered a symptom; as Haley (1981) tells us, symptoms are responsive behavior to a particular context. Furthermore, the learner with the symptom of reading disability cannot change unless the context of a relationship in which s/he lives also changes. Thus we need to look at context, perceptions, communication, and relationships. And it is these very factors that have emerged as significant in the case studies.

Part of what appears to be preventing a change from occurring for the students in the case studies is the double bind situation in which they find themselves in their relationships with school personnel. A paradoxical communication that essentially bankrupts choice itself is inherent within the LD metamessage. A student like James who has difficulty with reading attempts to respond to the social front of the teacher or specialist (fair, kind, helpful), but he may be greeted with a metacommunication of preconceptions, low expectations, and/or cultural bias. He knows this is a vital relationship, necessary for survival in the school, so he will not call the teacher unfair, prejudiced, or label happy. Instead he will deny his own correct perceptions and relate or communicate in terms of the social facade.

The LD or ADD metamessage consists of a communication of, "You cannot learn, but we will try to teach you," and a metacommunication of, "We do not feel you are fit for the mainstream." The learners can neither leave the field nor comment on the disparity of the communication. If they attempt to comment, they are termed "bad" or "mad" and, according to the Bateson group's (Watzlawick et al., 1974) theory, they are caught in the double bind of having to deny their own correct perceptions to maintain the needed relationship (they must see only what they *should* see). Eventually their self-expectations come down to match those that the teacher has for them. Caught in such a paradox, the students may choose "cognitive impairment" as the only reasonable response to an absurd context.

Watzlawick and coauthors (1974) suggest that, because of such communication and relationship problems as this, we need to attempt a new kind of change—one that transforms the system. Instead of the first-order, "more of the same" sort of change that leaves the system essentially intact and unchanged, we need to make a shift that lifts us out of the problem–solution paradox.

TOWARD AN ECOLOGICAL SOLUTION

If sociolinguistic and ethnographic research over the past decade has taught us anything, it is that all teaching, all learning, and all evaluation are social processes involving social interaction. Social interaction in teaching, learning, and evaluation defines who the participants are (competent, equal, or disabled), what they are expected to do (memorize fragments or learn concepts), and the relationships (teacher–student, parent–teacher, student–student) that support or undermine learning.

Teaching and evaluating are also political and interpretive processes, as Johnston (1989) describes, defining the learner and ultimately determining what kind of a society we will have. So we as teachers and evaluators must decide what kind of a society we would like to participate in building. There is no escape from our role in this. Our choices (particularly with respect to teaching methods, forms of evaluation, and classroom management schemes) and our day-to-day social interaction with students and their families all have serious political implications for the kind of society we will have.

From a broad ecological viewpoint, classroom environments, and ultimately the society of the future, are shaped by our (1) perceptions (about students, families, groups, materials, assessment, potential), (2) choices (what and how much to teach, to whom, for how long; what to test, for what purpose, how to interpret results), and (3) interactions with students and families (how they think we view them by our interactions; how they consequently will view themselves). If we want a multicultural, democratic society that allows for multiple perspectives, with both the rights and responsibilities to negotiate those perspectives, we will have to make choices that will lead us in that direction.

Most educators agree that they want students to be responsible, independent learners. Most agree that there should be more teacher ownership of the curriculum—curricula chosen, created, and controlled for quality by teachers. And most educators agree that the best kind of evaluation—the most real, important, and useful (for further learning) evaluation—takes place on a moment-to-moment, day-to-day basis between observant teachers and their students in the classroom.

So we need to look to the conditions that will optimize that kind of evaluation, teaching, and learning. For this we need five things.

1. Teachers and students as active learners, growing and learning together in an increasingly trusting relationship.

2. A valuing of teachers' own knowledge of curriculum and evaluation above other forms of evaluation and teaching. This means no linear skill testing of teachers (or students). Teachers do not need to be "Hunterized" into a rigid seven-step teaching sequence: They need validation and respect for their own experience and knowledge. It also means no threats of minimal competency testing, no coercion for teacher "programming," or other methods of undermining teacher confidence and competence.

3. A valuing of (and respect for) parents' knowledge of their children. This means the use of parent interviews that respectfully gather family literacy histories, as in *The Primary Language Record* (Barrs, Ellis, Tester, & Thomas, 1989), rather than prescriptive parenting programs in which "experts" dictate to parents, or other school workshops in which the teacher or school specialist is always the expert and the parent is always the learner.

4. A valuing of students' own knowledge, a respect for their individual ways of learning, a belief in their innate capacity to learn, and a deep commitment to leading them ahead. All children can indeed learn if we raise the level and quality of the curriculum and the evaluation methods, not lower them as we have in the past.

5. A collaborative, democratic community that includes teachers, parents, administrators, community members, and students as equally respected team members who read, talk, work, problem-solve, and learn together.

The models to follow in Chapter 9 include these vital conditions for optimal teaching, learning, and evaluation and for renewal and reform of the school system.

Peter Johnston (1989) reminds us that relationships built on threats and mistrust are never fulfilling. This is as true of the relationship between the administration or community and teachers as it is of the relationship between teachers and students. Teaching students to learn through threat and accountability does not make them avid readers and writers. What we have, then, is a relationship problem, which brings us full circle to the vital importance of social interaction in teaching, learning, and evaluating.

An ecological solution to this relationship problem would have to take into account the interaction of such school, family, and community dynamics as those described in detail in James's case study and reaffirmed in the inner-city study. It would focus on these interrelationships and avoid the fragmentation stemming from reductionist, positivist science solutions such as "ability" grouping, static (and culturally biased) tests, and nonintegrated curricula. An ecologically valid solution would also embrace multicultural understanding, celebrating linguistic and cultural differences and bilingual resources. And the process of coming to this solution would involve open discussion inclusive of the perspectives of all participants, and their voluntary agreement on shared ideals and goals.

Although such a democratic solution may appear at first to be utopian and impractical, it is no less ideal than the philosophies described by Thomas Jefferson two centuries ago and John Dewey a century ago, as well as those envisioned by Jurgen Habermas, Ann Lieberman, Linda Darling-Hammond, Deborah Meier, and a host of other educators and philosophers more recently. And, of course, it certainly beats Huxley's totalitarian alternative.

A CROSS-CULTURAL COMPARISON

Over the past few years there have been many comparative studies of education, particularly comparing education in Japan and the United States, with the former generally cited as outperforming the latter. Several hypotheses have been raised for this: Japanese mothers read to their children more; there is more family support and pressure for education in Japan; the symbol system of reading is easier to learn than the letter system; there is less control/more freedom in the early childhood program. But the most compelling hypothesis from an ecological viewpoint is that all Japanese students are expected to learn successfully in elementary school.

The Suzuki violin and piano methods are a reflection of this uniform (and equitable) expectation for early success. Parents and teachers of the

Suzuki piano method, for example, are told that any child can develop musical ability—there are no "disabled" learners.

> Musical ability is not an inborn talent, but an ability which can be developed. Any child, properly trained, can develop musical ability just as all children in the world have developed the ability to speak their mother tongue. (Shinichi Suzuki, 1978)

The implications of this simple, yet prophetic, statement of limitless expectations are profound. This same expectation can be found in schools in New Zealand and in China, with the same result—high literacy rates and few "learning disabilities."

All of this is not to say that there are no inherent differences in human beings. Certainly every person is unique, and certainly all good teachers find ways to treat each student as an individual. But the "solution" of differential ranking, slotting, and grouping by supposed ability or competence levels is too problematic to be continued unless our ultimate goal is enforced cultural uniformity, a large illiterate underclass, and an elitist, undemocratic government.

THE HETEROGENEOUS ALTERNATIVE

What happens if we focus on similarities and equality in educational opportunity instead of differences?

1. We can put individualization back into the hands of students and teachers, where it belongs. Each child can express, use, and develop individual responses, individual choices, and individual strategies in the context of a heterogeneous group. In addition, students can share their individuality with a diverse population of peers.

2. Teachers can also be free to develop their own individual teaching style and create their own materials and activities.

3. We can value the ecologically valid student evaluation by the teacher in the classroom, which puts value in the student instead of taking value out (see Barrs et al., 1989; Bartoli & Botel, 1988a, Chapter 11; Johnston, 1992).

4. We can allow teachers to integrate the classroom curriculum with concepts and connected themes, putting skill training back into perspective in meaningful, interesting, purposeful contexts; for example, writers' own manuals of conventions of language, personally chosen vocabulary lists, and

words studied in the literature, science, or math contexts from which they came.

5. We can allow all students to participate in a diversified community of learners, learning from and with each other and supporting each other's risk taking and growth in a trust-filled, democratic environment.

6. We can create a sense of community to help us build bridges of understanding and collaboration to link with the wider community beyond the school walls.

The Critical Experiences framework that can support such integration has been described in Lytle & Botel (1991), Seaver & Botel (1990), and Bartoli & Botel (1988a). This curriculum plan for Pennsylvania has been developed in collaboration with teachers and administrators across several states over the past 10 years and is rooted in Botel's (1977, 1979, 1981) framework for reading, writing, listening, and speaking across the curriculum. It is focused on integration of

skills within context and content,
concepts within subjects/content areas,
content areas with connecting themes,
learners with each other in a community of learners,
specialists with teachers in the classroom,
evaluation with the reading, writing, and learning processes, and
families with the school.

In this integrative model, individual differences are met within a collaborative classroom climate in which teachers, specialists, and other school personnel join together with students and their families to support better learning for all students. We can no longer afford to accept the assignment of a third of our future citizens to functional illiteracy, and another third to being "average" or minimally literate, if we are to survive as a participatory democracy. It is time to use the excellent resources that we have (teachers, specialists, parents, and students) to their fullest advantage.

We have many excellent, informed, dedicated teachers, specialists, administrators, and parents whose combined efforts can shape the kind of learning environment in which all children can learn and grow. The kind of fragmentation described in this chapter can be replaced by an integrative, ecological approach to learning in which teachers and specialists collaborate in the classroom to problem-solve together to meet the needs of students with difficulties and simultaneously build a stronger classroom curriculum for all students.

A NONIATROGENIC SOLUTION FOR READING PROBLEMS

The process for a student having difficulty with learning is described more fully in *Reading/Learning Disability* (Bartoli & Botel, 1988a), but I will briefly outline it here. The teacher first observes and documents anecdotally the student's classroom learning (see Appendix C). This, along with other teacher observations of the reading processes kept on note cards, a journal, a file folder, or in *The Primary Language Record* (Barrs et al., 1989), documents student behavior with respect to the experiences that are critical for learning. The specialist (reading/learning specialist, Reading Recovery teacher, Instructional Support Teacher, counselor, principal, social worker, or other support staff) is then invited to come into the classroom to also observe the student using the same Critical Experiences framework.

The teacher and specialist meet together as colleagues and problem-solve from their combined documentation of the student's learning processes. Classroom strategies are planned, tried out, and the student's learning is further documented by both the teacher and specialist. If they still have questions concerning what they have observed, and if the student continues to have difficulty with reading and learning, the parent is invited to come in to observe, learn about, and document the student's engagement in the Critical Experiences for learning. The teacher, specialist, and parent would then meet as colleagues to dialogue and problem-solve; and they would jointly arrive at plans both to work with the individual student and to adjust the classroom environment to meet the needs of the student (who could also be included in this dialogue for more ownership and voice in the learning process).

Again, there would be follow-up observations and dialogue among the teacher, specialist, parent, and student as the learning progresses. If the student continues to have difficulty with learning, another teacher or a specialist, counselor, administrator, social worker, or psychologist could be invited to observe in the classroom and continue the collaborative documentation, dialogue, planning, and follow-up process in cooperation with those already involved. A school team model (Comer, 1988) could also be used for particularly complicated learning problems. Continually involving the parent and the student as colleagues in the observation, dialogue, and problem-solving process is vital to the success of this approach.

Several important elements contribute to the nonproblematic/noniatrogenic quality of this model for helping students with difficulty in reading. First, all participants are collaboratively learning about and observing students in the actual process of reading and in the classroom context. This alone has the power to greatly enhance the knowledge base we have in the profession. We have too often substituted decontextualized testing of isolated skills for an in-depth understanding of students in their actual learning contexts. Neither students removed from their context nor skills removed from the whole reading/learning process can lead to valid conclusions and greater understanding.

Second, all participants are learning about and observing the Critical Experiences for learning as part of the process, which provides a common vocabulary and framework for better communication and understanding among professionals and between parents and the school. Lack of consistency and the proliferation of conflicting views of reading and learning have kept the field of reading from advancing for the past several decades. The field of writing has been less plagued by inconsistency and disagreement, and the consequent success of the national writing projects could serve as a model for the field of reading.

Third, all parties are drawn into collegial conversation with each other in support of the student, thus eliminating the artificial "expert"–client dichotomy typical of specialist–teacher, teacher–parent, or specialist–parent interactions. This collaboration also eliminates the fragmentation, isolation, and mistrust too often found in schools among teachers, specialists, counselors, social workers, administrators, and other support staff as they attempt to help students. If all participants, regardless of academic training, have access to a common framework and vocabulary, and are valued equally for the unique expertise, observations, and perspectives they have to bring to the solution of the child's difficulty, we will have come a long way in our goal of creating trusting, respectful communities of learners in our schools and in our society.

Examples of ecologically valid adjustments for a student found to be having problems with understanding or attending to literature activities, for example, might be

1. Provide more teacher scaffolding before reading: drawing upon prior experiences, concept/theme development, reading selected difficult spots aloud.

2. Provide more teacher mediation during reading, modeling a variety of meaning-making strategies.

3. Arrange for a partnering activity after reading in which a high progress reader would partner-read with the student having difficulty, mediate as they dialogue about the reading, and provide help with miscues in which the meaning was vital.

4. Structure a mixed progress group to include the student in an after-reading activity such as a dramatization, debate, mural, or diorama.

5. Have the reading or learning specialist do a think-aloud reading protocol with the student to understand more about specific strategies being used by the student.

6. Have an older student, a parent, or a peer tape record and jointly (with the student) transcribe a story told by the student. The student can then independently use this tape and the transcription for repeated practice in fluent reading.

7. Tape record some of the stories read in class so the student can listen to repeated readings at home to become more confident and fluent as a reader.

8. Use short-term (4 to 12 weeks) Reading Recovery (Clay, 1979, 1985) tutoring that uses a minimum of five texts in intensive, daily one-half-hour sessions.

The kinds of activities and interventions are limited only by the imagination of the teachers, specialists, administrators, parents, and students involved in the problem-solving process. Carini (1979) has devised a staff review for problem solving that could be used for particularly difficult problems that resist the best efforts of the teacher–specialist–parent team. The emphasis throughout Carini's process is on creating a stronger, more supportive classroom climate for the continued success of all students. And the resources to be used in the creation of this environment are the teachers, specialists, administrators, parents, and students who are already there. This cost-effective solution requires only a reorganization of already existing resources and the development of a new kind of collaborative professional.

THE NEW PROFESSIONALS

Over the past half century of "specialization," we have created innumerable specialists and experts in increasingly narrow fields. In schools we have reading specialists, learning disability specialists, curriculum specialists, speech therapists, tutors, aides, Chapter 1 basic skills specialists, school counselors and psychologists, and a variety of administrative positions, each with its prescribed areas of expertise and turf. In such a fragmented system it is possible to have a student being "helped" by five or more different specialists (with five different definitions of and solutions for the problem), none of whom ever confer with the others. Similar fragmentation is found within the social welfare and health care professions, so that a view of the whole ecology is quite rare for professionals in education, social work, psychology, or medicine.

A movement toward more cooperation and collaboration of professionals—a collegial sharing of knowledge and expertise focused on understanding the whole human being—would certainly be a good beginning for change. But efforts toward real change need to go beyond this. For "renewal" of schools, "empowerment" of learners and families, "reflective" practitioners, and "ownership" by communities that goes beyond clichés and buzz words, we need a different kind of professional: less "expert," less prescriptive, less authoritarian; and more inquiring, more collaborative, more facilitative, and more of an advocate for children and families—particularly for those who traditionally have been underserved.

This new (or renewed) breed of collaborating professionals would view students/families/clients as worthy of respect, and as able (not disabled or deficient) to take control of their own lives with the help (as needed) of a mediator or facilitator. Rather than serving people in ways that make them more dependent on the services, the new professional would mediate, facilitate, and lead the person ahead toward competence and self-control. This is a radically different approach from controlling people through drugs such as Ritalin, behavior modification techniques, or other forms of external manipulation by an "expert." The question would be, How can you and I together deal with this problem? rather than, What can I do for (or to) you to alleviate your problem? In the former stance, both the problem and the solution are jointly owned and shared. In the latter, the problem belongs to the client and the solution belongs to the professional.

The professionals who interacted with James, and the professionals in the inner-city study, were schooled in the traditional view of professional as independent expert rather than collegial facilitator, guide, or mediator. They were not trained to take a broader view of the problem of learning, or to look within the interrelated contexts of school, family, and community for the resources for solving problems. The reading and learning disability specialists, the counselors and psychologists, and the various administrators generally assumed that the problem was within the student (and/or family) and their job was to solve it within their behavioral frame of reference and training. In both the suburban and urban contexts, advocacy for families and children and linking with the community were not considered to be part of their professional responsibility. But let us look for a moment at the possibilities for real change that might come from this more collaborative approach to professionalism.

If professionals were to become advocates for children and families to overcome the inequities that affect their lives (in school, work, health care, and society), we might see more reflection on the part of teachers, specialists, counselors, and administrators concerning their own expectations, perceptions, and biases. This, in turn, might lead to removal of the assumptions and beliefs dictating the grouping, tracking, and labeling practices that separate the haves from the have nots. And such critical reflection would clearly point out the cultural biases of standardized tests that maintain the status quo, along with the diminished quality of the curriculum that one-right-answer, multiple choice tests maintain.

As child and family advocates, professionals in the school would link with families and communities to make use of the important resources across the ecology of the learner. Teachers and specialists would link with parents as respected colleagues to understand the learner more fully, and as partners in mediating in the learning processes of the student at home and at school. In schools with large cultural minority groups, such as the inner-city example, professionals would be co-learners with the families of a second language and culture, celebrating the many resources and strengths of the whole community and capitalizing on the opportunity for deeper multicultural understanding. Professionals in the school who can link with the community can foster a community for caring and for working toward the common good of society: a society that is concerned with all of our children—other people's as well as our own.

Professionals in business, health care, human services, colleges, and universities could join with schools to empower families and communities. They could facilitate with families and communities in defining their own problems, developing their own solutions, and directing their own efforts toward change. Collaborating professionals can work with families and communities in developing independence, competence, and confidence by helping to break down social and economic barriers to equality in housing, health care, employment, child care, and education.

This advocacy-oriented help may involve working toward equity in access to medical, dental, and psychological care; organizing and supporting the education of adults through courses, GED programs, or workshops (high school and language courses in particular, with provisions for child care) taught by community graduates; helping communities to organize more equitable child care—both nursery schools and day care with less racial and economic segregation; or serving as collegial consultants to build other structures that employ and empower communities and families. The college and university partnership models in Chapter 9 are examples of this kind of professional collaboration and networking.

The problems in our inner cities are immense, and they grow worse each year. They are not unsolvable, but their solutions will demand the very best collaborative efforts of professionals across all fields and institutions. If we are to make great strides toward a more equitable and humane society, the 21st century will not be the age of rugged individualism and self-serving competition. It will be the age of caring communities, collaborating professionals, shared leadership, and a renewed sense of the common good.

THE MOST FREQUENTLY ASKED QUESTIONS

There are, of course, a number of objections to a heterogeneous grouping arrangement in the school, the strength of which can be inferred from the fact that we have had the opposite arrangement (homogeneous "ability" grouping) for nearly half a century with little change in sight. Perhaps the most important reason for discontinuing ability grouping is that it is in direct conflict with our constitutional philosophy of democracy and equality for all. Beyond this moral reason, there is the practical problem of the growing numbers of functional illiterates who will constitute one-third or more of our population by the turn of the century. An increasingly technological, information heavy, global democracy cannot survive without a literate, informed, critically thinking citizenry.

But what of the questions raised by those both in and out of the school system concerning a more equitable arrangement in the nation's schools? What, beyond all of the political, economic, and personal vested interests, would people most object to if our schools embraced integration instead of differentiation by "ability" levels. Some of the most frequently asked questions follow, along with some possible answers to the reservations or misconceptions expressed.

1. How can we ever meet all of those individual needs within a heterogeneous classroom? What about all the different reading levels, skill levels, and I.Q. levels?

Response: Isn't there a range of abilities in classes now? Isn't there a range in the reading groups or remedial groups or disability groups as they now exist? Are not even these supposedly homogeneous groups characterized by a wide range of reading levels, motivation levels, and experience levels? Is it possible that the only major change we would actually be making would be the inclusion of more cultural diversity? And is this not an important addition for schooling in a democratic, culturally diverse society?

In many elementary schools social studies and science are taught to the whole, heterogeneous class, just as college and graduate school seminars are taught to a wide range of students of vastly differing backgrounds. In one of my first college composition classes I had among my class of 25 students a 45-year-old housewife taking her first college course, a 20-year-old college junior, a 29-year-old Korean veteran with 2 years of previous college experience, and an 18-year-old student fresh out of high school. Certainly there was a wide range in reading and writing levels, a wide range of personal experiences and backgrounds, and a wide range of needs and personal motivation. But somehow this enriched the discussions we had of readings by Socrates, Conrad, Twain, Baldwin, and Remarque. And I, as a teacher, was continually surprised at the diversity, complexity, and freshness of the oral and written responses of my students. Something in all of this was lost when I turned to teaching college preparatory English sections in a traditional, tracked high school.

Learning does not occur as the progressive, accumulative stages of development implicit in textbooks. Real learning is recursive, not linear. It may appear to regress as the mind circles back to reflect, link with prior experience, and assimilate something new, only to eventually leap ahead to a new level of understanding. Always we as learners return to previous experience and understanding to build new knowledge. We learn best from the risks we take and from our own mistakes as we explore the physical and conceptual environment, if we are allowed and encouraged to take those risks.

Unilateral reading, I.Q., and skill levels are products of positivist science's mistaken notion that there is a single right way of knowing the world. It is what Sternberg (1988) refers to as the executive style with set, generally man-made rules to execute. This "scientific" way of knowing is notoriously unfriendly to women's and children's ways of knowing and understanding the world, as Johnston (1989) has noted. Interpretation and exploration, which we now view as central to reading, learning, evaluation, and science, are negated in the "scientific" way of knowing. And several great teachers who have survived the test of time have suggested that the view of a little child may come closer to truth and validity than humanity's most exalted methods.

2. Well, what about the really "bright" students? Won't we be holding them back, waiting for the "laggards" to catch up?

Response: Without an artificial, superimposed linear developmental view, there is no such thing as "catch up" (or "laggard"). All children are gifted in various ways; and we are all individual, unique, lifelong learners progressing at various rates at various times. In one of my graduate classes, those registered included several doctoral candidates, a postdoctoral student, a new teacher with a bachelors degree, a previous state secretary of education, and a teacher with 30 years of experience plus a masters degree. All of them shared their personal knowledge and experience equally with each other, learned and grew together as colleagues, and built upon each other's knowledge to come to a deeper understanding of teaching, learning, and evaluation.

Even if there are, for instance, some low progress readers in a class who do not make the leap to automaticity on the same schedule as most of their peers, can't they still participate in discussions, group and partner activities, hearing texts read, and dramatizing texts? And isn't the higher progress peer who mediates and leads a fellow student ahead developing a higher level of cognitive abstraction in the teaching process? Perhaps the low progress learner should charge the high progress peer for the opportunity to enhance social interactional skills.

3. What will we do with the reading and learning disability specialists and teachers? Will they be out of jobs?

Response: This vital pool of resources is not being used in the most beneficial way (either to students or teachers) at present. Far too many students who need help are not served at all, and far too many who are getting services are not progressing well enough to move out of remedial or special education programs. Precious time is lost in transition and testing, vital class time (often reading time) is lost, many are misdiagnosed, and only the most "disabled" readers and learners are given services. Specialists need to be free to be the collaborative resources they can be to help classroom teachers build a stronger, more supportive classroom environment for all students. Specialists can lead the way to the vitally needed curriculum reform of regular education. It was the failure of regular education to meet the needs of a diverse population that began the differentiation into special and remedial education. But this solution, as we have described, has been highly problematic.

The call now is for (1) the integration of all students, with high expectations for the success of all; (2) a district-wide plan for teaching and evaluating rooted in the actual reading, writing, and learning processes of the student; and (3) a collaborative linking of professionals with each other, peers with each other, teachers with students, and families with schools to prevent further fragmentation. Specialists and teachers know the most about these problems, about previous problematic solutions, and about the choices only they can make that will begin to build the kind of democratic, literate society that we want to be a part of building.

4. Why change when what I am doing now works okay for me, it makes my teaching easier, and it has worked for lots of other teachers and students for the past 50 years?

Response: Did students learn because of, or in spite of, the fragmentation of skills from context, subjects from concepts, and able from disabled? Is the increasing segregation, disabling, alienation, and failure of our most vulnerable children a fair price to pay for maintaining the status quo? Or the loss of critical thinking ability in even our more able students? My colleague in teaching the language arts to prospective teachers at Elizabethtown College, Paul Rice, has noted that *all* students are disadvantaged by our current education system, even in the very best classrooms.

Some traditions, like participating in our democratic process or sharing our love of books and learning with children, are good and worth keeping.

But some, like soft drinks and donuts for breakfast, french fries and burgers for lunch, or chips, coffee, and cigarettes before bed, need to be reconsidered based on current research and knowledge.

AN ECOLOGICAL ALTERNATIVE

Entering a wide variety of classrooms on a weekly basis allows me the opportunity to see both the very good and the very bad in schools. I rejoice with teachers and students when teaching and learning are a celebration of our rich cultural diversity and the limitless potentials of all students. And I cry with them when children and teachers are frustrated and in pain after hours and days of standardized testing, or when teachers and students are disempowered by impoverished commercial textbook and workbook time fillers that have no resemblance to authentic teaching and learning.

In our schools there are children crying out in anguish and unable to make meaning in their highly charged, complex, emotionally depleted, and undersupported worlds of school, family, and community. When the treatment of choice of professionals in response to such problems is a higher dose of the amphetamine Ritalin—a favorite of heroin users—and when National Public Radio reports in 1994 that we cannot produce enough of the drug to keep up with the demand, I believe we have cause for serious reflection. And when the ultimate result of our desire for more order, more rules, and more control in schooling, particularly with poor children and children of color, may be the rapid growth of prison populations (in Pennsylvania the growth was from 8,243 to 22,325 between 1970 and 1980, with a 2000 projection of 33,154), we may be closer to the utopia that Huxley predicted for the year 2500 than even he could have imagined.

We return again to the central question: What kind of a society do we want to build—in our classrooms, in our schools, and in the community outside of our schools? Clearly our society, which the schools merely reflect, has problems with stereotypes and biases, inequality, fragmentation, developing trusting relationships, and building community. A careful examination of the problems in schools simply serves as a metaphor for the larger problem of inequity that is embedded in our culture and values—in the way we live our everyday lives.

I believe that those of us who inhabit schools have a choice. We can either choose to serve as a mere reflection of our contemporary society or choose to build a classroom community of learners and serve as a model for a renewed democratic society. Our society as a whole also needs to face its own problems and begin to collectively move forward toward meaningful change in all parts of the ecology. Acceptance of our own responsibility must come first, of course. This is not an easy task in the face of narrow-minded accountability measures that encourage blame placing and denial of individual responsibility.

Our best hope for meaningful transformation of the ecology of inequity lies in finding the multiple and complex ways that we may each be a part of both the problem and the solution. We can then work together to redefine our societal values and professional roles; participate in setting collaborative goals and creating nonproblematic solutions and strategies; and take responsibility for working individually and collectively toward these goals. This process will require democratic and creative leadership, knowledgeable vision, extended reflection, serious critical thinking, and a strong commitment to community service. We might consider these requirements as part of the future learning outcomes in our schools.

PART IV

Transforming the Ecology of Inequity

CHAPTER 8

Transformation Stories

Over the past 5 years I have had the opportunity to witness some encouraging transformations occurring in public school systems, including the inner-city site described in Chapter 4 and our present college–school partnership site. At the community level, there have been some promising developments in the Smalltown community that may serve as models for grassroots movements in other communities. And at the higher education level, we are developing an undergraduate teacher education model that has great promise for meaningful and lasting transformation of the school system.

This chapter will describe these public school, community, and higher education models for transformation that have promise as noniatrogenic, ecological solutions to the complex problem of learning to read and learning to learn in the U.S.A. Taken together, they address many of the recurring issues in the suburban and urban case studies; and they suggest possibilities for a second-order change of the educational and social system in our country.

TRANSFORMING THE PUBLIC SCHOOL: THE BASIS FOR HOPE

Reform, renewal, and restructuring of schools have been the subject of countless scholarly articles, texts, and conference presentations over the past decade, not unlike the wave of literature and workshops on whole language, thematic/integrated learning, portfolios, and alternative evaluation. And it is possible to find some model schools and classrooms that are examples of what is written and talked about, but the norm in public schools is too often more of the same—business as usual. And why is this?

Kenneth Tye (1992) suggests that much of today's restructuring rhetoric ignores the complexity of schooling, offering too many simple, safe answers for complex questions. The same, of course, is true for the reform of reading. His agenda for reform that goes beyond rhetoric includes

1. a reaffirmation of the importance of both excellence and equality for all students,

2. an examination of the deep structure of schooling (assumptions, expectations, values, unexamined practices),
3. school site curriculum and evaluation development,
4. changing management from bureaucratic accountability to collective responsibility and decision making, and
5. developing a focus—a small set of goals well articulated to the faculty and community.

Congruent with this agenda, Lieberman and Miller (1992) suggest the five building blocks of restructuring described in the second model in Chapter 9.

Restructuring and transformation require taking the risk of living on the edge of chaos where new ideas and innovations are "nibbling away at the edges of the status quo . . . where a complex system can be spontaneous, adaptive, and alive" (Waldrop, 1992, p. 12). The rewards are few, the risks are enormous, and the stress and frustration are overwhelming at this balance point between order and chaos; but the possibilities for change are limited only by human imagination, courage, and commitment.

Although the second law of thermodynamics tells us that the universe is governed by a tendency toward disorder and instability, we know also that the universe has brought forth such intricate structures as animal and plant life, the human brain, the planets, and the galaxies. And we know that complex, self-organizing systems in interaction with each other are capable of forming something that transcends themselves as individuals.

This, then, is our basis for hope: transcending ourselves as isolated individuals—forming a democratic community. We know that the world is not stable, least of all the marketplace or the school system, unless they are so autocratically controlled and static that real change and growth are impossible. But we also know that, collaboratively, people with intelligence, vision, and persistence continue to bring about change and create opportunities that were not thought to be possible. They are willing to wade into the complexity, live with it, breathe it, and stay with it until somehow certain patterns become clear. And they are committed enough to spend months and years clarifying these emerging patterns until the answers speak for themselves. They are the new kind of professionals—the collaborative, reflective, risk-taking leaders—and they are our hope for the future of schooling and the future of our democracy.

A COLLEGE–SCHOOL PARTNERSHIP STORY

My first transformation story involves the collaborative partnership between the Steelton-Highspire Elementary School and Elizabethtown College. The school is located in a multiracial and multiethnic steel town that has suffered from the economic decline of its steel company. Partly due to economic distress, previous patterns of bureaucratic management, and a host of yet to be understood social, cultural, political, historical, and economic factors, the school system and the community seem to reflect patterns of helplessness, resistance to change, powerlessness, low expectations, and hopelessness.

To counter this, the superintendent of the school district introduced a vision of democratic participation, professionalism, and vision building. Using the principles of shared decision making, community building, and strategic planning, he began to organize the school board, the school faculty, and community members into strategic planning teams and task forces to build a unified vision of education and learning.

Parents, students, and other community members were encouraged to join with teachers and administrators to develop a mission statement and strategic plans for change. Evening superintendent's coffees were held monthly to dialogue about school issues; a ministerium luncheon was held to invite further participation in the schools by church leaders; and an alumni group was begun to gather support for the school.

The superintendent also met regularly to problem-solve and dialogue with the administrative and school management team, and with the high school and elementary faculty. Carving out a new facilitative staff development role for superintendents, he led an on-site graduate course on reforming the curriculum for interested faculty members. The goals in all of this included better communication, building respectful relationships, and establishing a community of learners in the school and in the community.

The Deweyan participatory model of staff problem solving, strategic planning, and goal setting was new to the school district and community, so the process involved much facilitative leadership, hard work, persistence, and patience. But the faculty and community members involved in the process were empowered by the model: Teachers, parents, students, and community members appreciated having a voice in reforming curriculum and evaluation methods and in restructuring the school system. In time, as they continued to read, dialogue, attend workshops, visit other schools, and work together as colleagues, they began to envision possibilities for better teaching and learning, and for a renewed school district.

As this process was taking place, students and faculty members from Elizabethtown College had the opportunity to participate in a variety of ways. They attended faculty development seminars, school board meetings, and superintendent's coffees; they interviewed, observed, and collaborated with teachers and students at the school; and they were placed in classrooms for practicums in education, social work, and music therapy. Student teachers and junior practicum students in education were placed in classrooms with social work students to begin to build better relationships with the families of low achieving students.

Students and faculty members were involved as researchers in the classroom and in the community, and they had the opportunity to share their observations and questions with the superintendent and principal, who visited with them in their college classrooms to share their expertise on urban schooling and multicultural education. College students in my Schooling in Social Context course collaborated with teachers and parents to hold family holiday workshops for children and families at the elementary school. These included family storybook and card making, storytelling, music from a community children's choir, and a Kwanzaa demonstration by the College's African-American Cultural Society.

Several initiatives of the superintendent were particularly beneficial for our education students to learn about. One was a highly successful mediation and negotiation process with the teachers' union that prevented a possible teacher strike. Another was a badly needed school finance solution that involved a well planned, researched, and communicated bond issue. Restructuring efforts—instituting in-house professional development opportunities, adding a child and family support counselor at the elementary school, diminishing the discipline focus for young children, making better use of faculty for teaching, and reducing the number of pull-out programs—provided great opportunities for future teachers to see firsthand a variety of creative solutions to complex problems in schooling.

These were important firsthand experiences with the many possibilities that lie within reach of educators who have vision, who choose to work for change and renewal, and who are willing to take the risks demanded by the change process. The on-site professional development course, led collaboratively by college faculty and the superintendent, provided yet another opportunity for preservice and in-service teachers to learn together and to build a vision of school-wide reform and renewal.

Other college–school partnership opportunities involved teachers in workshop participation at the University of Pennsylvania (Penn Literacy Network Workshop), at Columbia University (the NCREST Conference), and at a New Zealand Approach Workshop at Elizabethtown College. There were also visits by college and school teachers to the River East School in Harlem and to PS 234, also in New York City. This was followed up by a return visit to our school site by a highly successful teacher, Dawn Harris-Martine, from the Mahalia Jackson School in Harlem.

The continuing research and development goals of our partnership include (1) better understanding of the "deep structure" of schooling—assumptions, biases, relationships, unquestioned practices that disadvantage students and families; (2) development of observant and reflective preservice teachers who are sensitive to cultural differences and the need for a multi-cultural curriculum; (3) collaboration of preservice and in-service teachers, administrators, and college faculty in the research, learning, and change processes; (4) better understanding of the broader family and community issues and relationships that foster or impede learning; (5) finding more inclusive and integrated ways to support the learning of all students; and (6) developing a collaborative model for systemic change and renewal of teaching and learning.

Community research is being conducted by Cindy Beyerlein and her students in a research methods class. Having gathered interviews and oral histories in the community and school, they will compile and present the voices of the community to add to our deeper understanding of the ecology of the learner at our site. They also presented their data at the Ethnography in Education Research Forum at the University of Pennsylvania (Beyerlein et al., 1994).

AN INNER-CITY STORY

National recognition, ongoing professional development and net-working, and invitations to presentations at other schools across the city and state are among the evidence of change at the inner-city site described in Chapter 4. What follows is a brief outline of this story. Further documentation of the successes at this site can be found in Bryan (1992) and Feinberg (1993).

1. The school received an IRA (International Reading Association) award for its school-wide reading program—one of 16 schools across the nation that received this award in recognition of excellence of the reading program.

2. The school also received national recognition for innovative use of Chapter 1 funds for school-wide improvement of learning that included staff development through the Penn Literacy Network and faculty task forces and teams focusing on evaluation and community involvement a nongraded approach in the first three grades; hiring a second school–community coordinator from the Latino community; use of portfolio evaluation and Botel Milestone Tests along with faculty reflection on evaluation practices; thematic unit approach as a focus for faculty development).

3. A site-based management team approach to school-wide change and reform continues to be used, with faculty choosing to participate in professional development and task forces.

4. Professional development both at the school site and in a variety of conferences and workshops is focused on more integrated reading, writing, and talking across the curriculum.

5. Faculty networking with other schools for broader change efforts, both in and out of the city, through faculty presentations at other schools and districts and through continued involvement (5 years) with the Penn Literacy Network.

COMMUNITY TRANSFORMATION EFFORTS

The Smalltown Oral History Project

In the spring of 1989, after an unsuccessful attempt to intervene on behalf of James's access to an equitable education (see Prologue and Chapter 3), I began to talk and meet with a group of community members to explore ways that we could encourage community-wide efforts to both understand and work to remove the racial inequalities in our schools, workplaces, and town. I had observed and documented a process of under-education for poor and minority students in the school district beginning in 1983, and I was finding the role of detached observer doing "pure" research untenable in the midst of failing children and continued inequity. The re-current themes in my observations were, as previously described, a lack of understanding, a lack of respectful, trusting relationships, and a lack of meaningful communication between the school and the Black and poor families.

Finding the school system a less than hospitable place to pursue the issues of racial equality, education for diversity, and improved home and school communication and relationship building, Bill Spraglin and I arrived at the idea of beginning a historical account of the Black Community in our town as told from the perspective of members of the Black Community. Bill knew a number of older people from the Black Community who would be veritable history books, and I had heard of a dynamic and committed sociology professor, Susan Rose, at Dickinson College, who was interested in community ethnography and oral history.

I talked with another ethnographer and friend, Andrea Fishman, who was teaching English in the town high school, and she said that she and some of her Black high school students would be interested in joining with us to explore both the problems of and solutions for racial inequality in the school and community. A Black teacher from the town also said she would join with us.

So, together with Reverend Jones, another concerned community member who was a minister of one of the four separated Black churches in the town (and who offered his church basement as a meeting place), we began in March 1989 what we called the "Smalltown Community Project:

An Interracial Collaborative." Our goals were to collect oral narratives to support the Black Community in writing its own history (hopefully to be used in the school curriculum) and to encourage other community-wide efforts to work toward more racial equality and understanding.

Our interracial group met together with community members, did interviews, explored issues and questions, analyzed interview data, and created three documents: Marianne Esolen's thesis paper on the Black Community, a copy of which was placed in the town historical library (which was sadly lacking in Black history); an article for the *International Annual of Oral History* (Palmer, Esolen, Rose, Fishman, & Bartoli, 1991); and a presentation of vignettes from the Black Community to the Ethnography in Education Research Forum at the University of Pennsylvania, parts of which were repeated at an open forum held in Smalltown.

Social Justice Committee and Social Justice Coalition

In the winter of 1990 I was approached for a contribution to the Smalltown YWCA building fund, and I inquired about the YWCA's one prime imperative: to eliminate racism. I was told by the director that the YWCA previously had a racial justice committee, but the chairperson died, and the director did not know if there was any interest in forming another committee. I suggested that she contact the ministers of the four Black churches, whose names and phone numbers I gave her, along with a few other interested community members whom I knew. She assured me that they would get something started again, and by the spring of 1990 the newly formed Social Justice Committee began meeting.

This committee had some success with challenging racial inequality in the social clubs in the town, but it had less success in challenging the more firmly entrenched systems of education, housing, and employment. Although the committee was initially set up to have interracial co-chairs, the leadership was white and limited by their lack of intimate understanding of the feelings and issues of the Black Community. Eventually many of the members from the Black Community stopped coming to the meetings, and the committee was finally discontinued in the spring of 1992.

During this time the director of the YWCA initiated the formation of a broader community group representing the town, to be called the Social Justice Coalition. Previous members of the Social Justice Committee were encouraged to join with this group in a larger effort to eliminate racism. Their first event was a forum on education that had been planned previously by the Social Justice Committee. In 1993 the Social Justice Coalition elected interracial co-chairs, and the prospects for continuation appear to be good.

African American Community Organizations

The Concerned African-American Parents and Supporters was organized by Curtis Thompson, an African American teacher and the director of the Local Action Center in Smalltown. The group began discussing the issue of education, sharing concerns of parents, drawing in resources for further education, and approaching the school system with their issues. Under Curtis's leadership, this group invited a professor of psychology, Dr. Rita Smith Wade-El, to share information on schooling for African American students. They also drafted a letter to the school superintendent that included a list of Black Community issues as shared by parents whose children, and who themselves, had experienced discrimination in the schools. In a May 1992 meeting, their issues included

> Ignorance of the problem—denial that racial issues exist
> Segregation of Black students from each other in the same classroom
> Use of slander (nigger, etc.)
> Low teacher expectations for African American students
> Teachers' fear of interacting with African American parents
> Inappropriate testing and use of drugs (Ritalin)
> Permanent tracking (if slow in kindergarten, slow through twelfth grade)
> Teachers taking over parental role
> Black parent responsibility (our problem)
> No policy for dealing with racism

Accompanied by Dr. Wade-El, we met with the superintendent to present our issues and concerns in August 1992. Since that time there have been many significant improvements, not the least of which was that the superintendent contracted with Dr. Wade-El to conduct workshops on interracial understanding and building a multicultural curriculum with the district personnel. Another session was open to the public in an effort to promote better interracial understanding.

A second group of Black Community members formed in Smalltown and organized an antidrug effort in the community. This group, some of whom attended Social Justice Committee meetings and the Local Action Center meetings, was called PUT, for People United Together, and they conducted a block march to protest drug dealing in the community. Their goals included opening a community center for tutoring, drug and alcohol counseling, social events for youth, and support for children and families in need. PUT was also working on interagency connections to better serve the families in the community.

Along with other community members, my husband and I have been involved with these grassroots groups, sharing and listening to ideas and concerns, and helping to formulate possible solutions to difficult and complex problems that have a long history in the community. This process of helping to link together people and agencies that can learn from and support each other requires patience and persistence from all of us. But it is one of the many ways that each of us can help build more cooperative relationships among community members—relationships that are rooted in deeper understanding, respect for each other, and trust.

As community members we sometimes helplessly wring our hands and say, "But what can I do?" in the face of seemingly intractable social problems. But individual people can contribute much to change efforts. My husband, for instance, has helped to paint and refurbish the community center building, and he has arranged to have the telephone company connect and donate the phones. A lawyer and a drug prevention agency director volunteered their time and expertise to help the group apply for grants to establish a community center with a paid director for drug and alcohol counseling, tutoring, agency referral, and other supports for underserved residents of the town. At the present time this group has a director and center, and is meeting together with other social service agencies to form a network of referral, information, and assistance for a wide variety of social, educational, health, employment, and housing problems.

HIGHER EDUCATION MODELS FOR TRANSFORMING THE SYSTEM

Over the past 4 years my colleagues and I have been developing an undergraduate teacher training model for transforming the learning environment for all children. We know that a strong preparation in critical thinking and integrative teaching before student teaching is important. Therefore we have been working toward a more integrated approach to teaching and learning that includes the Critical Experiences and a process for developing integrated, thematic units across all subject areas (Bartoli, Rice, Fox, & Bauman, 1992). Our junior year education students are required to develop integrated units and to teach parts of them during their junior practicum. In addition, students in my Reading and the Integrated Curriculum course are required to develop model curriculum plans for their low progress readers, based on their own observations and classroom analyses; and they are asked to synthesize their knowledge and experience into a personal philosophy of teaching.

Using the Critical Experiences framework and the SPITE themes (described in Chapter 1) as a basis for analyzing the learning environment, I ask my education students to observe and document the presence or absence of each of the Five Critical Experiences and SPITE (the social, personal, integrative, transformational, and ecological factors in the learning process). This has helped them to become closer observers of the reading and writing processes of students in the classroom in the wider context of the environment that is provided for learning.

After they have observed over time and documented the classroom learning environment, they are asked to carefully observe one student who is regarded by the school as a low progress reader. Their observations are to include their students engaged in reading and writing processes—the strategies the students use, the activities they are engaged in, and the quality of their learning experiences. This focus on the student in the actual process of learning to read in the classroom context allows undergraduate education students to develop their ability to observe and understand more about how students learn to read, what the barriers are to better learning, and how they as future teachers can construct an enriched learning environment for all children, particularly those who are having difficulty.

Part of one undergraduate student's classroom analysis using the Critical Experiences follows to illustrate the kind of understanding students gain from the use of this framework for observing. I have included Critical Experiences #1, #4, and part of #5 from a fourth-grade classroom analysis written by Michelle Principe.

Critical Experience #1: Transacting with Texts

The students in this classroom do minimal reading, and the reading they do participate in involves little transaction with the texts. The students are involved in reading groups, in which they read novels. The students are given some room to select the book they would like to read, but are more likely given a novel to read based on their past reading performance. The middle group is usually given a choice between two novels, but they are not given the choice to try the "higher" group's book. The highest group is usually given a novel to read whether they want to read it or not, and it is an implied privilege to be given this book, even if the students would rather read one of the other novels. The students do not complete response journals for their reading books, unless a topic concerning their book is given for them to write about in their journals. Often, the students are involved in thinking aloud about the book. The group is given a question relating their lives to the book (or vice versa), and all children are given the opportunity to respond. However, the children rarely share questions they have about the novels, and they are rarely motivated to pull something of more depth out of the book and discuss the idea. At the end of the book, the students are usually given some type of activity to do, such as role-playing, writing a sequel, etc. However, these assignments are more likely to occur in the top reading group than in the lower ones. Reading performance level is determined by the teacher; it appears to be based on the comprehension level of the child, but the level is also influenced by vocabulary, oral reading, and attention span. The students are not given the benefit of the doubt; it is not assumed that any child could read every book offered, and this may well be the case.

The students are taught the novel in question through before, during, and after reading activities. Some of these activities are better than others; for instance, sometimes the book is introduced only by having students look up vocabulary words in the dictionary, while at other times the book is introduced by showing the children where a place named in the story is on the world map. During reading activities always include vocabulary lessons and reflections, and, less often, writing or projects. After reading activities may include role-playing or writing, or simply a vocabulary quiz and a brief discussion of the plot. The level of the reading group has a direct influence on the types of activities done. Unfortunately, the lower reading groups, the members of which could use the activities most, usually end up doing boring, tedious work, such as straight vocabulary. The work with Critical Experience #1 is limited in this fourth-grade classroom.

Critical Experience #4: Investigating Language

Although most of it is not incidental [in the context of actual reading and writing], this in one area in which the students have a lot of practice. A spelling text is used, which is mandatory in the school, and many rules of spelling and decoding are given in the units. The words learned by the children are basically meaningless, however. The students do not learn these skills because they are needed to figure out words or phrases in a book; instead they "learn" the rules because they are introduced in a text. A lot of this information gets lost between the spelling homework the students complete, and the books the students are reading.

An English text is also used. Although lessons from this text are similar to the spelling text in that they are not used by students in reading, the English text does focus on writing and literature. Still, students do not apply the skills because they are so separated from what they are experiencing elsewhere.

The students also do what is termed "Daily Edit," although not daily. The students in this fourth-grade class know the edit marks and how to use them. About once a week, a passage is written on the board, which needs to be corrected. The students are to copy it and make necessary changes. The students are occasionally tested on this, and many of them do poorly. Again, they are not applying this technique to what they are actually writing.

The students in this class have experience with spelling, spelling rules, editing, mechanics, etc. Unfortunately, because the lessons are not incidental [in context], they probably will not carry this learning for long.

Critical Experience #5: Learning to Learn

The students in this class do not have to do a lot of critical thinking; most things they have to do are presented with explicit instructions and require one right answer.

I do not think that the children know various strategies for reading, writing, listening, and thinking. They have done the same processes for so long that if they ever knew other strategies, they have long forgotten them by now. For example, if a student needs to know the definition of a word, he/she will automatically look it up in the dictionary. In working with reading groups (of various levels), I have encouraged students to use the context to figure out the word, if possible. The students really have to think in order to do this, but often they figure out the definition. They also remember the words better when we figure out the word from context and talk about it. Given a choice, however, they will still go straight to the dictionary.

They are prevented from reading other material that is considered too difficult for them, but even when the students do attempt difficult material, they simply ignore the fact that they do not understand something. Until a difficult section is pointed out, the students just ignore it. In the same way, students do not question things, as far as I have seen. They move on, and miss a lot.

Problem solving is a weak area for these students. When given an open-ended science experiment, the students had a difficult time thinking of ways to get the desired result. When one student figured out a way of doing it, the rest of the class followed suit, and simply used that method without trying to think of alternatives. This has been the case in a few similar projects.

I have seen only a few instances of collaborative learning in this classroom, but in the times I have seen it, the students do not work together. Even when each child is given a specific task, the group members tend to work individually until they have to come together to pool their results. When working in pairs, the students end up with a final product, but the work is divided into halves instead of shared and worked on together. The focus is on individual work, even while in groups.

Classroom dialogue and conversation are limited. The majority of discussion is teacher led, and there is limited time for response, as the teacher is willing to "waste" only a few minutes on any topic that is incidental. The students do not get a chance to direct questions or comments to each other during whole class time. This is unfortunate, because the students could benefit from their classmates' experiences. The students do not listen to each other because the comment/question is always directed at the teacher. If there was more time allotted for whole class discussion, where everyone had to listen, the students would be more skilled listeners.

DEVELOPING REFLECTIVE TEACHERS

It has been well documented that student teachers tend to uncritically model the cooperating teachers to whom they are assigned, thereby perpetuating the status quo in teaching practice. Educators have suggested professional development sites, more careful selection of cooperating teachers, and more college/university seminars or workshops for cooperating teachers. A major goal of our college–school partnership is the collaborative development of reflective, continually growing preservice and in-service teachers. To accomplish this, an on-site graduate course (offered through the Penn Literacy Network) and other professional development opportunities were built into a federal grant project; and my students are continually encouraged to be teacher-researchers in collaboration with their cooperating teachers in the classroom.

The Penn Literacy Network at the University of Pennsylvania, under the direction of Morton Botel and Bonnie Botel-Sheppard, has similar goals on the graduate level. In over 75 school districts both in and out of Pennsylvania they collaborate with school districts, offer on-site professional development with graduate credit, and provide year-round learning opportunities for seminar leaders, participants, and school administrators. During week-long summer institutes they facilitate in developing the leadership within individual schools and establish a supportive network of change-oriented educators.

We are continuing to collaborate at the college and university levels as professors, refining our own teaching practice and challenging our students to do likewise. And we are continuing to build a multicultural professional development site where we can link meaningfully and collegially with teachers, administrators, students, and parents from diverse backgrounds.

For only they can help us to better understand the enduring inequities and complex challenges in the public school system. In this way we hope to contribute to the development of the next generation of reflective practitioners and creative leaders in the field of education.

Recently I asked some of my students who had participated in our college–school project about their views on building a partnership with a multiracial school and community for both research and development. I will end this chapter with one of my questions and a few of their responses.

Do you think that participation in this kind of collaborative research and intervention project will make a difference in your future teaching and your commitment to service in your own community?

- Absolutely. I am learning to speak out when people discriminate and oppress others. It's good to be offended sometimes.
- Yes, definitely.
- Yes. I perceive educators differently. I realize the impact they have on children. As a result I will be sure to work closely with teachers when I am working with a child. I believe I will also advocate for more school-based social service programs.
- Yes it does. I'm more aware of the problems that exist and the changes that need to happen. I'm no longer distanced from the problem but have experienced it. Because of this, it is no longer possible to ignore things going on in the community.
- Yes. It shows a person not only that there are problems but also that they can do something to help solve it. It's an encouragement to be further involved.
- Yes I do. I think that the satisfaction you get from doing some of these things is well worth the effort.
- Yes. Any interaction helps. One person can make a difference. Helping now will make me want to help in the future.
- Yes. It will go with me.
- Yes, I really do. I saw how much those children needed help and I believe it will greatly affect my commitment to community service.
- Yes, because I want to work to avoid it [prejudice], both as a teacher and as a human being. It has made me a more aware and caring teacher!!
- Yes I do. I feel that this placement has had an extreme impact on me. The children desperately need our help and I want to be there for them.
- Definitely!
- Yes, I am more empathetic and less selfish of my time to my community.

CHAPTER 9

Collaborative Models for Transforming Reading and Learning in the U.S.A.

Two models for transforming the ecology of inequity for students in U.S. schools are outlined in this chapter. The first model is a school–university partnership that Morton Botel and I developed at the University of Pennsylvania. The second is a partnership model that I developed at Elizabethtown College in collaboration with colleagues at the college and the administration and faculty of a multicultural school district. Our goal was to combine the resources of the college and the public school for the professional development of both in-service and preservice teachers.

Both models focus on the professional development of teachers, on opportunities for both teachers and students to engage in the Critical Experiences for learning, on linking with parents and families as vital resources in the school change process, and on taking a broader ecological view of the teaching, learning, and evaluation processes. And both models suggest ways that any college or university could link with underfunded and under-supported public schools to help provide more equality of opportunity for all children.

The first model focuses on more inclusion of all students in enriched, heterogeneous classrooms as a way to achieve both excellence and equity for all children. The staff development aspect of the model is a year-long, on-site graduate course: the Penn Literacy Network. The second model is a plan for collaboratively restructuring and reforming teaching and learning at both the public school district and college levels. The staff development aspect involves dialogue groups, preservice and in-service teacher research, and in-house use of in-service days for unified and continuous professional development designed by and for the staff.

MODEL I: A SCHOOL BUILDING MODEL FOR INCLUSION OF STUDENTS INTO REFORMED, ENRICHED CLASSROOMS

The purpose of this model is twofold: to provide a framework for integrating within a school building reading, writing, and talking across the curriculum; and to provide an ecologically valid alternative to the traditional school practices of labeling and segregating students into separate disability or remedial skill classes. The model is ecologically valid in that it meets four criteria: (1) It takes into account the vital importance of the interrelated systems of school, family, and community that shape the education of the student (systems that can operate either in support of or in opposition to learning). (2) It is not a problematic solution. (3) It is capable of lifting a school district out of its present problematic solutions. (4) It is capable of transforming the school system to include both excellence and equality for all students, thereby significantly reducing the number of long, sad stories, like that of James, of continued illiteracy and failure. Individual needs of previously labeled, separated, or at-risk students can be met in regular education classrooms with collaborating professionals using this field-tested model (Bartoli & Botel, 1988a; Botel, Ripley, & Barnes, 1993).

The model links the school district to the university for long-term staff development centered on developing more integrated, enriched, collaborative teaching and learning experiences for all students. The plan represents one conception of what might work best as a change model in a traditional U.S. school district. But adaptations unique to each school district are an inevitable part of the change process.

The plan is based on a strong commitment to allowing choice, personal voice, autonomy, and eventual ownership of the model for change in each individual school and school district. Anything less will eventually become a barrier to meaningful change and a loss of the unique potential of each district to create its own plan. There is a direct parallel here with the learning process itself: Unless we promote students' choice, voice, ownership, and responsibility for their own learning, we will limit their potential to become competent, contributing members of our democracy.

A project based on this model may be undertaken by individual schools or whole districts that choose to respond to the needs for less separation and labeling of students and more integrated, higher level learning environments for all children. Therefore the goal is a single-building model within the district—a goal that is reasonable within the limits of free choice and long-term staff development. If districts find that their entire staff eventually wishes to collaboratively unite for a district-wide plan, that would be the ideal.

Description of Model

This model is based on an approach that acknowledges both the complexity of classroom learning processes and the wider ecology of the student involved in the integration process. Attempts for reform toward more integration are often shortsighted, dealing inadequately with one of these areas, and the consequence has been more problematic solutions.

The central focus in dealing with classroom learning of students is toward more integration on a number of levels. The Critical Experiences curriculum framework is uniquely designed to provide optimal academic learning for heterogeneous groups of students. It includes integration of skills with meaningful content; integration of subjects with unifying concepts and themes; integration of reading, writing, listening, and speaking across the curriculum; integration of all students in collaborative, cooperative learning activities; and integration of regular, special education, and remedial teachers in collaborating teams to support students who are experiencing difficulty. Through a long-term collegial staff development program built on this theory-based and field-tested framework, teachers, specialists, administrators, and parents are assisted in analyzing and problem solving both in and out of the classroom to meet the needs of individual students, particularly those who are experiencing difficulty with learning.

A multitude of participants inhabit and influence the wider ecology of the student: the family system, including parents, siblings, and grandparents; the school system, including teachers, specialists, principals, and other administrators; and the wider community as represented by school board members, religious communities, social service and health practitioners, intermediate unit and state education department personnel, and state and federal policy makers. Without the informed support of all of these participants, the learning process may face insurmountable barriers. Therefore, both the design and evaluation methods of the model call for the collaboration of these participants in four major ways.

1. Monthly leadership meetings with representatives from each participating group (school administration, teachers, specialists, parents, community).

2. A collaborative approach to staff development in which the faculty chooses both participation and their own application of an integrative framework.

3. A parent program with two foci—the first on parents of children with learning difficulties, and the second on parents of all children.

4. Ongoing dialogue with faculty, administration, and parents through dialogue journals, consultation, leadership meetings, classroom observation, and continual responsive evaluation.

The ecological approach on which this model is founded views high failure, retention, disability labeling, and dropout rates in the inner city to be interrelated and interconnected in the wider ecology of the student: an ecology that is too often complicated by poverty, family distress, low expectations and strained relationships in school, teenage pregnancy, joblessness, drugs, and crime. Thus the model includes intervention and documentation in all parts of the ecology of the student—the school, the family, and the community.

Working through a shared governance process with the principal, school faculty, parents, and community, the university team makes a commitment to develop student potential through collaboratively building, refining, and documenting an ecologically valid model for renewing better education and strengthening families in the inner city. They link with other resources, so that this work is connected with and supported by a variety of agencies and supporting groups. This networking and alliance/partnership building are vital to the reform and renewal of inner-city schools and communities.

What follows is a description of the model's four-part ecological plan for developing the potential of inner-city students.

1. YEAR-LONG FACULTY DEVELOPMENT SEMINARS (THE PENN LITERACY NETWORK), WITH GRADUATE CREDIT, TO

• Study together and understand the problems associated with reading, writing, and learning across the K–5 curriculum; and integrate more reading, writing, and talking into the curriculum across all subjects using the Five Critical Experiences.

• Design and implement cooperative learning activities for more heterogeneous classroom grouping (partnering, small and large groups, peer tutoring, cross-age group collaboration).

• Link content material and all specialist and resource teachers with integrative themes across the content areas for higher level thinking to replace fragmented skill teaching by teachers isolated from each other.

• Develop congruent, ecologically valid evaluation methods such as student reading and writing portfolios, classroom observation, student self- and peer evaluation (for group activities), conferences, dialogue and academic journals, and other such process and product evaluation of learning.

• Meet one afternoon (3–5 p.m.) every other week with the school faculty for a 30-hour graduate credit course (on site at the school) to collaboratively accomplish the above objectives.

2. PLANNING AND PROBLEM SOLVING

• Meet with principal, teachers of special and remedial education, school–community coordinator, classroom teachers, parents, and other community members to collaboratively build plans for each year, learn the best resources for change, and understand local resources for and barriers to change.

• Present the plan to the entire faculty and invite interested faculty members to join the staff development seminar.

• Meet weekly with the school improvement team and pupil support committee to problem-solve, evaluate plans, and develop and refine plans and procedures for the process of better integration of labeled and at-risk students, and for better learning of all students.

• Develop methods for collaborating with reading and learning disability specialists and counselors to solve learning problems both in and out of the classroom.

• Implement and refine teacher–specialist collaboration methods for teaching at-risk, labeled, and remedial students in regular classrooms.

3. BUILDING LINKS WITH PARENTS AND THE COMMUNITY TO SUPPORT
   AND IMPROVE THE SOCIAL, EMOTIONAL, AND ACADEMIC LEARNING OF
   STUDENTS WHO ARE EXPERIENCING DIFFICULTY, THROUGH HOME VISITS,
   COLLABORATING AT HOME AND SCHOOL MEETINGS AND AT PARENT-LED
   WORKSHOPS; AND WORKING TOWARD ESTABLISHING A PARENT–CHILD
   COUNSELING CENTER WITH SOCIAL WORKER OUTREACH TO THE HOME.

• Begin to build more supportive and trusting relationships with key members of the community who understand the problems and needs of others in the community, and who desire change and more involvement. Learn from them, understand their world view, hear the voices of the community.

• Begin to plan parent workshops with key parents to share emerging ideas for better integrating labeled or remedial students into regular education, for developing the resources of the community, and for more academic and social success of all students.

• Explore resources and possibilities for an in-school family counseling service where students and their families could come for social services, emotional support, and ongoing counseling. Link this family counseling with the school's team approach for meeting the needs of individual students.

• Plan home visits by social work students from the Graduate School of Social Work, linked with the family counseling center. Gather information that will be useful in better understanding student and family strengths and resources for better learning. Link these resources with the school approach to better understanding the child (pupil support committee/child study team).

• Initiate teacher-specialist home visits and/or invitations for informal meetings to talk about the student's learning—beyond report card conferences that focus only on grades or poor behavior. Gather family academic histories and ask for their suggestions and ideas—find their strengths, potential, and resources.

• Plan and begin to build a parent–teacher resource collection of materials to be housed in the school library. Initiate reading and discussion groups linked with the faculty seminar, more holistic curriculum and evaluation methods, and multicultural, antibias education.

• Encourage parent–teacher involvement and relationship building through seminar projects, mini-grants, and the involvement of graduate students with a family literacy/family support interest.

4. Observation and collaboration in the classroom linked with
ongoing documentation/evaluation of the project.

• School faculty, staff development leader, project director, and doctoral research students plan observations in the classrooms of participating faculty to better understand problems and collaborate with faculty as they work toward change.
• Observations focus on labeled and at-risk students to more fully understand their problems in context and to collaborate with faculty as they implement in their classrooms new plans and methods developed in the seminar.
• The staff development leader and project director keep an ongoing record of the change process as it evolves throughout the year, documented with classroom observations, student and classroom evaluation methods, and teacher and specialist journals.

There are several advantages of this model that make its success more likely than more fragmented or narrowly conceived models. First, the long-term (5 to 7 years), in-depth staff development with course credit offered includes a broader vision of quality education, higher level thinking, fuller integration on many levels, and excellence that does not sacrifice equity. Second, the development, implementation, and evaluation of the model building plan are done in collaboration with the total school faculty and administration; and ongoing problem solving and collegial planning involve parents and community members as well as school personnel. Third, the model curriculum is accompanied by a collaboratively built evaluation plan that takes a broader view of both the learning and the integration processes; and it is responsive to a variety of audiences, providing continuous monitoring of student progress. And finally, it includes a strong parent involvement program.

The Objective: An Integrated Classroom Curriculum

The principal objective of the model is to successfully integrate students presently taught in separate learning/reading disability classrooms or programs, remedial reading resource or Chapter 1 rooms, or mixed category pull-out programs into reformed/enriched mainstream elementary classrooms for all subjects. Significant negative effects from the labeling process; concurrent teacher, parent, and self-expectations of the students; and the subskill curriculum predominant in the remedial and special education program are illustrated in the case studies in Part II of this book. Other studies of special education and remedial programs have had similar findings (Allington, 1991; Gartner & Lipsky, 1987; McGill-Franzen & Allington, 1993; Slavin, 1987; Ysseldyke & Algozzine, 1984; Ysseldyke et al., 1983), in addition to the general finding that few students (less than 2%) graduate from special education categories. There is also the vital equity issue of the overrepresentation of poor and minority students in all categories of learning difficulty.

For these reasons successful integration of LD or ADD labeled and remedial reading students into reformed regular education classrooms—heterogeneous classrooms providing the Critical Experiences for learning through the collaboration of the entire professional staff—is the best evaluation measure of the success of this model for optimal learning. Successful integration is interpreted by the success of the students' learning, as evaluated by student-centered observational, contextual and process-oriented methods (Barrs et al., 1989; Bartoli & Botel, 1988a; Johnston, 1992).

Without a shared, mutually owned curriculum for the full inclusion of all students into the mainstream—a curriculum built on the collaboration of teachers, specialists, and school leaders to meet the needs of diverse individuals within the general education classroom—there will be little long-term change in the labeling, grouping, tracking, and placement processes that presently segregate students in traditional schools across the country. Both the school district and the college or university will need to make, at a minimum, a 5- to 7-year commitment to the project to ensure the best possibility of a successful move toward fuller integration. Lazerson (1983) reminds us of the unsuccessful history of mainstreaming efforts over the past half century: only a long-term success, he notes, would be new.

This model has been documented in part in a textbook for teachers and specialists (Bartoli & Botel, 1988a), and it has been field tested in numerous school districts wherein faculty members documented the successful learning of LD labeled and remedial reading students in the regular classroom (Botel et al., 1993). In addition, the Critical Experiences framework for learning on which this book is based, *The Pennsylvania Framework,* has been endorsed by the Pennsylvania Department of Education, accepted by 440 of Pennsylvania's 501 school districts, used widely across the state, and documented as successful with low achieving students.

The Critical Experiences framework has been built in concert with the philosophy of 27 national organizations concerned with educating children (The Essentials of Education Consortium—see Mercier, 1981). Central to this framework is the question, What is critical for learning—for education in a democracy? The answer to this for the language arts curriculum is presented as the Five Critical Experiences for learning. (See Appendixes A and B for a description of the Five Critical Experiences.)

In this framework students are encouraged to express their own ideas both orally and in writing; build from their own experiences to greater understanding of concepts and connected themes; choose their own books and look to books for enjoyment as well as depth of understanding and growth as human beings; learn from literature about higher human values such as concern for and understanding of others, sharing, and cooperating; read texts for intention, tone, and purpose as well as for literal and symbolic meanings; take risks, challenge their own and others' thinking; critically analyze conflicting and contradictory material, information, and positions; make well-reasoned, intelligent, well-thought out and explored choices; and look beyond the present to past experience as well as future consequences. Learning to learn is the critical issue.

The growing number of students labeled as learning and reading disabled may well be one of the signs of the deficiency of our general education system to provide a critical, meaningful, and equitable education for all students. Another sign is the decline of higher level thinking decried by many critics who see students in the United States as less capable of the critical, analytic, exploratory, divergent thinking that is the life blood of a democracy.

Project Management

This model calls for both the project director(s) and the principal investigator to devote one-fourth of their time to the project. The director's time includes organization and collaborative planning, implementation, and evaluation of the project with the school district. In addition, the director would consult with the faculty both in and out of the classroom, make periodic classroom observations, and orchestrate the various activities of the project (staff development, parent involvement and workshops, participant observation, mini-grants for teacher and specialist projects, concerns/issues from monthly meetings, communication/publicity). The principal investigator's time would include monthly meetings, some of the staff develop-

ment seminars, and collaborative analysis/synthesis of the ongoing evaluation of the project as well as the final report.

Dialogue journals (Stanton, Shuy, Kreeft, & Reed, 1987) with the participants provide continual records of the success of individual students, implementation efforts of the faculty, their own issues and concerns, and their
understanding of key concepts. These journals are the major form of evaluation for staff development, and they provide for ongoing dialogue between
the school faculty and the university faculty. Teachers and specialists also
keep careful records of the progress of low achieving students as they move
toward full integration in the classroom.

Nurturing Parent Involvement

Concurrent with the staff development program is the development of
a model for parent involvement and participation as partners in the education of the student. Griffore and Boger (1986) describe the vital need to
encompass parents in the learning process, to build continuity between the
home and school, and to stress the parent's teaching role as equal to the
teacher's. A further comment on the separation of students from each other,
families from schools, and academics from vital relationships comes from
James Comer, associate dean of Yale's medical school. "Nothing is more
important to success in schools than the quality of relationships between and
among students, teachers, and parents. Yet many reformers treat learning as
a purely mechanical process" (1988).

The parents of each low achieving student integrated into the regular
classroom are informally interviewed at home by a teacher or specialist for
the purpose of better understanding the perspective of the family/parents
and establishing a more trusting, cooperative relationship. Parents are asked
to observe the student in the classroom and then meet together with the
teacher and specialist for collaborative problem solving. Further observations and meetings may be arranged as needed to continue planning the
individual education plan for each student, and to build a cooperative, congruent learning environment for the student in both the classroom and the
home.

As parents grow in their understanding of the learning processes of
their children, they can be asked to help with the planning of parent workshops. Parents and grandparents (who may share primary care responsibilities for students during part of their school years) are asked to come together
for three workshops in which they share ideas, learn more about the curriculum the teachers and specialists are building in the classroom, and
problem-solve together about ways to help the children with learning in
general and reading in particular. These workshops are collaboratively de-

signed by parents, teachers, and specialists, so that they have better involvement and commitment from the families involved. They are rooted in the very real needs and interests of the parents and families, and they reflect the school's willingness to respect the parents as partners in education.

A large proportion of families of students diagnosed as remedial readers, low achieving, LD, ADD, EMR, or SED are minority and poor families. Thus, a project based on this model would focus on a deeper understanding of poor and minority families so that fuller involvement and cooperation with the school would be possible. Often the extended family is involved in child rearing, particularly if the mother works, so the model encourages the involvement of grandparents and other relatives as well.

At present there often is an adversarial relationship between the family and the school, particularly in the cases of students with LD, ADD, and SED labels. There have been many due process lawsuits demanding that the district pay for private instruction and schools for students whose parents felt denied of appropriate help. And there is often little representation of poor, Black, Latino, Chicano, or Native American community members in parent advisory committees, parent–teacher associations, or such school functions as Back-to-School Night, making the gap between the school and these families even greater.

This model includes several ideas to ensure successful and realistic parent involvement in education, which have been suggested by Dorothy Rich (1986), President of the Home and School Institute.

1. Link parent involvement directly to the achievement of their children.
2. Provide ways for families to teach in complementary ways—opportunities for families to supplement and reinforce development of academic skill in the home.
3. Offer a variety of ways to participate, schedule around needs of working or single parents, have parents reach other parents, and continue involvement in middle and junior high school years.
4. Involve grandparents or other senior family members as volunteers in classrooms or as liaisons to the home.
5. Ensure that parent–community involvement is seen as important and necessary—an integral, vital part of the education program for the student, and not just a nice extra.

Turnbull and Turnbull (1986) provide another excellent resource for building partnerships between professionals and parents. They present general models of family functioning and the family life cycle to challenge professionals to think about the rich variation in the functioning of individual families. An excellent resource for understanding the perspectives of Latino parents is found in Toro-Lopez (1992). Kuykendall (1992) and Taylor and Dorsey-Gaines (1988) provide resources for understanding the perspectives of African American families.

Measuring Accomplishments

Three types of accomplishments are measured: (1) accomplishments of students (both labeled and nonlabeled), (2) accomplishments of staff development, (3) accomplishments of the parent education program. The first two types of accomplishments (student and staff) are calculated at the beginning, middle, and end of each year of the project. Parent involvement is assessed at the end of the year through both questionnaires and numbers attending the workshops.

Accomplishments of students. These can be calculated as number of minutes spent per day in each of the Critical Experiences for learning. The categories that follow are suggestive of some of the multiple options for documenting engagement in the Critical Experiences.

1. Time spent in reading/transacting with texts
   reading aloud to students
   reading activities
      before reading: total class instruction in strategies
      during reading: strategy instruction and pair reading
      after reading: small group tasks using strategies
   building world knowledge and discussing concepts
   connecting themes/linking ideas
2. Time spent in writing/composing
   writing original material
   oral composing (brainstorming, debates, storytelling, nonstop talking
      tasks, and other speaking activities)
   writing to learn subject matter—responding in writing to texts, written application, analysis, or synthesis
3. Time spent in independent reading and writing
   reading whole, connected texts of own choosing
   writing connected prose/poetry of own choosing
   journal and/or dialogue journal writing
   number of books read independently
4. Time spent investigating language
   problem solving, moving from whole text to parts or patterns in language, and back to the whole text

constructing writer's personal handbook of conventions (from inductively discovered patterns)
5. Time spent learning to learn
large group instruction in strategies
before reading: teacher modeling drawing upon prior knowledge and experience
during reading: large or small group predicting, summarizing, brainstorming, finding difficult/important text
after reading: large or small group discussion, analysis, dramatizations, debate to extend meaning
small group investigating using strategies
large group: What did we learn from this?

Note: The above increases should be accompanied by decreases in time spent with high, middle, and low reading groups and isolated workbook sheets on subskills of language.

Accomplishments of staff development. In addition to the above student accomplishments, the accomplishments of staff development can be measured in terms of the following increases in integration of learning and teaching:

1. More collaborative learning activities with heterogeneous groups of students
2. More integration of content areas with language activities: reading and writing to learn content
3. More integration of the curriculum with thematic units and unifying concepts across the curriculum
4. More integration of professionals: more time spent collaborating with other teachers and specialists; more observation, problem solving, and conferencing with each other; more co-instruction or planning together for individual needs of students
5. More integration of previously labeled, at-risk, and low achieving students in the regular classroom

Parent involvement accomplishments. The accomplishments of the parent program can be calculated in terms of the following kinds of involvement in addition to the questionnaire given at the end of the year:

1. Parents of low achieving children
number of homes visited for interviews
number of parents observing in the classroom

number of parents conferencing with teacher and specialist concerning their observations

number of parents involved in planning workshops with the teacher
and specialist

number of parents/grandparents volunteering to help in the
classroom

2. Parents of all children

number of parents attending the workshops

number of parents involved with the school

Ecological Evaluation

It has been well documented that test results do not, in fact, inform
policy making (Beard & McNabb, 1985; Congressional Budget Office,
1987; Linn, 1987; Petrie, 1987). The deficiencies of standardized tests in
identifying students with learning problems and in informing practice are
likewise well documented (Coles, 1978; Gartner & Lipsky, 1987; Hobbs,
1975; Johnston, 1992; Vinsonhaler et al., 1983; Ysseldyke & Algozzine,
1982). Thus, more ecologically valid evaluation methods are needed in
which teacher and specialist observations are most critical and contextual
information is gathered while the students are in the process of learning.

This ecological evaluation takes four major forms: (1) a richly descriptive qualitative account of the student engaged in the Critical Experiences
for learning, (2) an individual description focused on deeper understanding
of the student's world view (meaning-making) through interactive observational methods that include the student's experiences, (3) a reading and
writing portfolio of the student's finished work and work in progress representing critical learning experiences, and (4) more valid assessments of decoding, comprehension, and writing. A plan for preparing an individualized
education program that is congruent with the Critical Experiences framework can be found in Bartoli and Botel, 1988a.

Central to all of these forms of evaluation is the notion of teachers
and specialists as researchers and reflective practitioners. As they continually
observe in the classroom, reflect on their observations, share observations
with each other, and collaboratively seek patterns and themes in their data,
they become a part of the research community of qualitative scientists—
ethnographers of their own classroom contexts and their own students'
learning processes. This ongoing researching of their own settings allows for
greater understanding of the learner, greater understanding of themselves as
professionals, and a continuous improvement of the curriculum for learning
for individual students.

The individual (one-on-one) interactive observational methods are forms of oral and written dialogue, book conversations, reading protocols, and children's narratives. In the Vygotskian tradition of mediation, the teacher or specialist engages the student in the learning process; leads ahead through supportive encouragement, modeling, and other types of scaffolding; and mediates as the student builds on personal experience and knowledge. There is much agreement in education that an observant teacher can evaluate a child's learning progress more accurately than any test, but these one-on-one interactive methods allow the teacher and/or specialist to refine that evaluation even more. The methods are as instructive as they are evaluative, so there is no time loss and no threat to self-esteem.

Traditional testing too often has resulted in a fragmented curriculum of testable pieces of information. We often appear to be training specialized technicians for narrow areas of expertise rather than critical thinkers with broader, integrated knowledge. If we wish to allow more time for concept development, creative and exploratory thinking, and building upon the vital experiences of the learner, we need to use alternative forms of evaluation that are not separate from teaching. Such evaluation begins by assessing the classroom environment of the student, and it answers such questions as

> How and how well does the program allow for oral and written transactions with texts in all content areas?
> How and how well does the program allow for self-selection of books and opportunities for children to share what stands out for them in some of these books?
> How and how well does the program allow for children to write on topics of their own choice through a recursive process of prewriting, drafting, revision, and editing?
> How and how well does the program allow children to learn to decode and use standard English by studying language as an integrated, functional system?
> How and how well does the program enable children to learn to learn?

Evaluation of the Inclusion Process

The inclusion process will require the following:

1. The school leadership supports the program and invites participation from the faculty and parents.

2. Interested professionals and parents come together in the staff development program to work on the process of fully integrating children into regular education classrooms.

3. This is monitored continually through dialogue journals with the participants, observations, and interviews.

4. Participants document their use of class time for Critical Experiences at the beginning, middle, and end of the year.

5. Participants continually monitor the progress of students, who are evaluated in writing and decoding/comprehension at the beginning and end of the year.

6. Time use data, observational data, dialogue journal data, and student progress data are woven together into periodic reports at monthly leadership meetings.

7. Issues and concerns of various participants are subjects for continual problem solving (see Carini, 1979; Comer, 1988) and model refinement.

8. At the end of each year various forms of evaluation are collected by and from the participants. These include questionnaires for parents, teachers, specialists, administrators, school board/community members, and students to voice their evaluation of the success of the model along with their suggestions for improvement. Questionnaires ask for participant assessment of student progress, curriculum and evaluation methods, collaboration of professionals, and parent collaboration. Other evaluations include student performance levels, classroom evaluation (calculated as time engaged in the Critical Experiences and amount of integration), and evaluation of professionals (from observations of colleagues focused on the Critical Experiences framework).

MODEL II: SUPPORTING STUDENT AND TEACHER LEARNING IN URBAN SCHOOLS: A SCHOOL–COMMUNITY–COLLEGE DIALOGUE

This partnership model establishes a professional development site for preservice and in-service teachers in a culturally diverse urban school. The objectives are to

1. Organize teacher and parent dialogue groups to develop a unified vision of more inclusive, equitable, and integrated learning for all students.

2. Provide a range of opportunities for teachers for both on-site reflective professional development and off-site conferences, seminars, workshops, and school visitations.

3. Use preservice and in-service teachers as researchers in their own classrooms, documenting the full inclusion process for at-risk students (supported by a Community Resource Center, Reading Recovery, and a state Instructional Support Team model).

4. Link college/university resources with the public school and community in academic, music, and community service projects.

This model for systemic school reform and renewal calls for combining the resources of a multicultural public school, its community, a local college, two universities, and the state department of education. As a democratic, participatory model, it defines teachers as leaders, and parents as partners, engaging all participants in long-term dialogue, reflection, research, and development focused on (1) reforming teaching and learning processes, and (2) the impact of collaborative partnerships in facilitating systemic school change.

Need for Change

The pressing needs of students and teachers in urban schools are well documented in studies of U.S. schooling. High failure and dropout rates, economic and emotional hardships of single-parent families, scarcity of resources for schools and after school programs, racial and ethnic stereotypes and misunderstanding, and the continual frustration and burnout of teachers, parents, and students amidst all of this combine to present seemingly intractable problems.

A collaborative, interdisciplinary effort is needed to approach these complex problems. This model combines the resources of a multicultural school and community, a local college's education and social work departments, consultants from two universities, and the state department of education to begin to understand these problems at a deeper level and to work cooperatively toward system-wide change. Participants from the wider ecology of the learner—the school and classroom, the home and family, and the community and culture—work together to better understand the problems and to develop possible solutions.

Recently Robert Schwartz of the Pew Charitable Trust emphasized the need for a "massive investment in professional development" (Relic, 1993) and the concurrent need for preservice and continuing teacher education to assume a higher priority within our colleges and universities. The research of John Goodlad, Ann Lieberman, Linda Darling-Hammond, Theodore Sizer, James Comer, and Ernest Boyer echoes this need to go beyond shortsighted quick fixes to systemic change. This model avoids focusing on narrowly defined problems as a stimulus to begin staff development. Too often programs attempt to improve standardized test scores and to create accountability systems within schools. Staff development programs are often built around basal reading series with the accompanying unit tests, prescriptive exercises, and commercially produced tracking systems; or they may seek to improve teaching behaviors by sequencing lesson formats and regimenting supervisory practices.

Time is not allocated in these approaches for dialogue or communicating with peers. Hence, teaching becomes an independent activity, relying heavily on "hit or miss" techniques designed by the individual, leading to numerous homespun theories on how to teach and what is best for children (Lortie, 1975). Among the recurring ideas that support the need for the reflective dialogue approach to professional development are

1. Bureaucratic constraints hamper teachers in their work (Barth, 1990; Lieberman & Miller, 1992; Sarason, 1971).
2. Teachers, parents, and administrators view education differently (Barth, 1990; Dombart, 1985; Joyce & Showers, 1983; Lightfoot, 1978; Sarason, 1971).
3. Teaching often is viewed and undertaken as a private activity (Duke, 1984; Joyce & Showers, 1983; Lieberman & Miller, 1992; Lortie, 1975).
4. Teachers and parents work from individual and sometimes conflicting notions about teaching and learning (Dombart, 1985; Heath, 1983; Lightfoot, 1978; Lomotey, 1990; Lortie, 1975).

This research also suggests that a staff development program should include the following: collegial activity, ongoing efforts, broad perspectives in terms of what is hoped to be accomplished, collaborative opportunities, ownership, and participation. The image created is that teachers and administrators often lose sight of their primary responsibilities as they focus on going through motions, controlling student behavior, following the curriculum, or surviving crises rather than on educating individuals. Because they become so heavily involved in the "doing" aspect of teaching—following teaching manuals, covering the curriculum, assigning and grading workbook pages and skill sheets, disciplining students—the "thinking" aspect of teaching is forgotten. Staff development programs usually present different ways of "doing"; this model is designed to promote critical "thinking" about schools.

To become empowered to credibly uphold their unique positions and to become invested with a greater degree of trust and responsibility, all parties, according to this model, continually engage in activities to increase their understanding of education. This is accomplished by engaging parents and community members, teachers, administrators, and college faculty and students in professional readings and discussions. Greater understanding puts ideas behind practice; hence, practice results from educated decisions. Change is the goal of our research (Moll & Diaz, 1987).

The need to educate teachers for diversity is important in this model. Both preservice and in-service teachers, along with parents and community members, read texts such as Kuykendall's *From Rage to Hope* (1992), Taylor and Dorsey-Gaines's *Growing Up Literate: Learning from Inner-City Families* (1988), and Rose's *Lives on the Boundary* (1990), in addition to articles and texts on multicultural education, cultural competence, and developing an antibias curriculum (Banks, 1993; Derman-Sparks, 1989; Freire, 1970, 1981; Lomotey, 1990). Involving multiracial groups of parents, teachers, and community members in dialogue on racial understanding and on celebrating diversity also serves the important need of more interaction and relationship building between the school and its racially, ethnically, and economically diverse community.

Applying the Model: Beginning a Professional Development Site

This section describes how the model is being applied in a project that combines the resources of the Steelton-Highspire School District and the Steelton community; Elizabethtown College's Education, Social Work, Music Therapy, and Political Science Departments; consultants from two universities; and consultants from Pennsylvania's Division of Early Childhood and Family Education and the Bureau of Special Education. The model calls for linking the public school, community, local college, state, and university in collaborative, long-term research and dialogue on both the teaching and learning processes and the continuous process of school reform and renewal. College students and faculty, along with public school faculty, are teacher-researchers studying and researching schooling practices, observing and documenting student learning processes, analyzing and problem-solving, and developing or refining teaching processes on the basis of their observations.

At the professional development site in a low income, racially and ethically diverse community and school, participants in the project are working toward accomplishing the following objectives in support of more inclusive, equitable, and integrated learning for all students.

1. *Dialogue groups.* Dialogue groups comprising teachers, parents, community and college members, and administrators are being organized to (a) explore major issues in teaching, learning, and evaluation, (b) develop a unified vision of optimal education for all students, and (c) develop teaching and evaluation strategies that support a vision of integrated, equitable education.

The project director, principal investigator, and other consultants assist these groups and work with school faculty and college practicum students to facilitate and document the implementation of these plans in the class-room. The long-term goal is to have these dialogue groups co-facilitated by teachers and parents.

2. *Professional development.* On-site, continuous staff development is being developed that uses the resources of the school, community, state education department, college, and university. In-service days are being designed to offer ongoing staff, parent, and community development in multicultural literature, antibias curricula, reading and writing processes, integrated and thematic teaching and learning, alternative evaluation methods, child-centered and democratic discipline, children's book publishing, computer literacy and desktop publishing, and other topics suggested by the dialogue groups.

Both on-site and college site courses will be offered for the professional development of the school faculty, parents, aides, and college education majors. Some courses will be sponsored by the college and university, and others by the local intermediate unit or the department of education. There will be a reciprocal faculty exchange, with the project director teaching a course at the college and the principal investigator conducting classroom observations at the school; teachers serving as adjunct supervisors of student teachers; and college faculty serving as curriculum, evaluation, and re-search consultants.

3. *Supporting and documenting inclusion of students.* College students in education, social work, and music therapy are collaborating with teachers, specialists, counselors, parents, and community members to both develop and document the inclusion of at-risk and labeled (LD, ADD, Chapter 1, remedial) students in reformed and enriched regular education classrooms. A newly created Community Resource Center will use a combination of James Comer's (1980, 1988) model for a broadly based support system for children and parents in the school and two other methods of supporting low progress learners: Reading Recovery (Clay, 1979, 1985) and an Instructional Support Team model endorsed by the Pennsylvania Department of Education. The Reading Recovery and Instructional Support models are already in place in the school, and the Community Resource Center will be developed with the help of grant funds.

College practicum students in education and social work are doing ethnographic/ecological case studies of low progress learners who are included in regular classrooms, documenting the quality of the classroom curriculum (using the state's Critical Experiences framework—Lytle & Botel, 1990) and the actual learning processes of the child. Education and social work students are placed in the same classroom to observe, build a relation-ship with a child who is experiencing difficulty, and make a home visit to learn about the wider ecology of the child.

4. *Teacher-researchers*. Preservice and in-service teachers are collaborating teacher-researchers in their own classrooms, documenting and facilitating student learning, becoming both problem-posers and problem-solvers, and evaluating the school-wide change process.

Student teachers and their cooperating teachers are learning to use the Primary Language Record (Barrs, Ellis, Tester, & Thomas, 1989) and other observational methods to evaluate both the quality of the learning environment and the learning processes of the students. In addition, they will have monthly meetings with the principal investigator and other project team members to evaluate the classroom and school-wide change processes. The results of their research will be used to develop and refine curriculum and evaluation methods that better meet the needs of all students.

5. *Community service*. College students from a variety of academic disciplines are engaged with the school and the community in service projects that are jointly developed with community members and school faculty. With the assistance of the Pennsylvania Campus Compact and Diana Bucco to coordinate efforts, a coordinated plan of community and school service is being developed that links college students, administration, and faculty with public school students, faculty, and parents in a variety of collaboratively designed opportunities for students and their families. Family holiday workshops, Saturday morning workshops for children and families, after school music and art workshops, homework clubs, athletic clubs, computer clubs, college visits and overnights, pen pal programs, big brother/big sister programs, and habitats for humanity projects are both present and future activities.

The long-term goal for this project is to develop a replicable partnership model for democratic, teacher-led school reform and renewal in multicultural sites. The model includes the development of a college–school professional development site for both research and improvement that links college, public school, community, university, and state resources in support of both research and improvement of teaching and learning. With the full participation of the public school faculty and community, plans for reform are developed cooperatively, the change process is documented, the results are evaluated, and research findings are disseminated.

The process begins with dialogue groups that include public school and college faculty, parents, and students, along with community members who study, research, and reflect upon critical issues in teaching, learning, and evaluation. Participants are also involved in a variety of professional development opportunities to extend their thinking and learning, including in-service workshops, college and on-site graduate level courses, and professional conferences, seminars, and workshops.

As part of their practicum experience, college students collaborate with cooperating teachers to document the learning and full inclusion of low progress early childhood and elementary students in regular classrooms. Using an ethnographic teacher-researcher model (Cochran-Smith & Lytle, 1992; Erickson, 1987) students from education, social work, and political science document the ecology of the child, including the family, school, classroom, and community. Teams of public school faculty, parents, and administrators, along with college faculty and students, disseminate their research and development findings at conferences and workshops as well as in publications for the educational research community.

Project personnel. The principal investigator has conducted previous university and college partnership research and development studies, and she has both conducted and published research on the wider ecology of low progress learners (Bartoli, 1986b, 1989; Bartoli et al., 1991). She is working in collaboration with the school superintendent, the elementary principal and faculty, and community members.

Dr. Boyd Fox, one of the college consultants, has had 23 years of college curriculum teaching and student teacher supervision experience, including supervision at the Steelton Elementary School. He is taking a half-year sabbatical to facilitate in curriculum development and coordination, and also in classroom management at the school site.

A second college education consultant, Dr. Juan Toro, has done ethnographic studies of Latino parent attitudes concerning the education of their children, and he has developed and taught courses in early childhood education and multicultural curricula. He consults with the school staff and college students from time to time concerning cultural competence and education for diversity.

Dr. Vivian Bergel, chair of the college social work department, which is accredited by the Council on Social Work Education, has collaborated with the principal investigator in the linking of social work students with education students in the classroom to better meet the needs of children and families. She is also involved in developing the Community Resource Center, coordinating home visits, conferring with college students placed at the site, and consulting in the data collection and research analysis processes.

Dr. Cynthia Beyerlein trains social work and political science students in ethnographic research in the community. The students gather oral histories from the community, interview business owners for an economic profile of the community, and conduct a variety of research studies on the social, political, cultural, and economic contexts of the community surrounding the school site. She and her students presented their research on the Steelton community at the Ethnography in Education Research Forum at the University of Pennsylvania (Beyerlein et al., 1994).

Dr. Michael Rohrbacher supervises music therapy students at the site and provides workshops for interested faculty members. He will also supervise independent study students who may do school site practicums, work with students and parents in the Community Resource Center, organize a family multicultural music workshop/festival, or provide other family and child opportunities to become involved in music therapy.

Dr. Andrea Fishman, from West Chester University, is a Director of the National Writing Project and a Founding Director of the Literacy Project. She consults with teachers in the classroom and conducts workshops on writing processes and on K–12 literacy activities.

Dr. Rita Smith Wade-El, chair of the psychology department at Millersville University, and Rev. Edward Bailey serve as consultants to the school faculty, community, and college students in the development of cultural competence, multicultural curricula, and, in particular, deeper understanding of African American families. They meet from time to time with the school faculty to present workshops and to problem-solve in dialogue groups. In addition, they meet with students at the college and with parents in the community.

Educational value of the model. Given the traditional separation of public schools, parents, communities, and institutions of higher education, and the individual perspectives that each have regarding the operation of the schools, this model offers an opportunity to incorporate an approach in which community members, teachers, administrators, and college and university participants read, talk, and test solutions to problems that they themselves define. Studies of school reform, renewal, and restructuring processes provide the justification for the usefulness of this approach (Boyer, 1983; Darling-Hammond, 1992; Goodlad, 1987, 1990; Lieberman & Miller, 1992; Sirotnik & Goodlad, 1988; Sizer, 1984).

The professional development program engages community, school, and college members in collaborative, reflective dialogue. The process consists of a series of parent, teacher, administrator, and college faculty meetings to discuss issues and to create networks and continued opportunities for parents and educators to come together for the purpose of communicating, sharing, and thinking about educational issues above the plane of daily life in the classroom.

The process of involving all parties must stipulate that shared decision making is important; that dialogue is a means to involvement; and that the dialogue must be informed by ideas that are gained through professional study. Using Deweyan philosophy to guide his dialogue approach, Gibboney (1984, 1994) uses this approach to examine school issues through the reading of carefully selected books and articles. The essential characteristics of the dialogue process are voluntary participation; participants who are representative of all groups within the school; dialogue that is informed by ideas from carefully selected readings; a significant focus directing the group's work; time for understanding and growth; a rigorous, yet flexible structure; and a moderator who is knowledgeable in the content.

Congruent with the major objectives of this model, Lieberman and Miller (1992) describe the five building blocks of restructuring for systemic change.

1. Rethinking curriculum and instruction to promote quality and equality, such as through dialogue groups and opportunities to reflect upon and develop child-centered evaluation methods and antibias curricula.

2. Rethinking the structure of the school, including school-based management, shared decision making, and teacher leadership.

3. Focusing on both a rich learning environment for students and a professionally supportive work environment for adults, for example, through reflective professional development and teacher-researcher projects focusing on developing classrooms with the Critical Experiences vital to optimal learning.

4. Building partnerships and networks, exemplified by school, community, college, and university sharing of ideas, resources, experiences, and insights for the ultimate benefit of both student learning and the professional development of preservice and in-service teachers.

5. The increased and changing participation of parents and the community, leading to more respectful, supportive, and trusting relationships.

Many studies demonstrate that educators benefit by gaining ownership in the development of in-service and staff development opportunities, and by creating their own curricula (Little, 1993). Yet teachers have difficulty thinking about their role in terms other than "covering x amount of material in x amount of time" (Sarason, 1971). And since a program addressing only the daily functions of educators will maintain the status quo, this discrepancy points to the need to undergird the staff development process with research on teaching and learning.

Use of resources. The project underway calls for establishment of a Community Resource Center, with a publishing center as well as an informal family counseling center, both of which will make use of the combined resources of the community, the school, and the college for continuation. It also calls for a large investment in professional development of teachers, including seminars and workshops, retreats, and a variety of collaborative learning opportunities linked with parents and the community.

This is, at a minimum, a 5- to 7-year change process. The school faculty and administration as well as the college faculty and administration will have to continue to commit the time, energy, and resources necessary for a long-term change effort. In this project, resources are being contributed as follows.

COLLEGE CONTRIBUTION:

> Payment for supervision of student teachers and practicum students in education and social work (including mileage)
> Honorariums for cooperating teachers
> One half-time sabbatical for college faculty member
> Use of college facilities for task force meetings and retreats
> One-quarter time release for principal investigator in exchange for project director's teaching one course per semester
> Campus Compact and community service costs
> Payment of adjunct student teacher supervisors

SCHOOL CONTRIBUTION:

> Matching funds for teacher release/substitute teachers
> Renovations and construction of Community Resource Center
> Secretarial and office support
> Placements for and mentoring of college interns
> Matching funds for professional development of teachers and conference presentations by faculty and administration
> Facilities, supplies, and other expenses for dialogue group meetings

Evaluation plan. Qualitative evaluation of the school change processes, teacher and student learning processes, and the parent and community involvement process is conducted jointly by public school faculty, administration, parents, and students collaborating with college faculty and students.

Forms of student-centered evaluation methods include student portfolios (Bartoli & Botel, 1988a), descriptions of the classroom learning environment, analyses of the critical learning experiences, and inventories of reading and writing strategies (Barrs et al., 1989). In addition, parent questionnaires and interviews, teacher questionnaires and interviews, student questionnaires, interviews, and case studies are done by junior practicum students and student teachers at the site.

A combination of several site-based, internally conducted qualitative methods are used for program evaluation (Cousins, 1992; Oakes & Sirotnik, 1990; Patton, 1987; Spradley, 1979, 1980; Stecher & Davis, 1987; Szwed, 1981). Congruent with the design of the model, the key questions for the program evaluation are developed by the participants. The usefulness of both the evaluation and the model is ensured because questions and answers are rooted in the meaning perspectives and contexts of the participants. Stecher and Davis (1987) refer to this as a "user-oriented approach," while Goodlad and Sirotnik (1988) suggest that this promotes ecological validity.

At the forty-fifth ASCD Conference in San Antonio, Texas, Elliot Eisner suggested the need for evaluation that is congruent with teachers' most deeply held educational values. Good teachers do not view standardization as the greatest value: They value uniqueness, divergent thinking, personal responsibility for learning, individual creativity, and diversity in their students. Rather than using instruments that are incongruent with those values, and undermining both teachers' aims and goals as well as the students' learning process, the evaluation process in this model encourages teachers to generate the kinds of assessments that are congruent with their deeply held values and with current research on the teaching and learning processes.

The school essentially inquires about itself for the purpose of transforming the system. In collaboration with parents, community members, students, and college faculty, the school staff poses questions, tries out new ideas, reflects upon them, and refines them: a process that ultimately improves the learning of all participants.

The project team shares an ethnographic perspective that includes longitudinal observation and interviews conducted in the contexts of classroom, school, community, and family. In-depth documentation of both products and processes of teaching, learning, and evaluation is gathered and analyzed for connecting themes and issues. Likewise, ongoing documentation of the school change processes is analyzed by collaborating teams of teachers, administrators, parents, college faculty and students, university consultants, and state department consultants.

Drs. Bartoli, Toro, Beyerlein, and Fishman have conducted and published qualitative research studies; so the partnership team is well qualified in terms of congruent design, methodology and data analysis. In addition, both Drs. Bergel and Bartoli have experience with a school–family systems approach to framing both problems and solutions in their broader ecological contexts.

National significance. Several aspects of this project are of national significance in education. First, a collaborative, interdisciplinary approach is being used to address the vital issues surrounding student and teacher learning in urban schools. This approach uses teachers as researchers to both understand problems broadly and create solutions from within the individual school and community. Across the educational community there have been calls for a democratic, participatory dialogue model for change to replace the top-down mandates and controlled accountability schemes that have yielded little success, even less authentic, self-directed learning for teachers and students, and no second-order change.

Several other aspects of this project have national significance, among them:

1. Applied research on the development of a professional development site for multicultural education, documenting the process of preparing teachers for diverse classrooms.

2. Documenting the process of building a college–school partnership for school reform, renewal, and restructuring that includes a reflective, inquiry-based, useful evaluation plan.

3. Documenting the process of linking community service learning at the college and public school levels to benefit low income families and children.

4. Research and development in parent and community involvement in school reform and renewal, rooted in a broader view of the social, emotional, and cognitive development of children and families (Auerbach, 1989; Comer, 1988).

5. Documenting and facilitating the process of developing teacher-researchers at both the preservice and in-service levels, using observational research methods that guide and inform teaching and learning (Barrs et al., 1989; Clay, 1985; Cochran-Smith & Lytle, 1992).

6. Documenting and facilitating the process of full inclusion of previously labeled and at-risk students using a Community Resource Center and two other support models.

The collaborative nature of the project is also significant, as is its interdisciplinary breadth. The design and direction of the project are a joint effort, fully engaging the school, community, and college participants. In addition to ethnography/anthropology, the research, theories, and perspectives of several other disciplines are used in this project, including sociology (Glaser & Strauss, 1967; McLeod, 1987; Stack, 1974), language arts— reading/writing/talking—(Bartoli & Botel, 1988a; Calkins, 1986; Graves, 1983; Halliday, 1978; Vygostky, 1978), and history of education—with a focus on the critical pedagogy issues of race, class, and equity (Apple, 1988; Freire, 1980; Weis, 1988). This interdisciplinary breadth is necessary due to the complexity and urgency of the problems facing American education, and it is vital for pooling the best of current research, theory, and practice too often separated by discipline, methodology, and philosophical perspectives. The participants in this project hope that the collaboration across disciplines, schools, and agencies may serve as a model for successful collaboration linked with public and private education in our society.

At the turn of the 20th century John Dewey was writing about the aims and objectives of education being formulated on the basis of children's purposes, local conditions, social demands, and the knowledge needed to complete worthy projects. Nearing the turn of the 21st century we feel a renewed commitment to these aims. It was Dewey who said in 1899 that teachers must become learners with their students, planning with them and serving as guides and catalysts in helping children make connections and see relationships. And it was Dewey who viewed the function of the school as not only to fit the child to society, but to provide the means to change the society for the better.

Revaluing American Values

When we think about the United States, so many images come to mind. We may think idealistically of democracy, equality, freedom, and individual opportunity. We may envision the wealth of racial and cultural diversity that has always been the strength and greatest resource of our nation, held together by the ideal of unity in diversity, often hard won throughout our history, yet remaining a deeply held value.

Or we may think of less idealistic images: the burnings and riots in Los Angeles and other U.S. cities in 1965 and 1992; the disproportionate rates of poverty for children of color (one in two versus one in four of all U.S. children); the disproportionate school failure and disability labeling of poor and minority students; the continued social, political, and economic inequities that persist for African American, Latino, Mexican American, and Native American children and families; and a growing pattern of near genocide for some Native American groups and for young African American males.

The idealistic images of the United States are more often embraced by those who have been relatively successful in its educational, economic, social, and political systems. Having had success and having seen their families in the past achieving successfully, they can more easily maintain the images, values, and dreams of individual opportunity, equality, democracy, and freedom. They can, in short, imagine themselves and their families being successful.

IMAGES, VALUES, AND LEARNING

As human beings our motivation and potential for learning are shaped and limited by what we can imagine—by the person we can see ourselves to be. And this vision is further shaped and constrained by what others see in us, particularly those who are important to our own view of ourselves: our families, our teachers, our communities, our employers, and our leaders.

This book has been about some of these images, ideals, and values, particularly as they affect the lives of children, families, and educators in "good" suburban schools and "poor" urban schools. It details what I have come to term the ecology of inequity in learning to read in the United States for a Black student in a small, predominantly white town; and for Latino children and families in a large inner-city school.

What is perhaps most important about the experiences and perceptions of the students, families, and educators in two quite diverse environments is the striking similarities between them. Having gone to a major metropolitan city to explore the differences between suburban and urban schooling, I was amazed to find instead so many parallels. This suggests the pervasiveness of the ecology of inequity in the United States.

In both the suburban and inner-city studies I asked the broad question, What are the experiences, perceptions, images, assumptions, and values of these students, parents, grandparents, teachers, and administrators that may be related to learning to read and learning to learn? And as a participant observer in the various roles of colleague, parent, professor, researcher, community member, and friend, I listened as they told me their stories— stories that are richly descriptive of the complex ecology of learning and living in America.

Throughout this book the focus of understanding more about learning is on the perceptions or meaning-making of the people who make up the ecology of the learner, on the social relationships between and among the learner and others in the ecology, and on the quality of the environment for learning provided for the developing student in the schooling process. If we can come to more fully understand the interrelationships among these perceptions and social relationships, as well as the quality of the learning environment shaped by this social interaction, we will know quite a lot about creating an ecology for equity rather than inequity.

The case studies illustrate the vital importance of understanding how learners are perceived by teachers and others in the school and community. For it is these perceptions, beliefs, and assumptions that shape the social interaction that occurs in school, in the community, and between the home and school. Of course, perceptions themselves are shaped by the culture and society, and so they cannot be understood apart from that broader societal context. Likewise the stereotypes and biases of teachers, parents, and administrators cannot be understood apart from the racism and classism in the society that shapes and sustains them.

Quite different ecologies were created for James and the Latino students than were created for most of their white middle-class peers. And so we come to the central problem expressed throughout this book: The ecology of inequity created for these students is a denial of the fundamental values of equality, democracy, and individual freedom that have been the foundation of our nation. This is a tragic and dangerous waste of what we claim to be our country's most precious resource, and it is the primary barrier to meaningful, lasting change in the education system. A closer look at these traditional values that once united us, and perhaps can again, will help to define a better direction for saving the ecology of our children, for our children.

AMERICAN VALUES AND LEARNING TO READ

We begin with some of the images and values that are important in a reading of the stories of James and the inner-city school. Reading is trans-acting with text—making meaning in interaction with text as the reader connects with personal experience and knowledge and links this with new knowledge. As such, the reading of the case studies will (and should) be different for each individual depending on the knowledge and experience each brings to the text. The purpose of using a human values lens in reading the stories is twofold: (1) to give us a way of seeing similarities as well as differences among the participants in these stories—commonalities as well as uniqueness; and (2) to suggest a way that all of us can envision and pursue change or transformation of the ecology of inequity in schooling in the United States.

In their excellent analysis of the ways that Americans have failed their children, Grubb and Lazerson (1982) outline some of the ways that our traditional American values have turned into broken promises. Throughout the case studies in Chapters 3 and 4 it is tragic to see how the values of democracy, individual freedom, meaningful work, education for all citizens, and a caring community have been devalued and denied to Black American, poor white, and Latino students and their families.

Individual Rights and Freedom

The promise of individual freedom and liberty guaranteed by the Bill of Rights stands high as a symbol of fundamental American values. Central to this is the right of all citizens to be respected as equal human beings. But a resurgence of racism and self-seeking individualism, as well as a lack of concern for other people's children and the common good, has devalued and denied liberty and freedom for many poor and nonwhite children and families. Increasingly we are seeing problems with intolerance of and disre-spect for difference and diversity, abuse of those who differ from mainstream beliefs, overrepresentation of poor and nonwhite students in low achieve-ment and poor behavior groups, and other violations of individual rights to equal opportunity.

Reforms in education have replicated inequality rather than ensuring the equal rights of all individuals to develop their capacities. Low academic tracks, remedial classes, and disability labels ensure more controlling and warehousing in schools and other institutions for those labeled by the school and/or the society as disabled, disordered, at risk, remedial, or otherwise unfit to learn in the mainstream, rather than enhancing the freedom of individuals to learn to the limits of their potential.

Self-seeking individualism supports gifted, honors, and advanced placement classes for one's own children at the expense of equal opportunity for other people's children, or insists on the best teacher and school for one's own children regardless of the effect of these choices on other people's children. This is a denial of the individual rights of all children and families, and it is a denial of our social responsibility to care for everybody's children.

The future composition of our classrooms as well as our workforce demands that we learn to develop the individual potential of all of our children, celebrate and cultivate their individual differences, and begin to see the value of a more collaborative, rather than individually competitive, way of living and learning. The more cooperative cultural values of Latino and African American families can begin to lead us in a more profitable direction. And the Native American respect and reverence for both the human spirit and the earth are further resources for transforming the ecology of inequity.

Democracy

Democracy has been the backbone of our society, embracing the value of a classless society with citizens participating fully, equally, and actively in democratic decision making. Yet we find our nation too often divided by class and race, assuming blame and deficiency in families like James's because they represent stereotyped, misunderstood, and devalued cultural groups. These divisions create barriers to building trusting relationships, to equal participation, to shared decision making, and to the creation of self-governing communities that work together for the common good.

Powerless groups are alienated in a governing process ruled by self-interest, lobbying groups, and others who hold the greatest power. We have forgotten Jefferson's warning that democracy requires eternal vigilance, allowing the ideal of full participation to deteriorate into top-down mandates for accountability, elections of representatives by one-fourth of the voters, and important decisions about teaching and learning made outside the classroom and school. Without full participation and the educated, well-reasoned choices of all our citizens, we leave ourselves open to the rule of an elite few or to the subjugation and abuse of a charismatic dictator. Without the full participation of teachers and parents in the education of children, we permit a handful of textbook and testing companies to dictate a reductionistic, fragmented curriculum and testing system that stigmatizes, labels, and sorts some students while it limits the opportunities for authentic, critical learning experiences for all students.

We forget too quickly other lessons from history. It was the powerless, the poor, and those who had been stripped of their dignity and pride who were most willing to follow Hitler with complete obedience to his authority. And it is the powerless and the poor that we are training in our present schooling practices to follow prescriptive rules, to give unquestioning and passive obedience, and to learn to be controlled.

Morton Botel (personal communication, January 1994) shared with me his views on democracy when I asked him how and why he has continued to work toward change in school systems for the past 45 years.

> Democracy is so important, and you have to constantly work for it. It's so easy for it to slip away, and to have our lives controlled. We've got to make our institutions more democratic. That motivates me more than anything, coming from a background of totalitarianism where families were decimated and killed. One thing we've got to work for is this democratic society.

The Meaning of Work

The meaning of work has been a traditional American value since colonial times. The Puritans thought of work as "a calling" in which a person gains a sense of purpose and meaning through working. Work has been idealized as intrinsically satisfying and integral to understanding ourselves, while unemployment has been viewed as psychologically devastating, denying individual purpose and place in society.

Unemployment was an overwhelming problem for the Latino families in the inner-city study. Lack of success in the school system, language barriers, job discrimination, lack of affordable child care, and the sheer unavailability of jobs in the deteriorating inner city combined with other factors to produce a poverty cycle that was mired in hopelessness. Few jobs were available for Black Americans in James's small town, and similar evidences of hopelessness appear among Black and Latino youth: most notably, the interconnected problems of low motivation, school failure and retention, drug and alcohol abuse, juvenile crime, and teenage pregnancy.

Jobs that are available for the undereducated poor and minorities are often far removed from the lofty ideal of meaningful, self-fulfilling work. They are more often stripped of self-direction and creativity, monotonous, perhaps dangerous, and demanding of obedience in a structured hierarchy.

Intrinsic motivation is often replaced by money as the prime motivation for work.

The marketplace work-for-profit goal finds its way into the school system, particularly as applied to labeled or at-risk students. Behavior modification gimmicks, including money and tokens, are used with students labeled as LD, ADD, EMR, remedial, or behavior problem. A recent effort in James's school district to keep dropouts in school included paying them each term that they maintained a C average and stayed in school. Other study-for-pay techniques were being used in the city school district as well.

The underlying assumption is that learning is not and cannot be intrinsically satisfying to poor and minority students. That it is not, as the school system is presently structured, is unquestionable. That it cannot be is open to much-needed critical thinking and the concerted efforts of those who are working toward a transformation of the system. Erickson (1987) suggests looking beyond the school to the community and society for the roots of educational failure and success; his view of nonlearning as a form of political resistance is worthy of further exploration.

Unfortunately, obedience in lieu of creativity, critical thinking, and self-direction is favored in other parts of the school system as well. Teachers in the inner-city school were rewarded for obeying the mandates of the standardized testing and curriculum guidelines rather than for their attempts to challenge either the system or their own assumptions and biases. Their own creativity and voices, like those of their students, were too often left at the classroom door because of the tightly structured demands of the school system, stripping teachers' work of both meaning and personal responsibility.

In those instances where the environment for learning has included meaningful learning for every student, more decision making and choice for students as well as teachers, fewer class divisions, and less control from above, the learning of students and the work of teachers have taken on more significant, purposeful, and fulfilling dimensions. Students and teachers alike from the inner-city school in Chapter 4 have written glowing reports of their successes with writing workshops rooted in a writing process approach, for instance, and with a wide variety of creative reading activities rooted in meaningful transactions with good literature and content-rich texts.

Education for Critical Thinking

This leads us to another traditional American value that is suffering from devaluation: the education of a free people to be literate, critical, intellectually independent thinkers capable of comprehending the threats of tyrants or manipulators of truth. Education in a democracy should prepare people to participate in the democratic political process of building a community and a common purpose. It should be liberation education designed to free people to think, understand, choose, and take responsibility and ownership: education to be liberated from authoritarian mind control, from isolation and segregation, and from narrow views, bias, and prejudice.

The twentieth-century devaluation of education has too often reduced the process for poor students and students of color to preparing them for the labor market. Even the most current reform rhetoric is filled with references to production, work skills, vocational training, and competition in the global marketplace. Economic value has replaced the intrinsic value of education, and the education system has served to extend class divisions through such practices as "ability" grouping, tracking, testing, and labeling.

If we are to re-establish education as a critical and creative process, we need to define it as something other than social control, individual gain, or rate of return. Incremental gains on standardized tests, comparative scores on minimal competency tests between schools or states, and other myopic measures of education will have to be replaced with portfolios of student work over time, student exhibits and projects, research reports, student essays and speeches, community service proposals and reports, collaborative research, and other educationally valid evaluation measures that reflect a broader view of education in a democracy.

The safety of our democracy depends on well-educated citizens capable of making choices among candidates, critical thinkers who can vote on important issues facing humanity in the twenty-first century, and citizens who can look to the future and plan for generations to come. Citizens of the next century will need to have a broad knowledge of the interrelationships among complex processes, concepts, trends, and issues to address such problems as conservation of our resources (including the educational, social, emotional, and physical well being of our children), a stable food supply, world peace, protecting the ozone layer, and preventing ground, water, and air pollution.

Learning experiences in U.S. schools need to be Critical Experiences, rich in intellectual challenge and personal interest, and linked with excellent literature and important concepts. And, if we are to truly educate for critical thinking, these Critical Experiences must be provided across all subjects, throughout each day, and to all students equally.

A Caring Community

Our nation's growing underclass reminds us of a final traditional American value that is being devalued: a caring community of citizens dedicating their energy for the good of all. At its best the value of a caring community embraces the ideal of social responsibility and concern for others in a society in which all members respect, identify with, and appreciate each other.

These separate social class groupings with homogeneous values that are structured in our schools and communities do not lend themselves to mutual responsibility and dedication to the common good. Such separation prevents the trusting relationships that can be built only through mutual understanding and respect. Such segregation also prevents collaborating as equals; so instead of cooperation in the classroom, workplace, and community, we have individual competition that only rarely leads to public responsibility for those who are poorer, less educated, or otherwise in need of our collaboration.

Classrooms can become model caring communities, with heterogeneous groups of students working collaboratively as a community of learners. Those who need help may receive it from their peers in partner tasks, during a small discussion group, or in a heterogeneously arranged project group. They may also receive help from collaborating teachers and specialists, collaborating teachers and parents, or a cooperating administrator, counselor, or social worker—all within the classroom community of learners. Exclusionary goals that consider only the self-interests of a few selected individuals are superseded by goals that promote the learning of all, leaving no one behind to fail.

Trust could be built within this kind of classroom: the kind of trust needed for cultural understanding and meaningful relationship building, and the kind of trust needed to risk learning. Erickson (1987) reminds us that learning demands trust at the "edge of risk" and that "it is essential that the teacher and the students establish and maintain trust in each other" (p. 344). With the cultural understanding that would flourish from the social relationships built within this caring community of learners, the African American and Latino students in the case studies would not be denied their cultural identity and pride. The classroom community model could serve as a model for the larger community and for the society as a whole. And it could lead us to renew the basic values on which our country was established: individual freedom, democracy, meaningful work, education for all citizens, and a caring community.

The failures in our schools cannot be viewed apart from the failures of the society that has created the schools, because schools are essentially a microcosm of the society, teaching the values, beliefs, and hopes that it has. But if the fault lies within ourselves, then the hope for change is there as well. This then suggests great potential for the next century. We have many traditional values to build on, which gave birth to our society and which sustain us as a democracy. Confronting and examining these established values is critical for education: "An education system that fails in this task fails in its mission, no matter how good a technical preparation it offers" (Spiegler, 1992).

WASTED RESOURCES

One of the most important resources presently being wasted in our society is the vitality, energy, and creativity of our culturally diverse citizens. The great diversity of ideas, cultures, heritages, languages, ideals, and dreams has always been the life blood of our society. This vital human energy has historically kept us open to new ideas and innovation, and willing to take the risks necessary to learn, change, and grow. But our rich diversity has become seriously endangered due to homogenizing, standardizing, devaluing trends in our schools and in the society they reflect.

The integrity of the individual voice of students like James is not valued for its potential to contribute in the classroom community of learners, nor is the cultural heritage of James's family and community. The rich bilingual resources of the Latino students and families in the inner city are rarely celebrated and used to their full capacity. Worse yet, this diversity is often labeled as negative difference, deficit, or disability, signaling sure death to the cultural and linguistic pride that is vital for further learning.

By such homogenizing techniques as separating young learners into reading "ability" groups and homogeneously grouped kindergarten, pre-first/transitional, or first-grade classes; segregating students into various levels of academic tracks; labeling some students as LD, ADD, EMR, gifted, or remedial; or otherwise separating the "fit" from the "unfit" and the "disordered/disabled" from the "able," we are not only narrowing our vision of education in a democracy, but we are cutting ourselves off from the human diversity that historically has led to our best thinking and kept us growing as a pluralistic nation, united in all our diversity.

When what is valued in a person is reduced to one-right-answer, multiple choice, standardized testing formats from kindergarten through college and beyond, we have severely diminished the integrity and potential of individual human beings. And when those who find fault with the system are labeled as "oppositional" (James's last diagnosis) and removed by that system, we are endangered as a democratic society. It is not our "underclass," but the ecology of inequity we have created, that is to blame for the fact that we are regressing.

The fault also is not in the field of special education, although many references are made to labels and problems of pedagogy and evaluation in special education classes. Regular education has the same problems with deficiency labels, fragmented pedagogy, and invalid evaluation methods—and had them before the field of special education came into existence to try to solve the problems created by regular education's "solutions."

In the 1990s we are experiencing a state and national movement to return students to the mainstream—but not for the right reasons, and not with the necessary support. Students cannot be returned to the same classrooms from which they failed to learn, without, at a minimum, (1) removing the curricular and evaluative constraints on teachers that prevent them from both using and further developing their best professional judgment and expertise, (2) building into the system the kind of long-term, reflective staff development described in Chapter 9, (3) critical reflection on personal and societal assumptions and biases, and (4) serious efforts to build respectful relationships with all families and children. If students with reading or learning difficulties are returned to classrooms that have not been reformed, and to teachers who have not been given the opportunity to reflect on and renew their own teaching practices, then the current efforts toward full inclusion, Instructional Support Teams, and reintegration will only produce more problematic solutions.

The staff development needed in every school across the nation to ensure the optimal learning of all students should include at least three crucial elements: (1) a focus on renewal in pedagogy and assessment, (2) a re-examination of personal assumptions and biases—particularly with respect to poor and minority children and families, but also in reference to learning to read and write, and (3) a commitment to building respectful and trust-filled relationships with every child and every family. We cannot afford any more clichéd efforts at home and school cooperation, new methods, and innovative approaches. What is critical are serious efforts to build classroom communities of learners, collaborative faculty networks for ongoing problem solving, and home–school relationships rooted in honesty, trust, and respect for all individuals, and equality for every child and family in the nation.

If the real barrier to change is our self-created ecology of inequity, then we should be able to create an ecology of equity as well by using an ecologically valid plan for systems change. This book has been an attempt to define the problems in learning to read in the U.S.A., to better understand the problematic solutions we have created, to redefine education and learning more broadly, and to create a plan for meaningful and lasting change. With the continued collaborative efforts of teachers, parents, and students, and with the support of administrators, community members, and higher education working toward renewed definitions of education and learning in a democracy that embraces the value of leading forth—a process congruent with Vygotsky's (1978) theory of interactively leading ahead through personal mediation in the learning processes of every student in our nation—we will see a transformation of our educational system to an ecology of equality for all of America's children.

And what is the hope for this transformation? I look to my African American and Latino friends for inspiration and for the basis for hope. Many of them have experienced a lifetime of struggle toward equality, as have their parents before them, only to see what appeared so hopeful in the 1960s subverted in the 1980s and 1990s. They have experienced an increase of covert racism that has subverted employment, housing, and educational opportunities; and they are seeing an appalling resurgence of acts of overt racism as well. Just this past year a cross was burned on the lawn of an African American family who moved to a white neighborhood in Smalltown. And a Ku Klux Klan march was held in a neighboring town.

The persistence, tolerance, strength, forgiveness, faith, and hope of our African American, Latino, Native American, and Mexican American citizens is a lesson for us all—and certainly one that should enter every classroom across the country. We have the resources to transform the ecology of inequity: We need only to stop wasting them.

Afterword

Jill Bartoli wants to transform her readers' approach and she has succeeded. I'm not sure what I would have given yesterday as my answer to the question, "What is a teacher?" but I know a common answer is, "A facilitator," or, "A creator of a literate community," or, "A responder."

Regardless, today I have a new answer, "An advocate." What a difference that answer makes! Thanks, Jill.

To look at ourselves as advocates means we stop looking at our students, their families, and communities as people and places that present us with problems to be solved. Instead, we look at ourselves as the advocates of our students, their families, and communities. Yes, that shift in perspective represents a transformation in my thinking.

Unequal Opportunity represents Jill's abandonment of a neutral role as a researcher to one of an advocate. She cares deeply about James, the Black American who kept her informed about his life situation between the ages of 10 and 20. His mother, grandparents, and other members of his community share their souls and reveal the insidious games the larger society and the school play with their small minority in a middle-class white town. Jill also cares about the other students she studied: inner-city Latino students, their families, and their community. Why can't the mothers bring their little children into the school building as they always did in Puerto Rico? Why was one entire first grade retained?

The inequity in the U.S.A., in local communities, in schools, and in classrooms upsets Jill. She is hopeful, however. We must act. Jill, an expert in reading instruction for students who have difficulty learning to read, begins her action by collaboration with everyone you can think of. She says James's problems are the responsibility of the local druggist, the school board members, his grandfather, and James himself. She would include all of them and many others in a plan for James's instruction. We must consider the entire context in which a student lives, plays, and learns.

Jill tells her story with many compelling quotes from interviews and explains her follow-up actions as part of projects in which community members, students, administrators, parents, teachers, and university personnel work for years to change the large picture in which students in James's town and the inner-city Latino students will learn.

There will be no elitist tracks or groups, no dumb tracks or groups. Everyone will be together, helping, sharing, caring, and celebrating. There will be no multiple choice tests seeking to eliminate complexities of thinking. What is missing in test scores is the child as a whole—"a complex, thinking, feeling human being with interests, motivation, emotions, and important personal relationships." At present, evaluation systems imply that personal relationships don't count; such interactions are never mentioned, evaluated, or recorded.

As educators we've not kept close contact with the communities, parents, and students we teach. Educational issues that have become disconnected from their "wider ecology have resulted in shortsighted, unsuccessful, and inequitable approaches to schooling." We've created a "highly destructive system of labeling and separation of children from their constitutional right to education. . . . We are moving toward a permanent underclass of one-third of our population by the twenty-first century."

Over the past decade the number of students given labels of reading and learning disability (e.g., LD, ADD, remedial, Chapter 1) has tripled. The number of children living below the poverty level is one out of four, and one out of two for African American children. These statistics show our failures. It's too late to change. We need a transformation of our values, not tougher standards and better tests, not cosmetic changes in the present system. We need to reposition ourselves.

This book can transform our thoughts about learning to read, learning to learn, and learning to live together in the U.S.A. We must reconsider our stance in relation to both "individual freedom and community responsibility."

Jane Hansen
University of New Hampshire

The Five Critical Experiences in Theory

1. READING: TRANSACTING WITH TEXTS

• Bringing prior knowledge and experience to construct/compose meaning; encountering texts with different purposes, concepts, and structures; using a repertoire of reading strategies for a variety of purposes; exploring similarities and differences in meaning and response; responding in a variety of ways: discussions, enactments, writing, and the use of other media; learning to read one's own texts and the texts of other students.

2. WRITING: COMPOSING TEXTS

• Using a wide range of kinds of discourse: expressive, informational, and poetic/imaginative; acquiring a repertoire of composing processes; selecting the writing strategies most appropriate for different kinds of discourse, audiences, and purposes for writing; learning about relationships between oral and written language; using writing to learn content, to engage actively in the study of a discipline; using writing to make sense of and affect the world.

3. INDEPENDENT READING AND WRITING

• Empowering oneself to become a more independent and self-reliant learner (student ownership of learning); choosing among options what to read and write both in and out of school as a part of the regular program of education; using reading and writing to satisfy personal and social needs; developing a variety of independent strategies depending on the text, context, and one's own purposes.

4. INVESTIGATING LANGUAGE

• Exploring language in the context of language in use rather than as a separate set of skills; building upon one's own prior knowledge and intuitions about language; acquiring metalinguistic awareness—knowledge about language and how it works—including relationships of parts and social rules; doing problem-solving tasks with whole texts, dealing with language parts within a meaningful context; understanding and appreciating cultural and linguistic diversity, and the relationships between language and culture.

5. LEARNING TO LEARN

• Building knowledge or awareness of one's own thinking processes and of various aspects of the processes of reading, writing, listening, and speaking; using this knowledge to orchestrate one's own thinking and learning; developing a repertoire of learning strategies for different tasks such as note-making, studying, and generating questions; learning to function both independently and interdependently; learning to pose as well as solve problems; taking risks in learning, and learning from one's own mistakes; learning to collaborate with others.

The Five Critical Experiences in Classroom Practice

CRITICAL EXPERIENCE #1—READING—TRANSACTING WITH TEXTS

When teachers provide this experience students are:
> listening to literature read aloud on a daily basis
> reading whole books (starting in first grade)
> reading trade books for information and research
> responding to reading with many opportunities to write
> working with other students cooperatively on book projects, and
> learning to be flexible and strategic in reading skills.

CRITICAL EXPERIENCE #2—WRITING—COMPOSING TEXTS

When teachers provide this experience students are:
> learning the writing processes of brainstorming, organizing, drafting, revising, and editing
> learning to make decisions about topic choice, revising, editing, and publishing
> learning the spellings and usage for words in their own writing
> writing for different purposes and for different audiences, and
> learning to write for sustained periods of time.

CRITICAL EXPERIENCE #3—INDEPENDENT READING AND WRITING

When teachers provide this experience students are:
> learning to select, read, and share books of their own choice
> learning to read for longer periods of time
> learning to observe, reflect, and express themselves through writing in connection with class readings or assignments through a dialogue journal or class learning log, and
> developing the lifetime reading habit.

CRITICAL EXPERIENCE #4—INVESTIGATING LANGUAGE

When teachers provide this experience students are:
>   connecting vocabulary meanings to class readings
>   connecting spelling to writing or reading
>   learning the correct forms of mechanics, usage, and grammar in the editing stage of their writing, and
>   learning how language use changes with different cultural and social settings.

CRITICAL EXPERIENCE #5—LEARNING TO LEARN

When teachers provide this experience students are:
>   learning to be knowledgeable, reflective, and strategic about their learning
>   learning how to take notes and how to organize them to learn
>   learning how to ask critical questions
>   learning key study skills
>   learning how to research a question and present it to others, and
>   learning to work collaboratively with partners and groups.

Ways to Observe Critical Experience #1 (Reading) in the Classroom

Observe and record the following CE #1 activities provided by the teacher in the classroom, noting the frequency:

4 Daily   3 Weekly   2 Monthly   1 Sometimes   0 Never

_____ 1. Reading aloud to students several times a day.

_____ 2. Choosing texts to read aloud that interest and motivate students to read on their own.

_____ 3. Providing opportunities for active student engagement in the texts (e.g., dramatizing, echo/choral reading, music).

_____ 4. Inviting a variety of student responses to the texts (e.g., personal feelings, descriptions, analyses, interpretations, questions, evaluations).

_____ 5. Encouraging students to link with their own personal knowledge and experiences to "transact" with texts.

_____ 6. Exploring texts through a variety of strategies, such as:

    _____ a. Brainstorming and reflecting

    _____ b. Student questioning and predicting

    _____ c. Reporting and reviewing

    _____ d. Keeping journals

    _____ e. Illustrating or making a collage, diorama, timeline, chart, graph, map, sculpture, or other artistic exhibits

    _____ f. Summarizing or retelling/rewriting

    _____ g. Using films and videos

_____ 7. Using both informational and literary texts to supplement (or replace) textbooks to deepen concept learning.

_____ 8. Leading students to discover similarities and differences in meanings gained from texts.

_____ 9. Exposing students to the wide diversity of viewpoints and cultures found in our pluralistic democracy.

_____ 10. Arranging heterogeneous large and small groups for reading/ transacting with text activities.

_____ 11. Using partners for some reading activities, including cross-age reading pairs.

_____ 12. Including parents in the reading activities, both in and out of the classroom.

_____ 13. Including a variety of before, during, and after reading activities.

References

Ada, A. (1988). The Pajaro Valley experience: Working with Spanish-speaking parents to develop children's reading and writing skills in the home through the use of children's literature. In T. Skutnabb-Kangas & J. Cummins (Eds.), *Minority education: From shame to struggle* (pp. 224–238). Philadelphia: Multilingual Matters.

Adelman, H. (1989). Toward solving the problems of misidentification and limited intervention efficacy. *Journal of Learning Disabilities, 22,* 608–612.

Agar, M. (1980). *The professional stranger.* New York: Academic Press.

Allington, R. (1983). The reading instruction provided readers of differing reading abilities. *Elementary School Journal, 83,* 558–569.

———. (1991). Children who find learning to read difficult: School responses to diversity. In E. Hiebert (Ed.), *Literacy for a diverse society* (pp. 237–252). New York: Teachers College Press.

Allington, R., & McGill-Franzen, A. (1989). School response to reading failure: Instruction for Chapter 1 and special education students in grades two, four, and eight. *Elementary School Journal, 89,* 529–542.

Apple, M. (1980). Curriculum form and the logic of technical control: Building the possessive individual. In L. Barton, R. Meigan, & S. Walker (Eds.), *Schooling, ideology and the curriculum.* Brighton, England: The Falmer Press.

———. (1988). Redefining equality: Authoritarian populism and the conservative restoration. *Teachers College Record, 90,* 167–184.

Ashton-Warner, S. (1963). *Teacher.* New York: Simon & Schuster.

Auerbach, E. (1989). Toward a social-contextual approach to family literacy. *Harvard Educational Review, 59,* 169–181.

Banks, J. (1993). Multicultural education. *Review of Research in Education, 19,* 3–50.

Barrs, M., Ellis, S., Tester, H., & Thomas, A. (1989). *The primary language record.* Portsmouth, NH: Heinemann.

Bart, D. (1984). The differential diagnosis of special education: Managing social pathology as individual disability. In L. Barton & S. Tomlinson (Eds.), *Special education and social interests* (pp. 81–121). New York: Nichols.

Barth, R. (1990). *Improving schools from within.* San Francisco: Jossey-Bass.

Bartoli, J. (1985a). Metaphor, mind, and meaning: The narrative mind in action. *Language Arts, 62,* 332–342.

———. (1985b). The paradox in reading: Has the solution become the problem? *Journal of Reading, 28,* 580–584.

———. (1986a). It is really English for everyone? *Language Arts, 63,* 12–22.

————. (1986b). *Exploring the process of reading/learning disability labeling: An ecological systems approach.* Ann Arbor, MI: University Microfilms International.

————. (1989). An ecological response to Coles' interactivity alternative. *Journal of Learning Disabilities, 22,* 292–297.

————. (1990a, February). *The barriers to multicultural and anti-racist education in an inner-city elementary school.* Presentation at the Ethnography in Education Research Forum, Philadelphia.

————. (1990b). On defining learning and disability: Exploring the ecology. *Journal of Learning Disabilities, 23,* 628–631.

Bartoli, J., & Botel, M. (1988a). *Reading/learning disability: An ecological approach.* New York: Teachers College Press.

————. (1988b). *A school building model for educating students with handicaps in general education settings.* Proposal submitted to U.S. Department of Education, Office of Special Education and Rehabilitative Services.

————. (1989). *Developing potential in the inner-city: An ecological approach to a school/ university/community partnership.* Proposal submitted to U.S. Department of Education, Secretary's Fund for Innovation in Education.

Bartoli, J., Palmer, M., Esolen, M., Rose, S., & Fishman, A. (1991). "I haven't anything to say": Reflections of self and community in collecting oral histories. In R. Grele (Ed.), *International Annual of Oral History, 1990* (pp. 167–189). New York: Greenwood Press.

Bartoli, J., Rice, P., Fox, B., & Bauman, D. (1992, November). *Integrated language arts at the college and elementary levels.* Presentation to the Pennsylvania Council of Teachers of English Conference, Harrisburg, PA.

Bateson, C., & Bateson, G. (1987). *Angels fear.* New York: Macmillan.

Bateson, G. (1972). *Steps to an ecology of mind.* New York: Ballantine Books.

————. (1979). *Mind and nature: A necessary unity.* New York: Ballantine Books.

Bateson, G., & Ruesch, J. (1951). *Communication: The social matrix of psychiatry.* New York: Norton.

Beard, J., & McNabb, S. (Eds.). (1985). *Testing in the English language arts: Uses and abuses.* Rochester: Michigan Council of Teachers of English.

Bellah, R., Madsen, R., Sullivan, W., Swidler, A., & Tipton, S. (1985). *Habits of the heart.* New York: Harper & Row.

Bernstein, R. (1983). *Beyond objectivism and relativism: Science, hermeneutics, and praxis.* Philadelphia: University of Pennsylvania Press.

Beyerlein, C., Anderson, M., Bekelja, K., Derenzo, C., Lisi, J., Marks, M., McCall, B., Moll, T., Patton, P., & Rubinkam, M. (1994, February). *The gathering of history: The economic revitalization of Steelton-Highspire, Pennsylvania.* Presentation at the Ethnography in Education Research Forum, Philadelphia: University of Pennsylvania.

Botel, M. (1977, 1979, 1981). *A comprehensive reading and communication arts plan.* Harrisburg: Pennsylvania Department of Education.

————. (1993a). *Toward congruence of holistic learning and assessment.* Philadelphia: University of Pennslyvania.

————. (1993b, May). Address to Penn Literacy Network Conference, Philadelphia: University of Pennsylvania.

Botel, M., Ripley, P., & Barnes, L. (1993, September). A case study of an implementation of the "New Literacy" paradigm. *British Journal of Research in Reading*, 16, 112–127.

Boyer, E. L. (1983). *High school*. New York: Harper & Row.

Bredekamp, S. (1987). *Developmentally appropriate practice in early childhood programs serving children from birth to age 8*. Washington, DC: National Association for the Education of Young Children.

Bredekamp, S., & Rosegrant, T. (1992). *Reaching potentials: Appropriate curriculum and assessment for young children*. Washington, DC: National Association for the Education of Young Children.

Britton, J. (1970). *Language and learning*. New York: Penguin.

———. (1988). *Writing and reading in the classroom*. (Tech. Rep. No. 8). Berkeley: University of California, Center for the Study of Reading.

Bronfenbrenner, U. (1979). *The ecology of human development*. Cambridge, MA: Harvard University Press.

———. (1986). Alienation and the four worlds of childhood. *Phi Delta Kappan*, 67, 430–436.

———. (1988). Foreword. In A. Pence (Ed.), *Ecological research with children and families*. New York: Teachers College Press.

Bruner, J. (1973). *On knowing: Essays for the left hand*. New York: Atheneum.

———. (1984). Language, mind, and reading. In H. Goelman, A. Oberg, & F. Smith (Eds.), *Awakening to literacy* (pp. 193–200). Portsmouth, NH: Heinemann.

———. (1986). *Actual minds, possible worlds*. Cambridge, MA: Harvard University Press.

Bryan, P. (1992). *A narrative of change through teacher development and literacy networking in an urban elementary school*. Philadelphia: University of Pennsylvania.

Calkins, L. (1986). *The art of teaching writing*. Portsmouth, NH: Heinemann.

Carini, P. (1979). *The art of seeing and the visibility of the person*. Grand Forks: North Dakota Study Group on Evaluation, University of North Dakota.

Cazden, C. (1981). Social context of learning to read. In J. Guthrie (Ed.), *Comprehension and teaching: Research reviews* (pp. 118–139). Newark: International Reading Association.

Clay, M. (1979). *Reading: The patterning of complex behavior*. Portsmouth, NH: Heinemann.

———. (1985). *The early detection of reading difficulties*. Portsmouth, NH: Heinemann.

Cochran-Smith, M., & Lytle, S. (1992). *Inside/outside: Teacher research and knowledge*. New York: Teachers College Press.

Coleman, J. (1987). *Public and private high schools: The impact of community*. New York: Basic Books.

Coles, G. (1978). The learning disabilities test battery: Empirical and social issues. *Harvard Educational Review*, 48, 314–340.

———. (1983). The use of Soviet psychological theory in understanding learning dysfunctions. *American Journal of Orthopsychiatry*, 53, 619–628.

———. (1987). *The learning mystique*. New York: Pantheon.

Comer, J. (1980). *School power: Implications of an intervention project*. New York: The Free Press.

————. (1988). Educating poor minority children. *Scientific American, 259,* 42–48.

Congressional Budget Office. (1987, August). *Educational achievement: Explanations and implications of recent trends.* Washington, DC: U.S. Government Printing Office.

Cousins, J. (1992, November). *The case for participatory evaluation.* Paper presented at the annual meeting of the American Evaluation Association. Seattle.

Cummins, J. (1986). Empowering minority students: A framework for intervention. *Harvard Educational Review, 56,* 18–36.

Cushman, P. (1990, May). Why the self is empty: Toward a historically situated psychology. *American Psychologist,* pp. 599–611.

Daniels, H. (1993). Whole language: What's the fuss? *Rethinking Schools, 8*(2), 4–6.

Darling-Hammond, L. (1992). Achieving our goals: Superficial or structural reforms? *Phi Delta Kappan, 72*(4), 286–295.

Darling-Hammond, L., Lieberman, A., & Miller, L. (1992). *Restructuring in policy and practice.* New York: Teachers College, Columbia University, National Center for Restructuring Education, Schools, and Teaching.

Delpit, L. (1986). Skills and other dilemmas of a progressive Black educator. *Harvard Educational Review, 56,* 379–385.

————. (1988). The silenced dialogue: Power and pedagogy in educating other people's children. *Harvard Educational Review, 58,* 280–298.

Derman-Sparks, L. (1989). *Anti-bias curriculum: Tools for empowering young children.* Washington, DC: National Association for the Education of Young Children.

Dewey, J. (1899). *The school and the society.* Chicago: University of Chicago Press.

————. (1910). *How we think.* Lexington, MA: Heath.

————. (1916). *Democracy and education.* New York: Macmillan.

————. (1938). *Experience and education.* New York: Macmillan.

Dombart, P. (1985, November). The vision of an insider: A practitioner's view. *Educational Leadership, 43,* 70–73.

Donaldson, M. (1978). *Children's minds.* New York: Norton.

Donovan, D., & McIntyre, D. (1990). *Healing the hurt child: A developmental-contextual approach.* New York: Norton.

Duffy, F. (February, 1987). Personal communication to Morton Botel.

Duke, D. L. (1984). *Teaching—the imperiled profession.* Albany: State University of New York Press.

Eisner, E. (1992). Educational reform and the ecology of schooling. *Teachers College Record, 93,* 610–627.

Elsasser, N., & John-Steiner, V. (1977). An interactionist approach to advancing literacy. *Harvard Educational Review, 47,* 355–369.

Erickson, F. (1987). Transformation and school success: The politics and culture of educational achievement. *Anthropology and Education Quarterly, 18,* 335–355.

Feinberg, P. (1993, February). *Trying on a new lens for literacy acquisition in an inner city elementary school: A view from the resource room.* Presentation at the Ethnography in Education Research Forum, Philadelphia.

Feuerstein, R. (1979). *The dynamic assessment of retarded performers: The learning potential assessment device, theory, instruments, and technique.* Baltimore: University Park Press.

————. (1984, May). Reuven Feuerstein makes every child count. *APA Monitor,* pp. 18–20.

Feuerstein, R., Rand, Y., & Rynders, J. (1988). *Don't accept me as I am: Helping "retarded" people to excel.* New York: Plenum Press.

Fine, M. (1991). *Framing dropouts.* Albany: State University of New York Press.

Freire, P. (1970). *Pedagogy of the oppressed.* New York: Continuum.

————. (1980). The adult literacy process as cultural action for freedom. In M. Wolf, M. McQuillan, & E. Radwin (Eds.), *Thought and language/language and reading* (pp. 363–381). Harvard Educational Review, Reprint Series, No. 14.

————. (1981). *Education for critical consciousness.* New York: Continuum.

————. (1983). The importance of the act of reading. *Journal of Education, 165,* 5–11.

Fullan, M. (1991). *The new meaning of educational change.* New York: Teachers College Press.

Gartner, A., & Lipsky, D. (1987). Beyond special education: Toward a quality system for all students. *Harvard Educational Review, 57,* 367–395.

Geertz, C. (1973). *The interpretation of cultures.* New York: Basic Books.

Gibboney, R. A. (1984). *Toward intellectual excellence.* Philadelphia: University of Pennsylvania.

Gibboney, R. A. (1994). *The stone trumpet: A story of practical school reform, 1960–1990.* Albany: SUNY Press.

Glaser, B., & Strauss, A. (1967). *The discovery of grounded theory.* Chicago: Aldine.

Goldberg, S. (1993, March 10). Commentary. *Education Week,* p. 29.

Goodlad, J. (1984). *A place called school: Prospects for the future.* New York: McGraw-Hill.

————. (1987). *The ecology of school renewal.* Chicago: University of Chicago Press.

————. (1990). *Teachers for our nation's schools.* San Francisco: Jossey-Bass.

Goodlad, J., & Sirotnik, K. (1988). The future of school-university partnerships. In K. Sirotnik & J. Goodlad (Eds.), *School-university partnerships in action* (pp. 205–225). New York: Teachers College Press.

Goodman, K. (1988, May). *The place of evaluation in whole language.* Paper delivered at International Reading Association Conference, Toronto.

Gould, S. (1980). *The panda's thumb.* New York: Norton.

————. (1981). *The mismeasure of man.* New York: Norton.

Granger, L., & Granger, B. (1986). *The magic feather.* New York: Dutton.

Graves, D. (1983). *Writing: Teachers and children at work.* Portsmouth, NH: Heinemann.

Gray, P. (1992, May). Lie society. *The Washington Monthly,* pp. 36–40.

Griffore, R., & Boger, R. (Eds.) (1986). *Child rearing in the home and school.* New York: Plenum Press.

Grubb, W., & Lazerson, M. (1982). *Broken promises: How Americans fail their children.* New York: Basic Books.

Haley, J. (1981). Towards a theory of pathological systems. In J. Haley (Ed.), *Reflections on therapy and other essays* (pp. 94–112). Washington, DC: Family Therapy Institute.

Halliday, M. (1978). *Language as social semiotic: The social interpretation of language and meaning.* Baltimore: University Park Press.

Hansen, J. (1987). *When writers read.* Portsmouth, NH: Heinemann.

———. (1994). Literacy portfolios: Windows on potential. In S. Valencia, E. Hiebert, & P. Afflerbach (Eds.), *Authentic reading assessment: Practices and possibilities* (pp. 26–45). Newark, DE: International Reading Association.

Harman, S. (1991, November 13). The basal 'conspiracy.' *Education Week, 11,* p. 32.

Heath, S. (1982). Questioning at home and at school. In G. Spindler (Ed.), *Doing the ethnography of schooling* (pp. 102–131). New York: Holt, Rinehart & Winston.

———. (1983). *Ways with words: Language, life and work in communities and classrooms.* New York: Cambridge University Press.

Hobbs, N. (1975). *The futures of children.* San Francisco: Jossey-Bass.

———. (1978). Families, schools, and communities: An ecosystem for children. *Teachers College Record, 79,* 756–766.

Hoffman, L. (1981). *Foundations of family therapy.* New York: Basic Books.

Huxley, A. (1932). *Brave new world.* New York: Harper/Collins.

Jencks, C. (1992). *Rethinking social policy: Race, poverty, and the underclass.* Cambridge, MA: Harvard University Press.

Johnston, P. (1984). Assessment in reading. In P. D. Pearson (Ed.), *Handbook of reading research* (pp. 147–182). New York: Longman.

———. (1989). Constructive evaluation and the improvement of teaching and learning. *Teachers College Record, 90,* 509–528.

———. (1992). *Constructive evaluation of literate activity.* White Plains, NY: Longman.

Johnston, P., McGill-Franzen, A., & Allington, R. (1985, April). *The practical problems of reading failure: Pedagogy and research.* Paper presented at the annual meeting of the American Educational Research Association, Chicago.

Joyce, B., & Showers, B. (1983). *Power in staff development through research on training.* Alexandria, VA: Association for Supervision and Curriculum Development.

Kozol, J. (1985). *Illiterate America.* New York: Anchor Press.

———. (1991). *Savage inequalities.* New York: Crown.

Kreeft, J. (1984). Dialogue writing—bridge from talk to essay writing. *Language Arts, 61,* 141–151.

Kuykendall, C. (1992). *From rage to hope: Strategies for reclaiming Black and Hispanic students.* Bloomington, IN: National Educational Service.

Labov, W. (1972). *Language in the inner city: Studies in the Black English vernacular.* Philadelphia: University of Pennsylvania Press.

———. (1982). Competing value systems in the inner-city schools. In P. Gilmore & A. Glatthorn (Eds.), *Children in and out of school* (pp. 148–171). Washington, DC: Center for Applied Linguistics.

Lafferty, T. (1988). *Professional growth through cooperative educational planning.* Philadelphia: University of Pennsylvania.

Lazerson, M. (1983). The origins of special education. In J. G. Chambers & W. T. Hartman (Eds.), *Special education policies: Their history, implementation, and finance* (pp. 15–47). Philadelphia: Temple University Press.

Lieberman, A., & Miller, L. (1992). Restructuring schools: What matters and what works. *Phi Delta Kappan, 71*(10), 759–764.

Lightfoot, S. (1978). *Worlds apart: Relationships between families and schools.* New York: Basic Books.

Linn, R. (1987). Accountability: The comparison of educational systems and the quality of test results. *Educational Policy, 1,* 181–198.

Little, J. (1993). *Teachers' professional development in a climate of educational reform.* New York: Teachers College, Columbia University, National Center for Restructuring Education, Schools, and Teaching.

Lomotey, K. (1990). *Going to school: The African-American experience.* Albany: State University of New York Press.

Lortie, D. (1975). *School teacher: A sociological study.* Chicago: University of Chicago Press.

Lytle, S. (1982). *Exploring comprehension style: A study of twelfth-grade readers' transactions with text.* Ann Arbor, MI: University Microfilms International.

Lytle, S., & Botel, M. (1990). *A Pennsylvania comprehensive reading/communication arts plan II.* Harrisburg: Pennsylvania Department of Education.

———. (1991). *The Pennsylvania framework: Reading, writing, and talking across the curriculum.* Harrisburg: Pennsylvania Department of Education.

Marmor, T., Mashaw, J., & Harvey, P. (1992). *America's misunderstood welfare state: Persistent myths, enduring realities.* New York: Basic Books.

Mayer, M. (1966). *They thought they were free.* Chicago: University of Chicago Press.

McDermott, R. (1974). Achieving school failure: An anthropological approach to illiteracy and social stratification. In G. Spindler (Ed.), *Education and cultural process* (pp. 82–188). New York: Holt, Rinehart & Winston.

———. (1987). The explanation of minority school failure, again. *Anthropology and Education Quarterly, 18,* 361–364.

McGill-Franzen, A., & Allington, R. (1993). Flunk 'em or get them classified. *Educational Researcher, 22*(1), 19–22.

McLeod, J. (1987). *Ain't no makin' it: Leveled aspirations in a low-income neighborhood.* Boulder, CO: Westview Press.

McNeil, L. (1986). *Contradictions of control: School structure and school knowledge.* New York: Routledge & Kegan Paul.

Mehan, H. (1980). The competent student. *Anthropology and Education Quarterly, 11,* 131–152.

Mellon, J. (1981). Language competence. In C. Cooper (Ed.), *The nature and measurement of competency in English* (pp. 21–64). Urbana, IL: National Council of Teachers of English.

Mercier, L. (Ed.). (1981). *The essentials approach: Rethinking the curriculum for the 80's.* Washington, DC: U.S. Department of Education, Basic Skills Improvement Program.

Minuchin, S. (1974). *Families and family therapy.* Cambridge, MA: Harvard University Press.

Moll, L., & Diaz, S. (1987). Change as the goal of educational research. *Anthropology and Education Quarterly, 18,* 300–311.

Napier, A., & Whitaker, C. (1978). *The family crucible.* New York: Harper & Row.

Oakes, J. (1985). *Keeping track: How schools structure inequality.* New Haven: Yale University Press.

Oakes, J., & Sirotnik, K. (1990). Evaluation as critical inquiry: School improvement as a case in point. *New Directions for Program Evaluation,* No. 45, 37–59.

Ogbu, J. (1980, July). *Literacy in subordinate cultures: The case of Black Americans.* Paper delivered at the Library of Congress Conference on Literacy, Washington, DC.

———. (1986). The consequences of the American caste system. In U. Neisser (Ed.), *The school achievement of minority children* (pp. 19–55). Hillsdale, NJ: Lawrence Erlbaum.

Paley, V. (1983). *Mollie is three: Growing up in school.* Chicago, IL: The University of Chicago Press.

Palincsar, A., & Brown, A. (1984). Reciprocal teaching of comprehension fostering and comprehension monitoring activities. *Cognition and Instruction, 1,* 117–175.

Palmer, M., Esolen, M., Rose, S., Fishman, A., & Bartoli, J. (1991). I haven't anything to say: Reflections of self and community in collecting oral histories. In R. Grele (Ed.), *International Annual of Oral History, 1990* (pp. 167–189). New York: Greenwood Press.

Patton, M. (1987). *How to use qualitative methods in evaluation.* Newbury Park, CA: Sage.

Petrie, H. (1987). Introduction to evaluation and testing. *Educational Policy, 1,* 175–180.

Postman, N. (1980). The politics of reading. In M. Wolf, M. McQuillan, & E. Radwin (Eds.), *Thought and language/language and reading* (pp. 355–362). Harvard Educational Review, Reprint Series No. 14.

———. (1985). *Amusing ourselves to death.* New York: Penguin.

Purvis, A. (1981). Competence in English. In C. Cooper (Ed.), *The nature and measurement of competency in English* (pp. 65–94). Urbana, IL: National Council of Teachers of English.

Relic, P. (1993, October 20). Commentary: Part of—not apart from. *Education Week, 13,* 52.

Rhodes, W. (1967). The disturbing child: A problem of ecological management. *Exceptional Children, 33,* 449–455.

Rich, D. (1986). Focus for education reform: Building the home-school synergism. In R. Griffore & R. Boger (Eds.), *Child rearing in the home and school.* New York: Plenum Press.

Rist, R. (1970). Student social class and teacher expectations: The self-fulfilling prophesy in ghetto education. *Harvard Educational Review, 40,* 411–451.

Rist, R., & Harrell, J. (1982). Labeling the learning disabled child: the social ecology of educational practice. *American Journal of Orthopsychiatry, 52,* 146–160.

Rose, M. (1990). *Lives on the boundary: The struggles and achievements of America's educational underclass.* New York: Penguin.

Rosenblatt, L. (1978). *The reader, the text, and the poem.* Carbondale, IL: Southern Illinois University Press.

———. (1980). What facts does this poem teach you? *Language Arts, 57,* 380–388.

Sarason, S. (1971). *The culture of the school and the problem of change.* Boston: Allyn & Bacon.

———. (1982). *Schooling in America: Scapegoat or salvation.* New York: The Free Press.

Sarason, S., & Doris, J. (1979). *Educational handicap, public policy and social history.* New York: Macmillan.

Sass, L. (1988). Humanism, hermeneutics, and the concept of the human subject. In S. Messer, L. Sass, & R. Woolfolk (Eds.), *Hermeneutics and psychological theory: Interpretive perspectives on personality, psychotherapy, and psychopathology* (pp. 222–271). New Brunswick, NJ: Rutgers University Press.

Saunders, W. (1992). The constructivist perspective. *School Science and Mathematics, 92,* 136–141.

Schrag, P., & Divoky, D. (1975). *The myth of the hyperactive child: And other means of child control.* New York: Pantheon.

Seaver, J., & Botel, M. (1990). *Literacy Network handbook.* Levittown, PA: Morton Botel Associates.

Sirotnik, K., & Goodlad, J. (Eds.) (1988). *School-university partnerships in action.* New York: Teachers College Press.

Sitkoff, H. (1993). *The struggle for Black equality.* New York: Hill & Wang.

Sizer, T. (1984). *Horace's compromise: The dilemma of the American high school.* Boston: Houghton Mifflin.

Skrtic, T. (1991). The special education paradox: Equity as the way to excellence. *Harvard Educational Review, 61,* 148–194.

Slavin, R. (1987). Making Chapter 1 make a difference. *Phi Delta Kappan, 69,* 110–119.

Smith, F. (1987). *Insult to intelligence.* Portsmouth, NH: Heinemann.

Spiegler, G. (1992). Address to the Board of Trustees. Elizabethtown College, Elizabethtown, PA.

Spradley, J. (1979). *The ethnographic interview.* New York: Holt, Rinehart & Winston.

———. (1980). *Participant observation.* New York: Holt, Rinehart & Winston.

Stack, H. (1974). *All our kin.* New York: Harper & Row.

Stanovich, K. (1986). Matthew effects in reading: Some consequences of individual differences in the acquisition of literacy. *Reading Research Quarterly, 21,* 360–405.

Stanton, J., Shuy, R., Kreeft, J., & Reed, L., Eds. (1987). *Interactive writing in dialogue journals: Practitioner, linguistic, social, and cognitive views.* Norwood, NJ: Ablex.

Stecher, B., & Davis, A. (1987). *How to focus an evaluation.* Newbury Park, CA: Sage.

Sternberg, R. (1988). *The triarchic mind: A new theory of human intelligence.* New York: Viking.

Sutton-Smith, B. (1982). The importance of the storytaker: An investigation of the imaginative life. *The Urban Review, 8,* 82–95.

Suzuki, S. (1978). *Suzuki Piano School, Volume I*. Tokyo, Japan: Zen On Music Company.

Szwed, J. (1981). The ethnography of literacy. In M. Whiteman (Ed.), *Writing: The nature, development and teaching of written communication*. Hillsdale, NJ: Lawrence Erlbaum.

Taylor, D., & Dorsey-Gaines, C. (1988). *Growing up literate: Learning from inner-city families*. Portsmouth, NH: Heinemann.

Thomas, L. (1974). *Lives of a cell*. New York: Viking.

————. (1992). *The fragile species*. New York: Scribner.

Toro-Lopez, J. (1992). *Perceptions of parental competence among four Puerto Rican families living in the continental United States*. State College: Pennsylvania State University.

Turnbull, A., & Turnbull, H. (with Summers, J., Brotherson, M., & Benson, H.) (1986). *Families, professionals, and exceptionality: A special partnership*. Columbus, OH: Merrill.

Tye, K. (1992). Restructuring our schools: Beyond the rhetoric. *Phi Delta Kappan, 74*, 8–14.

Vellutino, F. (1987). Dyslexia. *Scientific American, 256*, 34–41.

Vinsonhaler, J., Weinshank, A., Wagner, C., & Polin, R. (1983). Diagnosing children with educational problems. *Reading Research Quarterly, 28*, 134–164.

Vygotsky, L. (1934). Thinking and speech: Psychological investigations. Cited in J. Wertsch (1985), *Vygotsky and the social foundation of mind*. Cambridge, MA: Harvard University Press.

————. (1962). *Thought and language*. Cambridge, MA: MIT Press.

————. (1978). *Mind in society*. Cambridge, MA: Harvard University Press.

Walberg, H., & Tsai, S. (1983). Matthew effects in education. *American Educational Research Journal, 20*, 359–373.

Waldrop, M. (1992). *Complexity*. New York: Simon & Schuster.

Walker, L. (1987). Procedural rights in the wrong system: Special education is not enough. In A. Gartner & T. Joe (Eds.), *Images of the disabled/disabling images* (pp. 97–115). New York: Praeger.

Watzlawick, P., Beavin, J., & Jackson, D. (1967). *Pragmatics of human communication: A study of interactional patterns, pathologies, and paradoxes*. New York: Norton.

Watzlawick, P., Weakland, J., & Fisch, R. (1974). *Change: Principles of problem formation and problem resolution*. New York: Norton.

Weis, L. (Ed.). (1988). *Class, race, and gender in American education*. Albany: State University of New York Press.

Will, M. (1986, November). *Educating students with learning problems: A shared responsibility*. Washington, DC: U.S. Department of Education, Office of Special Education and Rehabilitative Services.

Wilson, J. (1987). *The truly disadvantaged*. Chicago, IL: University of Chicago Press.

Woodbury, J. (1993, August 23). Interview with Wilbert Rideau. *Time Magazine, 142*, 33–35.

Ysseldyke, J., & Algozzine, B. (1982). *Critical issues in special and remedial education*. Boston: Houghton Mifflin.

————. (1984). *Introduction to special education*. Boston: Houghton Mifflin.

Ysseldyke, J., Thurlow, M., Graden, S., Wesson, C., Algozzine, B., & Deno, S. (1983). Generalizations from five years of research on assessment and decision-making: The University of Minnesota Institute. *Exceptional Education Quarterly, 4,* 75–93.

Index

About the Author

Jill Sunday Bartoli is an associate professor at Elizabethtown College in Pennsylvania where she involves her students in collaborative research and development projects connected with urban schools. After earning her Ph.D. in language arts and family literacy at the University of Pennsylvania, she co-authored a book on more inclusive language arts teaching, *Reading/ Learning Disability: An Ecological Approach,* with Morton Botel. Before coming to Elizabethtown, she combined research in inner-city schools with teaching Penn graduate courses in learning disabilities and reforming the curriculum. Her recent federal grant project links both Penn and Elizabethtown College with an urban school in support of a multicultural professional development site for preservice and in-service teachers.